CATHOLIC DIVORCE

CATHOLIC DIVORCE

THE DECEPTION OF ANNULMENTS

Edited by
Pierre Hegy
and
Joseph Martos

Continuum
New York London

2000
The Continuum International Publishing Group Inc
370 Lexington Avenue, New York, NY 10017

The Continuum International Publishing Group Ltd
Wellington House, 125 Strand, London WC2R 0BB

Printed in the United States of America

Library of Contress Cataloging-in-Publication Data

Catholic divorce : the deception of annulments / edited by Pierre Hegy and Joseph Martos.
    p. cm.
    Includes bibliographical references and index.
    ISBN 0-8264-1228-9
      1. Marriage—Religious aspects—Catholic Church. 2. Divorce—Religious aspects—Catholic Church. 3. Pastoral theology—Catholic Church. 4. Catholic Church—Doctrines. I. Hégy, Pierre, 1937– II. Martos, Joseph, 1943–

BX2250.C29 2000
261.8'3589'08822—dc21

                  00-029540

Contents

Introduction

BEFORE INTRODUCING THE CONTENTS OF THIS BOOK, it may be worthwhile to look at the context in which it is written. The year 2000 is the twenty-third in the pontificate of Pope John Paul II. The longest papacy in recent history was that of Pius IX, who reigned from 1846 to 1878. Pope Pius steered the church into religious and political conservatism through his rejection of many modern ideas (summarized in his 1864 *Syllabus of Errors*) such as freedom of speech, freedom of conscience, and separation of church and state. By the end of his pontificate, there were few bishops left who had been nominated before his reign and who did not have the approval of his conservative curia.

Much the same can be said about John Paul II: he is conservative, and his lengthy tenure in the papacy has allowed him to appoint like-minded bishops throughout the Catholic world. Today, few bishops remain who do not owe the current pope their promotion to the episcopacy. The Catholic Church is becoming increasingly more conservative.

THE CHURCH UNDER JOHN PAUL II (1978–)

What are some of the important developments that have occurred in Catholicism during the past twenty years and more? Among other things, the rate of Catholic weddings is down, while the rate of Catholic annulments is up. Sacramental practice continues to diverge from sacramental theory (as it has since the 1960s), typified by declining weekly mass attendance and a chronic shortage of priests. Dissent from papal teaching has become a central issue, culminating at times in power struggles between hierarchy and clergy and between hierarchy and laity. Let us review some of these issues.

1

Catholic Weddings and Divorces

The numbers speak for themselves. There were 327,317 Catholic weddings in 1950, or 11.4 per 1,000 registered Catholics in the United States. In 1995, only 302,919 marriages were recorded in Catholic churches, or 5.0 per 1,000 Catholics, a decrease of 55 percent over 45 years. (These data are from Joseph Claude Harris in *America*, April 10, 1999.) Between 1950 and 1995, however, the number of Catholics in the United States doubled from 28.6 million to 60.3 million, and the marriage rate in the general population remained constant. Had all the Catholics who married in 1995 done so in the Catholic Church, there would have been about 687,000 Catholic weddings instead of 303,000. What happened to the missing 384,000 newlyweds who did not show up in Catholic parishes?

Is it that "many Catholics apparently do not choose to be married in a church," as J. C. Harris suggests? Not exactly. Knowing that approximately 45 percent of all marriages in the United States are second marriages involving at least one divorced person, and knowing that between 80 percent and 90 percent of divorced Catholics do not obtain annulments so they can remarry in the Catholic Church, we can be virtually certain that many of the missing 384,000 were prevented from having a Catholic wedding by the church's marriage laws. If this situation continues, the U.S. Catholic Church will be losing perhaps half of its newlyweds every year. Moreover, since rejected divorced Catholics are less likely to foster the Catholic faith in their children, the church is likely to lose the children of these marriages as well.

Catholic Annulments

The number of annulments granted by diocesan tribunals to divorced Catholics rose from 368 per year in 1968 to about 40,000 in recent years. During the same time period, the rate of annulments granted by civil courts remained relatively low and did not appreciably change. Why is this?

An annulment, whether it is granted by an ecclesiastical court or a civil court, is a recognition that a marital contract is invalid. For example, if a person was mentally impaired (e.g., drunk) or under duress (e.g., a "shotgun wedding") when getting married, he or she could ask to have the marriage contract annulled because a valid contract requires the free consent of both parties. Likewise, if the bride or groom discovered after the wedding that the other party was already married to (and not legally divorced from) someone else, she or he could ask to have the marriage contract nullified. Indeed, both civil and church law recognize this second situation as bigamous and illegal.

If Catholic annulments increased so drastically in a short amount of time, something must have happened. In fact, what happened was a revision of the definition of marriage in the early 1970s, which opened the door to tens of thousands of Catholic annulments annually. The Second Vatican Council had spoken of marriage as a covenant and an intimate relationship, and this addition to the Catholic understanding of marriage enabled canon lawyers in the church to argue that the ability to enter such a relationship was required for a sacramental marriage. Since many people in our society do not have the self-awareness or relationship skills to enter into a deep relationship of this sort, it has been relatively easy for marriage tribunals to find grounds for annulment for almost all Catholics who have sought to obtain one.

This expansion of the grounds for annulment and the relative ease with which divorced Catholics can obtain them gives the impression that annulments have become Catholic divorces that can be obtained more or less on demand. While all this is going on, however, the church steadfastly refuses to reexamine the legal structure that makes annulments necessary for divorced Catholics, it refuses to acknowledge the pastoral problems that this legal structure precipitates, and it refuses to consider the possibility that a covenant theology of marriage, such as the one suggested by Vatican II, is ultimately incompatible with the older contract theology that thinks in terms of validity and nullity. In other words, the pope and the bishops seem to be in denial about the state of marriage in the Catholic Church.

One reason they can do this is that 70 percent of all annulments granted in the world take place in the United States. To the pope and others in Rome, it may seem as if they are "holding the line" against divorce and remarriage in the rest of Catholicism. This is not necessarily the case, however, since anecdotal evidence from Europe and elsewhere suggests that, like the majority of divorced Catholics in the United States, divorced Catholics in the rest of the world simply ignore the annulment process altogether and remarry outside the church. In any event, the state of denial persists and it is real.

Shrinking Numbers of Priests and Parishioners

The dwindling number of priests is a common experience in many parishes. By 2005 there will be 40 percent fewer active priests in the United States than there were in 1966, according to Richard Schoenherr, who has dedicated most of his career to this study (*Full Pews and Empty Altars* [University of Wisconsin Press, 1993]). Why is this happening? One reason was a mass exodus of priests from active ministry from the mid-sixties to the late seventies by men who wanted to marry, who did not want to continue working in an authoritarian church, who wanted to minister in ways that their superiors would not allow, who perceived the gap between church teaching and church practice as hypocritical, and so on. For many of the same reasons, the number of men in seminaries training for the priesthood dropped by 59 percent between 1966 and 1993, making it impossible to replace many of the priests who died, retired, or resigned during those years. During the same period, as mentioned above, the number of registered Catholics has doubled. The result is that there are almost three times as many Catholics per priest in the United States today.

The situation would be worse than it is, except for the fact that fewer Catholics are practicing their faith than used to. Weekly mass attendance in the United States is now about 30 percent, down from 75 percent in the 1950s. While this is three times better than the 10 percent attendance rate in most European countries, it is nonetheless the worst decline in centuries. Moreover, the decline is continuing. If one surveys Catholic parishes from Maine to California, one discovers that most of the people at mass in many places are gray-haired. Where are the young people? Where are the children? And what will happen to the church when the elderly parishioners die?

The church's response to this dual decline has been a massive amount of inertia and inactivity. Dwindling church attendance has meant dwindling revenues, and this in turn has meant the closing of parishes and schools—except in places where the Catholic population has been increasing due to internal migration (e.g., Catholic retirees and white-collar workers moving to Florida) or international migration (e.g., Latin American blue-collar workers moving to California). It has also meant the closing and consolidation of diocesan offices, making the church even less able to cope with the ever-worsening situation.

An Ideological Rather Than a Pastoral Response to the Crisis

Ironically, the Catholic Church is responding to this crisis the same way it did to a similar crisis in Europe a century ago. In the late nineteenth century, Catholic intellectuals attempted to demonstrate the compatibility of modern ideas with the Catholic faith. Their attempts were labeled "modernism" and were dismissed as heretical, and, until the papacy of John XXIII, Catholic priests had to take an oath disavowing any allegiance to modernism. Innovative pastoral solutions to problems facing the church among the working classes in Europe (e.g., the worker-priest movement in France) were suppressed. The result is that few people in European countries today consider themselves more than nominally Catholic, even in countries such as Spain and Italy, which were once almost entirely Catholic.

Today, Catholic thinkers are trying to show that the church can and should come to terms with postmodern ideas and realities, but under Pope

John Paul II these voices are being ignored or suppressed. Outstanding theologians such as Karl Rahner and Edward Schillebeeckx, whose writings were the intellectual underpinnings of many of the newer ideas that found their way into the documents of Vatican II, are being passed over in favor of more traditional thinkers such as Walter Kasper and Hans Urs von Balthasar. Innovative pastoral efforts involving lay people and especially women in liturgical roles are being tolerated at best, and even efforts by the clergy (e.g., the use of general absolution in places with few priests) have been suppressed for not adhering to the letter of church law. As a result (although there are undoubtedly other causes as well) more and more Catholics are being alienated from the church to which they once belonged.

In Central and South America, for a brief time following the Second Vatican Council, the church took up the cause of the poor, promoted the creation of lay-led small Christian communities, and encouraged the development of liberation theology in the face of political oppression. Under Pope John Paul II, the members of the hierarchy have retained the rhetoric of the "preferential option for the poor" but they have done little to implement such an option. In addition, they have discouraged small communities in favor of traditional large parishes controlled by priests, and they have closed seminaries where liberation theology was taught.

The church's response to the situation of divorced Catholics falls into this pattern. During the 1970s, U.S. bishops took the initiative in allowing expanded grounds for annulments. During the 1980s and 1990s, however, recently appointed bishops began making it more difficult to obtain an annulment or to obtain one quickly in the hope of preserving the Catholic doctrine that marriage is indissoluble. Statistics prove that this has done nothing to slow down the rate of Catholic divorce and remarriage; it has only increased the number of Catholics who remarry outside the church in which they were raised. Nonetheless, this ideological answer to the solution is the only one that is currently acceptable to the Catholic hierarchy.

The Struggle over Dissent and Dialogue

With the condemnation of dissent in *Ad Tuendam Fidem* (*To Defend the Faith*) in 1998, Pope John Paul II clearly defined the hierarchy's position with regard to debate and discussion within the church. In summary, the church reserves the right to decide which issues are debatable and which ones are not, which teachings can be dissented from and which ones cannot, which questions can be discussed and which ones cannot.

According to the pope, there is only one acceptable answer to the question, Can one be a good Catholic and disagree with the church's position on birth control, women's ordination, or divorce and remarriage? In fact, it is no longer acceptable even to raise these issues. For the majority of American Catholics, however, the issues are real and the need for dialogue is pressing.

The need is real, but there is no longer any forum for discussion of these and other issues within the institutional church. Nonetheless, discussion must continue if Catholicism is to remain morally healthy and intellectually viable. And if discussion cannot continue in institutions controlled by the Catholic hierarchy, it can at least continue in the church at large, that is, among the people who constitute 99 percent of the Catholics in the world.

It is to that discussion that this book hopes to make a contribution.

THE CHAPTERS IN THIS VOLUME

Because divorce among Catholics is a complex issue, it needs to be looked at from a variety of perspectives, and indeed, it requires research in a range of academic disciplines. This book combines previously published articles and newly written chapters that together cover the topic without going into every aspect in depth.

Following an initial chapter by Pierre Hegy, Charles Davis presents letters written to the *National Catholic Reporter* in response to a call for reform in the church's position on divorce, remarriage, and annulments. These letters speak of the pain and suffering of Catholics in divorce situations and raise questions that cannot be ignored. The remaining chapters can be divided into three parts. The first deals with biblical texts on divorce, the second with historical developments, and the third with alternative theologies and practices.

Exegesis of Biblical Texts on Divorce

"Christian Marriage and the Human Reality of Complete Marital Breakdown," by Edward Schillebeeckx, was first published in 1970 and appears here for the first time in English, translated by Daniel Thompson. Schillebeeckx sees marriage as cultural phenomenon that is historically conditioned, not as an institution created by God in paradise in the form of Western monogamy. The permanence of marriage has always been a scriptural ideal, yet the possibility of divorce in certain cases has at the same time been a historical reality.

"Disputed Biblical Interpretations about Marriage and Divorce," by Pierre Hegy, reviews the literature on biblical interpretations of the New Testament texts on marriage and divorce. For centuries, disagreements about these texts divided Eastern (Greek) Christians from Western (Latin) Christians. Since the Reformation, similar disagreements have divided Catholics from Protestants in the West. The Catholic theology of marriage as indissoluble is based in part on an interpretation of biblical texts that is no longer tenable.

Theological Histories of Divorce

The two most ancient Christian traditions originated during the time of the Roman Empire, which, for administrative purposes, was divided in the fourth century into the Latin-speaking West with Rome as its capital and the Greek-speaking East with Constantinople (later Istanbul) as its capital. After the fall of the Western empire, the Latin church continued as a major force in European culture and remained centered in Rome, eventually becoming known as the Roman Catholic Church. The churches in the East during the same period retained much of their cultural diversity and eventually became known as Eastern Orthodoxy.

In a real sense, the Eastern or Orthodox tradition is the older of the two because its liturgy, theology, and practices—including those surrounding marriage—have remained relatively unchanged since the eighth century. The Western or Roman Catholic tradition, on the other hand, continued to evolve through the Middle Ages, although it has remained relatively stable since the twelfth century.

From this historical perspective, therefore, the Eastern tradition is treated first. "The Indissolubility of Marriage in Orthodox Law and Practice," by Bishop (now Archbishop) Peter L'Huillier, concludes that in the East the marriage bond was never considered to be absolutely indissoluble, and so remarriage after divorce was always a possibility. "Catholic Marriage and Marital Dissolution in Medieval and Modern Times," by Joseph Martos, looks at the evolution of marriage in Western Europe and argues that the doctrine of absolute indissolubility, developed in the Middle Ages, is based on theological assumptions that most Catholics today would question or even reject.

Alternative Theologies and Practices

From its beginning, Anglicanism had to wrestle with the question of divorce. The church of England broke from the church of Rome precisely over the issue of King Henry VIII's desire to remarry in order to secure a male heir to the royal throne. Protestantism likewise has had to come to terms with divorce both pastorally and theologically.

"Not Made in Heaven: Marriage and Divorce in the Anglican Tradition," by William Swatos, explains why Anglicans today do not have one official position about marriage and divorce. Although some church policies have been shaped by historical and political forces, the Anglican communion (including the Episcopal Church in the United States) is a union of national churches that allows for diversity in practice and pluralism in theology.

The topic of divorce and remarriage in Protestant denominations is so vast that an adequate treatment would require a volume in itself. "Divorce among Protestant Clergy," by Adair Lummis, looks at a single facet of that topic, and one that is unique to churches with a married clergy. Like divorce in general, divorce among the clergy is a relatively recent development in Christianity. Although divorce is obviously not a problem that can affect celibate Catholic priests, divorce among lay ministers will undoubtedly become a more pressing issue as the Catholic Church increasingly relies on nonordained professionals for many of its ministries.

In his reflections on "Church Teaching on Sexuality and Marriage" (first translated here into English), Schillebeeckx offers conclusions that can be applied to church teaching on divorce. Most prominent in importance is the distinction between "convictions of the church" and "opinions of the church." History shows that what passes as conviction of the church may be no more than theological opinion a few generations later.

The concluding chapter, "Divorce and Remarriage as Second Chances," by Pierre Hegy and Joseph Martos, first reviews the preceding chapters from the perspective of deception. After turning to attachment theory to understand marital breakdown in contemporary society, the chapter proposes a theology of second chances within which divorce and remarriage can be viewed as a process of personal growth.

1

Catholic Divorce, Annulments, and Deception

PIERRE HEGY

Clearly the church deplores divorce. . . . But once the conjugal union has been broken and this rupture has been legally ratified, it is difficult to pretend that the marriage continues to subsist in the abstract.

Archbishop Peter L'Huillier (1988:218; reprinted below, p. 120)

WHEN A MARRIAGE HAS BEEN DULY CERTIFIED as dead by a divorce court, "to pretend that the marriage continues to subsist in the abstract" would be deceitful. But how can Peter L'Huillier, a canon lawyer and archbishop, say something that most or all Catholic archbishops would reject? The answer is simple: he belongs to the Greek Orthodox Church, not the Roman Catholic Church. Here is the deception of annulments: canon law claims that a marriage is still alive even when the parties involved, common sense, and the judgment of a civil court have declared it dead. L'Huillier agrees with common sense; official Catholic teaching does not. It is refreshing to see Rembert Weakland, the archbishop of Milwaukee, recognize that for "middle-ground" Catholics, annulments "border on dishonesty and casuistry of the worst kind. . . . They would prefer some kind of more humane and helpful solution and are surprised that other alternatives are not openly discussed"(*America*, April 18, 1998, p. 13).

In this chapter I am interested mainly in deception and its effects. Let us begin with a definition. I understand deception as *unintentionally misleading*, often with the best of intentions. To deceive is to make a person (or oneself) believe something that may only be a partial truth—in short, to mislead. Examples of self-deception include the alcoholic who calls him/ herself a social drinker, the obese person who sees himself as pudgy or herself as pleasantly plump, the anorexic whose self-image is that of being overweight.

I differentiate deception from lying. A lie is something objective that can be proven by comparing words and deeds. Deception, in my use of the term, cannot be proven; it is a subjective *judgment* about reality, not an objective conclusion. Both deceptions and lies are ethical failures; lying is a moral failure because telling the truth is a moral virtue. Deceiving, on the other hand, is an intellectual failure, a failure of judgment. If lying is morally reprehensible, then to be naïve and deceptive is intellectually reprehensible. Unfortunately in our culture—and in authoritarian societies—to be moral but intellectually submissive is often seen as a virtue.

Let me take an example emphasizing the importance of judgment. When fifteen to seventeen hours of weekly class time become eight to ten hours of real class time, and the thirty to forty hours of homework become five to ten hours of studies, then a full-time student can also hold a full-time job. But there is a fine line when a full-time student is no longer a full-time student, and when higher education is no longer higher education. Students may feel they have been deceived by the education they have received. The same can be said about most things: conservatives in their pursuit of an integral faith can become narrow-minded integralists, and liberals in their pursuit of social justice can become shallow political activists. Both the conservatives and the liberals can deceive themselves. Deception is a question of judgment, not of facts. Not to see the fine line between an alcoholic and a social drinker, or a conservative and a zealot (or not wanting to see it) is self-deception; and besides deceiving ourselves, we can also deceive others.

Deception is often applied to relationships. We feel deceived when we realize that others have hidden part of themselves from us, have presented a partial or false self, maybe with the best of intentions. Don Juan is obviously deceiving when he swears eternal love to every new lady he meets. Spouses may deceive one another when they hold back their inner self, maybe to protect the other.

More generally put, to present a partial or even false picture of reality (even with the best of intentions) can be deceitful. Thus, to teach only Catholic theology in a religious studies department would be seen as deceitful today (most Catholic colleges now have courses on non-Catholic beliefs). To teach only Thomist philosophy in a philosophy department would be seen as deceitful today, although before Vatican II this was the norm. Generally speaking, for a theologian to be a propagandist rather than a teacher would be seen as deceitful; for church authorities to be propagandists rather than teachers would similarly be seen as deceitful. According to a recent Vatican instruction, the official task of theologians is only that of "presenting and illustrating the doctrine of the faith" as established from above. There is no room for public dissent. (See "Instruction on the Ecclesial Vocation of the Theologians," #22, *Origins* [July 5, 1990].) Most scholars in theological and religious studies oppose such a view as obsolete. Even John Paul II has retreated from integral traditionalism: he is not essentially a Thomist, and his social philosophy borders on radicalism. Yet, on divorce, official Catholic teaching is as one-sided and partial as ever: only the strictest traditional view is presented. There has never been any public discussion of divorce before, during, or since Vatican II. One might say that divorce is a taboo, along with the ordination of women and sexual morality. While in the past such practices were seen as pastoral, today we increasingly see them as deceitful.

Let me turn to annulments. In the United States, annulments rose from 368 in 1968 to 58,000 per year in the 1984–1994 period (see Coleman 1988; Vasoli 1998), down to about 40,000 in recent years. Most contemporaries view with alarm the doubling of the divorce rate in twenty years, but what about the hundredfold increase of annulments in the same time period? The existence of about four hundred annulments in fifty million Catholics is quite plausible. Since civil courts also may grant annulments, how plausible would it be if the number of annulments in the civil courts were to increase one hundred times? A hundredfold increase in the number of invalid marriages is highly implausible. If four hundred annulments are plausible, 40,000 annulments are not; hence they are likely to be divorces under a different name. Realizing that 80 percent to 90 percent of all petitions for annulments are granted, 40,000 annulments a year seems like annulment-on-demand.[1] To use the same label when the content has changed is deception. I will develop this point below.

In summary, this chapter is an invitation to the reader to make judgments about common deceptions. I will conclude this chapter with a discussion of healing from public deception.

THE DECEPTION OF THE CREATIONIST/ABSOLUTIST VISION OF MARRIAGE

It is my thesis that a major source of deception about annulments comes from the creationist/absolutist conception of marriage. In this view, marriage is an unchangeable divine institution to be understood literally like the creation of the world in seven days; this view is said to be based on Scripture.

Most generally, the creationist view holds that "God himself is the author of marriage" (*Gaudium et Spes* §48.1). This formula is vague and misleading: What kind of marriage did God create, polygamy (the patriarchs were polygamous) or monogamy? If monogamy, did God also create patriarchy (the universally accepted form of marriage in Judaism and the Roman Empire)? One might indeed say that God created birds and butterflies if it is assumed that God also created evolution. One might say that God created the American Constitution if it is assumed that God created human intelligence. Indeed, God created males and females, thus making possible both marriage and celibacy in their various forms. The pious sacralization of human institutions can be self-serving, and the purpose is to oppose change.

The creationist/absolutist philosophy of marriage has been incorporated into canon law, but it is only implicit, as if taken for granted. In the first canon on marriage, it is stated that this institution "has been raised by Christ our Lord to the dignity of a sacrament" (canon 1055). This canon assumes implicitly that marriage was first instituted by God. But marriage became recognized as a sacrament in both East and West only in the thirteenth century; hence it is *the church*—not the Lord—that raised marriage to the dignity of a sacrament. Is the sacrament of marriage absolutely necessary? A recent commentary on canon law (Coriden et al. 1985:741) raises the issue: "Although there is no scriptural evidence of direct institution by Christ, the sacramentality of marriage is grounded in His saving work." Not only is it acknowledged that there is no "scriptural evidence for direct institution"; it is also implied that since all sacraments are grounded in Christ's saving work, the church might have instituted more than seven, or maybe fewer than seven sacraments. In such a perspective, then, sacraments are social constructs, not God-created institutions, as implied in the first canon on marriage.

"The essential properties of marriage are unity and indissolubility, which in Christian marriage obtain a special firmness in virtue of the sacrament" (canon 1056). Because of its divine institution, marriage must be, by virtue of philosophical necessity, monogamous and indissoluble. The practice of the patriarchs' polygamy is not seen as an objection here. In light of a theory of theological "development" (the equivalent of the secular theory of progress) later stages of development are seen as higher than previous ones; hence today's monogamy must be seen as superior and absolute (this philosophy of religious progress is also often presented as divine pedagogy). The same reasoning applies to Christian marriage as perfecting natural marriage: it enjoys "special firmness." What this "special firmness" is, is left unsaid; it is contradicted by the fact that Christian marriages in the West (United States, United Kingdom, Scandinavia, Germany, France, etc.) are less "firm" than non-Christian marriages in the Far East if measured by divorce rates.

What we have in the above canons is an absolutist vision of marriage based on a literal interpretation of the Genesis text. According to the creationist view, all species—birds and butterflies—were directly created by God and have remained such ever since. Similarly in a creationist view of marriage, the institution of marriage is God-made and has never changed; social customs are corruptions or deviations from the divine plan. Hence there is no need to refer to the variety of marriages around the world, especially since most marriage systems include forms of divorce, and in a few cases, limited forms of polygamy.

Marriage is defined as a "marital contract" (canon 1055, 2). A marriage contract is "brought about by the consent of the parties. . . . Matrimonial consent is an act of the will . . ." (canon 1057). Furthermore, "A valid marriage between baptized persons is called . . . consummated if the parties have performed . . . the conjugal act" (canon 1061). These canons extend the absolutist vision of marriage as (1) a contract, (2) an act of the will, and (3) as consummated by intercourse. This absolutist vision can be seen at work in traditional and/or authoritarian societies such as China and India, where a marriage contract comes into existence by the will of the parents (rather than the parties) and is consummated by intercourse, at times coerced. In the West (and East), however, marriage as a contract consummated by intercourse is obsolete. Such a view is likely to be seen as deceptive.

Finally, following *Gaudium et Spes*, marriage is defined as a covenant (canon 1055). To explain such a view, commentators follow two lines of thought; the marriage covenant is compared to either the Yahweh–Israel covenant, or the covenant between Christ and the church.

According to Scripture, the covenant at Sinai between Yahweh and "his" people was one of fear and inequality. On the third day, when Yahweh was to appear, "there were peals of thunder and flashes of lightning . . . the people in the camp were all terrified" (Exod. 19:16). Moses explains to the people that fear "is to keep you from sin" (Exod. 20:20), a very traditional teaching ever since. Ten centuries later, when the church became the new bride, the "marriage" between Yahweh and Israel became bigamous (Origen's expression). Clearly the covenant between Yahweh and Israel does not illustrate well even the absolutist vision of marriage as a free contract, brought about by the consent of the parties themselves. The covenant between Yahweh and Israel was not really free, nor was it ratified except in fear. Hence in our times of gender and political equality and great aversion to all forms of coercion, religious and otherwise, the patriarchal image of one-sided covenant is not very appealing to egalitarian couples.

Many commentators (e.g., Coriden et al. 1985:740) see the covenant between Christ and the church as the ultimate model for Christian life. This view can be seen as a development of Eph. 5:25: "Husbands love your wives as Christ loved the church." However, this development turns the *sacramentum* of marriage on its head. In Eph. 5:31–32, it is the union of husband and wife that is the *sacramentum* of the union of Christ and the church, not the other way around. The author of the epistle uses a metaphor, that is, a figure of speech that explains the unknown by that which is known. It is through metaphors that God can be known, according to scholasticism and Scripture. According to Rom. 1:20–21 God's "invisible attributes, that is to say, his everlasting power and deity, have been visible ever since the world began." It is through the visible signs of creation that the Creator can be known. By putting this metaphor on its head, one comes to say that creation is best known through its invisible divine attributes. Are the divine attributes of Christ's relationship to the church our best model for everyday life, according to the author of Ephesians? Clearly not, since the author writes in continuation: "Husbands should love their wives as they do their own bodies. He who loves his wife loves himself" (Eph. 5:28). Reference is made here to a common saying about loving oneself and one's body. This text refers to common knowledge, not an inverted metaphor.

Marriage as covenant understood as a reversed metaphor is a form of mystical Platonism that posits the invisible attributes of God as norms for the visible reality. It may give rise to flowery rhetoric, but in practical terms its content tends to be empty and unreal. This point is of great importance, since much Catholic devotional and exhortational literature is based on reversed metaphors. To wit: it is martyrs and confessors, holy monks, priests, and nuns who were (are) the traditional devotional models of religious life, and by default, of married life. Reversed metaphors allow for easy devotional rhetoric but offer no concrete models for life.

The above leads us to express fundamental questions. Could there be more than seven sacraments? Could there be fewer than seven? Are there major and minor sacraments? Are some sacraments (e.g., confession, anointing of the sick) mainly devotional practices? In what sense is marriage a sacrament? What is the special firmness that differentiates sacramental from nonsacramental marriages? What would be a meaningful theory of sacraments today? I will come back to these issues in the conclusion. Let me now turn to two deceptive claims: that Scripture and tradition are definite about divorce, and that Christian marriages cannot be dissolved by any human power.

THE NEW TESTAMENT TEXTS AND THE COUNCIL OF TRENT
ARE NOT DEFINITE ABOUT INDISSOLUBILITY

I can only summarize here what will be said more at length later. In short, the New Testament contains no clear and definite statement on indissolubility. Two major texts in Matthew contain an exception clause that remains unsettled among scholars since early Christianity. Although Jesus condemned divorce unequivocally, this is not the issue: no known society ever praised divorce; all newlyweds want their marriage to last forever. Moreover, what needs to be explained convincingly is the meaning of Jesus' teaching on marriage and divorce: Is it an ideal? an evangelical counsel? a mandate? a commandment?

The Synoptics did not address the issue of what to do when a marriage fails. Paul's conception of marriage as "concession" (1 Cor. 7:6–9) does address the question. In case of marital breakdown between a pagan and a Christian, Paul does not oppose divorce; "in such case the Christian husband or wife is under no compulsion"; they may remarry (1 Cor. 7:16). There were probably no divorced Christians in the early Christian communities; hence, Paul has no advice for them. It is likely, however, that he would have applied his principle, "it is better to marry than to burn," to the divorced (see 1 Cor. 7:9). Is it better to burn than to remarry? The Catholic Church persistently refuses to address the question. According to an editorialist, "The church's willing sacrifice of the 90 percent of divorced Catholics who don't bother with annulments is a tragedy" (*CFFC* [Summer 1997]: 42). The church prefers to look the other way. This is blindness; in view of the editorial just quoted, "Many of these Catholics, estranged from their church, either go to other denominations, or forgo church completely."

Such was not the case in early Christianity. We know from Origen (185–253) that certain churches permitted remarriage while the spouse was still alive, although the ideal of one marriage per lifetime (even after the death of one's spouse) was vehemently championed by others. In case of adultery, remarriage was usually allowed for the innocent spouse, because of the early Christians' understanding of Matthew's exception clause. In 401 Jerome wrote the funeral eulogy of Fabiola, who had dismissed her husband for immorality and remarried. Jerome justifies her deed in reference to Paul's principle: "it is better to marry than to burn," and Paul's similar advice (1 Tim. 5:14–15) to young widows to remarry rather than become grounds for gossip. How much concession should be allowed? This question is pastoral and cultural. Not too strangely, it is about how much concession should be allowed in celibacy, marriage, and divorce that Eastern and Western churches parted, and, centuries later, Protestantism and Roman Catholicism.

Divorce under precise circumstances was accepted by a few early councils and fathers of the church. Eastern Christianity as a whole never banned divorce, and Orthodox Christianity is again in communication with Rome. The Council of Florence (1438–1439) did not see divorce in the Eastern churches as an obstacle to the reunion with Rome. The Reformers came to similar conclusions about divorce on the basis of their own understanding of Scripture, more particularly of Matt. 19:9.

The Council of Trent did not settle the issue. The bishops of Segovia and Modena even expressed the view that indissolubility was a question of discipline, not doctrine. Thanks to the intervention of the representative of Venice, a moderate view prevailed. In canon 7 the council fathers accomplished the nearly impossible task of condemning the Reformers without condemning the early fathers and Eastern Christians. Canon 7 condemns those (Reformers) who reject the *church's right* to teach "that the bond of marriage cannot be dissolved because of adultery of either spouse." The contention is on power and discipline, not doctrine: the Catholic Church claims to have the *right to teach* and administer authoritatively in the sphere of marriage; the Protestants denied such a right; the question of doctrine was thus bypassed. The text also implicitly acknowledges that the Eastern churches' traditions accepting divorce may equally be "in conformity with evangelical and apostolic doctrine."

At the end of his three volumes of inquiry into the theology of marriage, Theodore Mackin comes to the same conclusion, calling "inconclusive" the official Catholic position (1989:659).

CHRISTIAN MARRIAGES CANNOT BE DISSOLVED BY ANY HUMAN POWER: NOT ACCURATE

According to canon law (canon 1141), ratified and consummated marriages between persons who are baptized "cannot be dissolved by any human power or for any reason other than death." The "baptized" referred to here include not only Catholics but also, according to one commentary on canon law (see Coriden et al. 1985:811), "most Protestants and all Orthodox." But it is false to say that Protestant and Orthodox marriages cannot be dissolved in and by their own churches,[2] and legitimately so. The Orthodox churches with which Paul VI reestablished communication obviously can, but from a Roman perspective they *should not,* allow divorce and remarriage. The same can be said about Protestants: they *should not,* according to canon law, recognize divorce among baptized believers. Hence the meaning of *cannot,* in reference to Protestants and all Orthodox, is *should not.*

Unknown to the fathers of Trent was the development of the Petrine privilege, which allowed marriage dissolution in special cases, for example, in foreign missions. In the constitutions *Altitudo* in 1537 and *Romani Pontifices* in 1571, the papacy recognized itself as having the right to annul nonsacramental marriages, even when the person requesting the annulment neither was nor intended to become Catholic, as in the 1959 case when Pius XI in 1924 granted a dissolution "in favor of the faith" to an American from the state of Montana, a foreign mission at the time (see Mackin 1984:15). This made big newspaper headlines. The Petrine privilege rests on the distinction between sacramental and nonsacramental marriages. All marriages, Christian and non-Christian are said to be indissoluble, but marriages between non-Christians (e.g., a man asking for baptism but married to several wives) can be dissolved by Petrine privilege (Mackin calls this "dissoluble indissolubility," a paradoxical term and reality). All sacramental marriages among Christians, Catholics and non-Catholics, are theoretically indissoluble, but non-Catholic marriages are commonly dissolved as a matter of fact. Moreover, the indissolubility of sacramental marriages among non-Catholics is often denied in practice: a Catholic wanting to marry a divorced Protestant need not worry: the Protestant party's previous marriage and divorce are simply considered invalid, as having never existed. Hence, the traditional Catholic distinctions as well as the traditional practices are not convincing today, as suggested by the very abrogation of the Petrine privilege proceedings (five thousand petitions for dissolution from the United States alone were pending in 1970 when the practice was abruptly suspended; see Noonan 1972:366).

It would be a moderate position to say that the Roman Church does not recognize itself as having the power to dissolve sacramental marriages. If the church has no power to divorce, however, *it is false to say that "no human power" whatsoever,* religious or secular, has such a power (the claim of canon 1141) because civil authorities grant divorces quite frequently. It may be presumptuous to speak in absolute terms about the power of the Catholic Church to grant divorce (e.g., the church *never has and never will* have this power). In more relative terms I would say that *so far* the church of Rome has neither recognized itself as having the right to grant divorce, *nor has it in modern times ever considered this issue seriously and openly,* in an ecumenical dialogue. Before we address the deception of annulments, we must consider what seems to be the crux of the matter: theological pluralism.

THE CRUX OF THE MATTER:
THE HIERARCHY OF TRUTHS VERSUS INTEGRISM

The reader may have noticed my occasional critique of canon law or even Vatican II. On what grounds can one criticize evangelists, council documents, papal statements, or canon law? This question cannot be eluded.

One of the most revolutionary insights of Vatican II—indeed *the* most revolutionary one in my view—is the proclamation of a hierarchy of truths. "The unique church of Christ which in the Creed we avow as one, holy, catholic, and apostolic . . . subsists in the Catholic Church . . . although *many elements of sanctification and truth* can be found outside of her visible structure" (*Lumen Gentium* 8; emphasis added). If *many* elements of truth subsist outside Catholicism (more in some religious bodies than in others), and if some of the most important truths subsist in Catholicism (rather than the other way around), then there is a hierarchy of truths. The text also assumes a hierarchy of ethical values and practices ("elements of sanctification").

Unfortunately Vatican II did not elaborate the notion of a hierarchy of truths. A few years later, at the first meeting of the international theological commission in 1969, Karl Rahner developed the thesis of pluralism in the church (text in *IDOC International Documentation*, No. 13). This statement came in the aftermath of *Humanae Vitae* (1968) on birth control. Now Pandora's box was wide open. What opened the box is this: Vatican II had implicitly proclaimed a hierarchy of truths, and the magisterium had failed to explain it in concrete and practical terms. In the context of *Humanae Vitae*, everyone had to create their own hierarchy of truths, on birth control first, sexual morality next, and later, about the authority of the church itself.

In relationship to Scripture, tradition, and the teaching of the magisterium, there are only two possible alternatives: integrism (or integralism), which holds that all truths are equally valid (the pre-Vatican II position), or a hierarchy of truths, which holds not only that some truths are more important than others but also that choices are possible, if not necessary. Pandora's box has been opened; there is no way to close it again. It would be regrettable if the church at large were to follow the second alternative and the magisterium the first.

Without the notion of a hierarchy of truths, orthodox Catholicism can be compared to Orthodox Judaism. There are 613 commandments in Jewish law; they include prescriptions about health, diet, ritual, as well as moral behavior. Orthodox Judaism recognizes no hierarchy among them; one must obey *all* the commandments of the Lord, from first to last. Similarly, without a hierarchy of truths, traditional Catholicism is a complex set of beliefs and practices which include dogmas, the rosary, Lourdes and Fatima, the miraculous medal, the Sacred Heart, the First Friday mass, filial devotion to pope and bishops, and so on. Similarly, without a notion of hierarchy, all the texts of the New Testament are equally normative, all conciliar documents, all papal statements are equally important. In such a perspective, all biblical, conciliar, and papal documents can be (and have been) itemized, from birth control to smoking, and used for didactic teaching. Then the faithful (and the lower clergy as well) become the passive recipients of the latest papal or episcopal pronouncements.

Both theological pluralism and the notion of a hierarchy of truths are generally accepted today. Unfortunately, the magisterium has failed to provide guidelines for interpretation. In the absence of the latter, one has to make one's choice. Thus it seems to me that the logia of Jesus are not on the same plane as the social philosophies of Paul or Peter (e.g., about women and obedience to the Roman emperor). Similarly, not all papal documents, not all council statements, not all canons of canon law are equally insightful; some seem obsolete and unenlightened. Many papal documents betray the social philosophy of their time, making them obsolete decades later. Without a hierarchy of truths, papal documents would be a dull encyclopedia about the evils of the time. But with a hierarchy of truths, lost insights can be retrieved, and new life can be given to ideas found in obsolete forms of expression.

About marriage and divorce, the council's statement about the preservation of truth outside the Catholic Church should make us rediscover some of the truths lost in Catholicism. Some practices of compassion toward divorced people found in the early church may well have survived in orthodoxy and found a new life in Protestantism.

THE DECEPTION OF ANNULMENTS

New guidelines for annulment were introduced by Paul VI and later institutionalized in the 1983 Code of Canon Law. To the traditional grounds for annulment (insanity and impotence prior to marriage, insufficient use of reason, impairment of judgment through coercion or addiction—also accepted by most civil courts) were added psychological grounds such as the inability "of assuming the essential obligations of matrimony due to causes of psychological nature" (canon 1095, 3). In an important decision the Rota called this "emotional immaturity"; it consists of "gross and sustained impairment in social relationships, e.g. lack of appropriate affective responsibility, inappropriate clinging, asociability, lack of empathy" (Coriden et al. 1985:778). But with such vague terms as "emotional immaturity" or "lack of empathy," no marriage is safe anymore. The Catholic Church has opened its gates to the pro-divorce culture.

The introduction of no-fault divorce in the 1970s is often considered the beginning of the pro-divorce culture in the Unites States. Not only is there no need of grounds for divorce, but also and more importantly, one spouse can divorce the other without the other's consent. This view is now quasi-universally accepted in the United States, on the basis that marriage is not a prison, and that one person cannot be coerced to stay in a relationship against his or her will. Such is also the Catholic practice: either spouse can introduce a petition for annulment; the cooperation of the other spouse is desirable but not mandatory. In some extreme cases, annulments have been granted without even the knowledge of the other party.

Although there are great similarities between "irretrievable differences" and "emotional immaturity," and between divorce-on-demand and annulments-almost-on-demand, there is one fundamental difference: while civil courts conclude that the marriage is dead, Catholic tribunals always conclude that the marriage never existed. Although one can easily understand that an insane person cannot contract a valid marriage (something obvious to most educated observers), the claim that an emotionally immature or socially unempathetic person cannot contract a valid marriage is not obvious at all.

One major ground for annulment is a "grave lack of discretion of judgement concerning the essential matrimonial rights and duties" (canon 1095, 2). According to Terence Tierney (1993:44) this lack of judgment "does not mean that a person is suffering from any specific psychological problem. . . . It refers specifically to a person's lack of discretion of judgment about the special and lifelong obligations of marriage." Among the various obligations of marriage the author mentions "oblatory love" [sic] (pp. 14–15), respect for conjugal morality (pp. 16–18), and responsibility in establishing conjugal friendship (pp. 21–22).

In the course of an annulment proceeding or trial, implicit rather than explicit definitions of psychological and/or emotional immaturity are used by the judges to come to a decision. Because what is immaturity to one judge may not be immaturity to another, the working definitions are likely to be influenced by casuistry, that is, the case-by-case analysis of annulments. Since the marriage of an annulment petitioner has already be dissolved by a divorce court, the ecclesiastical court is likely to corroborate the conclusions of the civil court and conclude that the marriage was invalid. The notion of immaturity may also convey guilt and shame. The procedure may be compared to the treatment of prison inmates who in order to be paroled must acknowledge that they are psychologically sick. However, by acknowledging psychological and/or emotional immaturity, the petitioner is led to believe that he/she should seek psychological treatment rather than spiritual guidance; in other words, when a religious court of law becomes a court of psychological maturity, at least one of the parties is likely to leave shameful, empty, and disillusioned.

How efficient is the new law? Not very. Out of 262,683 Catholic divorces granted in the United States in 1992, only about 13 percent applied for an annulment. The numbers are even lower elsewhere: only 4 percent of divorced French Catholics applied for an annulment (Orsy 1997:12). Clearly something is not working. Having lost during the last century most of its secular power in national and international affairs, the church is holding to its judicial power over the faithful in dissolving marriages. This need for power is obsolete, but the need for pastoral service to the divorced is real.

PASTORAL APPROACHES TO DIVORCE

There are many aspects of divorce which deserve our attention but which will not be addressed here. For instance, in the United States we live in a pro-divorce rather than a pro-marriage culture (see Popenoe 1996; Whitehead 1997). The Catholic Church contributes to it through its policy of quasi annulments on demand (at a 90 percent acceptance rate, according to Coyle-Hennessey 1993:164). This change is mainly due to the no-fault divorce laws. Among Americans, however, very few want to return to the pre-1970 legislation.

Divorced people are often confronted with the feeling of failure. It is important to distinguish between psychological flaws (e.g., wrong attitudes) and moral failures (wrong deeds or sins). Socially, divorce sanctions the failure of a relationship, not a moral failure. Rather than pointing the finger at who is to be blamed (the traditional grounds for divorce), it is important to find out what went wrong at the psychological level. This psychological dimension is also a spiritual one. Hence its importance in a religious context.

Most generally speaking, a relationship can be seen as a struggle to find a balance between communion with others and separation from them, or, in different terms, between intimacy to the point of fusion and identity to the point of isolation from others (Rice and Rice, 1986). Fused with the mother at birth, the child must learn to differentiate without becoming estranged. Spouses must learn to be one, without being fused to one another. We must immerse ourselves in professional activities without loss of self. When a relationship falters (with or without divorce), it is often due to intimacy and/or separation problems.

The relationship between the church and world can also be analyzed in these terms. The church needs to be of this world without fusing with it. The early church quickly adapted to the Roman culture; it did so well that twenty centuries later the Catholic liturgy was still in Latin. The church immersed itself in the medieval culture so well that it often still thinks in medieval deductive schemes. The papacy indulged in Renaissance art and Counter-Reformation authoritarianism so well that it has a hard time outgrowing its past. The local church, too, goes through phases of inculturation and eschatological separation from regional cultures.

Any failure (including relationship failures) can be an experience of grace and growth and the occasion for a better balance between identity and separation. For the time being, by rejecting pastoral solutions to the problem of divorce, the Catholic Church stands as judge, not as healer; this is unfortunate, for only a healer can help one find grace and growth.

If any failure can be an occasion for grace and growth, the church must learn to heal its failures. John XXIII's appeal for *aggiornamento* through listening to the outside world may now mean that we must listen to the church's internal problems. How many divorced and remarried Catholics accept to live as "brothers and sisters" as required by Catholic teaching? Are there any at all? Let us listen to the stories of divorced Catholics and their healing or nonhealing in new marriages. What do women have to say about the impact of the male leadership on marriage teaching? It is only by listening that the church will be able to heal from its failures and to make these very failures an occasion for grace and growth.

CONCLUSION: THE HEALING FROM DECEPTION

The pastoral dimension of this book will be the healing from the deception of misleading church teaching. Whether this deception is due to selective listening on the part of the faithful or to unintentionally misleading teaching on the part of leaders is not our concern.

Catholic teaching is deceiving when the basic issues allowing for a variety of interpretations are not addressed. Here are some basic issues.

- What is marriage? What is the difference between a Catholic and a Protestant marriage? between a marriage of Catholics in front of a justice of the peace and one witnessed by a priest? What is the essence of marriage? Is it spousal love, *affectio maritalis,* as in Roman law and for most of our contemporaries in the West? Is marriage essentially a contract? Is it a contract that can be terminated by the decision of both parties? If not, why not? Is marriage "two in one flesh" as in intercourse? Is marriage more than intercourse? Is marriage "two in one" because, as in ancient Judaism, the married woman had no social or economic identity apart from her husband's? Should the Hebrew "two in one flesh" be translated as "two in one love"?

- What do biblical texts say about marriage and divorce, according to scholarly and nonpartisan (nondenominationally biased) research? How relevant for us today is Paul's position on marriage as concession to "those who cannot control themselves"? Is it better to burn than to remarry, or better to remarry than to burn? To what extent was the medieval theory of marriage borrowed from Roman stoicism and determined for centuries by Augustinian pessimism?

- In light of the Vatican II vision that the catholic truth of Jesus Christ subsists in various ways in all Christian denominations, what can Roman Catholics learn from past and present practices in Orthodoxy and Anglicanism?

- How meaningful are annulments-almost-on-demand at the rate of forty thousand per year? How can the grounds for divorce in a civil court become grounds for the nonexistence of marriage in an ecclesiastic court?

- What do surveys say about the beliefs of bishops, priests, and lay people on marriage, celibacy, and divorce? Do Protestant ministers experience divorce? Do marriage counselors experience divorce? If so, what is the meaning of divorce over the life cycle?

- Is there a positive view of remarriage as "second chance"? The imagery of God's marriage to a "new bride" for a "new covenant" is pervasive in both the Jewish and the Christian Scriptures. What can be done to make remarriage really a second chance? Our answer will be faith, both theological and institutional, or a better balance between the two.

Let us briefly turn to personal testimonies of pain, resentment, and deception, before we tackle the theoretical issues of Catholic divorce.

Notes

1. "Annulments are not difficult to obtain, given the streamlined procedures of the church's *Code of Canon Law* and the expanded psychological grounds for nul-

lity. In the last twenty years, there has been an explosion of petitions for annulments and, today, nine out of ten petitioners who complete the process receive a declaration of nullity" (Coyle-Hennessey 1993:164).

2. Orthodoxy does not dissolve marriages; the Orthodox Church only recognizes the fact that given marriages have become spiritually dead. It is only when marriages are seen as contracts, as in the West, that they must be dissolved when they are actually dead.

WORKS CITED

Coleman, Gerald D.
     1988   *Divorce and Remarriage in the Catholic Church*. New York: Paulist Press.
Coriden, James A., Thomas J. Green, and Donald E. Heintschel
     1985   *The Code of Canon Law: A Text and Commentary*. Mahwah, N.J.: Paulist Press.
Coyle-Hennessey, Bobbi
     1993   *Once More With Love*. Notre Dame, Ind.: Ave Maria Press.
L'Huillier, Peter
     1988   "The Indissolubility of Marriage in Orthodox Law and Practice." *St. Vladimir Theological Quarterly* 32, no 3.
Mackin, Theodore
     1984   *Divorce and Remarriage*. Mahwah, N.J.: Paulist Press.
     1989   *The Marital Sacrament*. Mahwah, N.J.: Paulist Press.
Noonan, John T., Jr.
     1972   *Power to Dissolve*. Cambridge, Mass.: Harvard University Press.
Orsy, Ladislas
     1997   "Marriage Annulments: An Interview with Ladislas Orsy." *America*, October 4, 1997.
Peterson, Richard R.
     1996   "A Re-Evaluation of the Economic Consequences of Divorce." *American Sociological Review* 61 (June).
Popenoe, David, ed.
     1996   *Promises to Keep*. Lanham, Md.: Rowman & Littlefield.
Rice, Joy K., and David G. Rice
     1986   *Living Through Divorce*. New York: Guilford Press.
Tierney, Terence E.
     1993   *Annulment: Do You Have a Case?* New York: Alba House.

Vasoli, Robert H.

1998   *What God Has Joined Together: The Annulment Crisis in American Catholicism.* New York: Oxford University Press.

Weitzman, Lenore

1985   *The Divorce Revolution.* New York: Free Press.

Whitehead, Barbara Dafoe

1997   *The Divorce Culture.* New York: Knopf.

2

Testimonies: Letters Mailed to Catholics Speak Out

SELECTED BY CHARLES N. DAVIS

MOM SHOULD HAVE BEEN ALLOWED
TO REMARRY

M Y EARLIEST MEMORIES OF FAMILY LIFE are positively idyllic. I loved my parents and wanted to please them, but I felt especially close to my Dad. He was a truant officer and he'd take me on his rounds with him while my mother stayed home with my two sisters.

When he enlisted in the Army during World War II, he came to my room to say goodbye. I was very unhappy and very worried. I was afraid he would get hurt and never come home. He was very reassuring and minimized the danger. He promised to come home but never did really.

My first premonition that something was not quite right occurred on the morning of my First Holy Communion. Dad told me he had forgotten to fast, so he wouldn't be receiving communion. He was living at Fort Sheridan and began his career in the Regular Army.

Nana, Mom's mother, came to live with us after she was widowed. Mom needed her help since Dad was away. I remember years of financial difficulty. Dad's visits became fewer and fewer. Finally they stopped. Mom acted really strange. She cried a lot and grandmother tried to keep us from bothering her. Mom and Nana argued a lot, and we girls fought with them and

The letters in this chapter were first published in the *National Catholic Reporter,* July 4, 1997. For more about their origin, see p. 46 below.

with each other. Nana admonished us to be nice to Mom because of what she was going through trying to support all of us.

It was not till seven years later . . . when I asked Mom if she and Dad were considering a divorce. She looked so sad. That night she told all of us that Dad had divorced her a number of years ago. We were shocked, hurt, and very angry.

She explained that Dad had started dating a girl who was in the Women's Army Corps on a military base and got her pregnant. She threatened him with his career. In those days the Army wouldn't put up with scandal. His career meant more to him than his marriage did. It didn't help to hear that she was the daughter of a Protestant minister. She proved to be mentally unbalanced and felt that he should be divorced from his daughters too. She made his life miserable but bore him three children. She managed to keep him from visiting with us most, but not all the time. We'd see him about once every seven years.

Nana wasn't Catholic, and she felt Mom should get on with her life and that she probably would be happier if she could marry again. She urged Mom to date. Mom was reluctant. She was a convert to Catholicism, and she was faithful to the rules of the church. She knew she wasn't allowed to remarry. However, she did see a few men. One man, in particular, became a strong candidate. Then Mom had a dream about him with lobster claws. She was afraid to let him touch her. She never dated after that.

We kids were older by then, and somehow Mom managed to send us to Catholic schools. We knew Mom wasn't supposed to remarry even though she had not been the one to seek the divorce. We used that as an excuse to give her a rough time. We didn't want her to remarry. Perhaps we were still hoping Dad would come back.

We were very competitive and unruly at times. Even Mom's friends told us we were to blame for her unhappiness. I felt very betrayed by Dad and blamed Mom for Lord knows what. I was still crazy about Dad, and he could do no wrong I guess. I was confused. Mom had at least stayed with us and supported us; it seemed we were just an unpleasant duty to her.

Mom would go to confession and tell the priest that she didn't know if she could go on, and the priest would tell her that at least she had her children. Then she would cry a lot and tell us what he had said, obviously resenting it deeply. She would spend hours at our bedroom door, explaining her situation and pleading for us to behave. Then she'd cry. I did feel awful for her, and I was convinced that I was an awful, even sinful, child.

She was so depressed that she begged Nana to put her in an institution. We used to call this a mental breakdown in those days.

I feel the Army did us no favor by being the righteous enforcer of morality, forcing Dad to make a choice between us and his career. And I feel the church was dead wrong to deny my mother a chance for happiness. Yes, you should work at a marriage, but why would God or the church not want Mom to get on with her life and find happiness in a second marriage if that's what would make her happy? Didn't Christ come to bring us life and bring it more abundantly? Instead, she held a torch for my Dad for years and kept expecting he would come back, and she did this way past the time when it was rational or healthy.

Mom was looked upon as a divorced woman, and she encountered outrageous and undeserved suspicion and exclusion at work and even at church. We moved to a small town after Nana died. At times, the abuse became very pronounced. Mom had found work as an industrial nurse. It was a good job and it paid well. Eventually, Mom acquired a reputation for kindness and compassion; and she was much loved. But it didn't have to be that difficult. We didn't need to endure wounds made worse by Army regulations and church rules.

I have come to believe that to marry legally or in the church is less important than to commit to each other's well-being and that of one's children. What is important is mutual respect, love, understanding, and a commitment to the relationship. Mom's marriage to Dad ceased to have those characteristics. It was no longer a marriage. It was not fair to expect Mom to hold up her end of the contract/commitment when the other end was no longer there. Was she supposed to cast herself upon the funeral pyre? Why? Was this a ruling that gave witness to any of the attributes of our loving Father? I would challenge you to name one.

THE PAINFUL ANNULMENT PROCESS

This letter is from a nurse practitioner, married in 1970 and separated in 1991. Her marriage was annulled in 1996.

I am the one who chose to end the twenty-one-year marriage. The best explanation that I can give for the marriage ending is to say that one of the people in the couple grew and changed and the other refused to grow and change. I am the one who changed. There were many factors that promoted my growth and development: ongoing higher education, the birth of my children, family crises, and my own personal choice to understand my own behavior better. For me and my former spouse, the marriage was initially salvific; we had each desperately needed someone and because our dysfunctional families were so alike in many ways the pairing was a naturally occurring event that stabilized both people for quite some time.

Eventually, the marriage became unmanageable. Our children were witnesses to and part of an abusive cycle where their father would go for weeks and not speak to me. When conversation occurred, it was usually in argument or confrontation, and toward the end there were a few instances of hitting and shoving. The tension in the household over the final four years of the marriage was so intense that both of our children are able to reflect and say that these were the worst of times. I stayed in the marriage as long as I did out of fear and monetary constraints. When I left, I was able to pay three months' rent on a townhouse, including a deposit, and I had a car and credit cards in my name. These latter things came about over time as I quietly prepared to leave.

After I left, I had an immediate sense of relief. There was also a part of me that hoped that my estranged husband would look at his behavior (or the lack of it) and want to do something to get us back together again. I waited four years to file for divorce; the separation agreement was signed before I left the marital household (attorney's advice), and that agreement is what became part of the divorce decree.

Both of my children were/are aware that I have dated. At some point, my son informed me that unless I received an annulment from the Roman Catholic Church, I would not be following the rules of the church and I couldn't consider myself a Catholic in good standing. (I had tried to raise both of my children in the Catholic/Christian tradition and they knew that I had an old saying which basically was—you must play by the rules of an organization if you want to be considered a functional member of that organization.) So, with thoughts of my children in mind, I decided to explore the annulment process; this was long before the divorce was final. I went to several workshops and presentations and read what I could find on annulment. Eventually, I concluded that the process wouldn't be that bad and that it might enable me to write to the issues at hand and get rid of some more "baggage." Also, I really did believe that my former husband and I were "set up" as a couple to not be successful in a long-term marriage because of the dysfunctionality in our families of origin. So, initially it seemed all right to say that we were not really capable of knowing what we were doing when we got married because neither of us had any role model for what a good marriage should look like.

My divorce was final in August of 1995; the day after the decree was granted, I filed my annulment papers. In preparation for this event, I had six meetings with a deacon at St. Mary of Sorrows; this parish "sponsored" my annulment, and this deacon accompanied me to the annulment hearing. In addition, I met with a friend (priest) who had served on the tribunal for many years. One point became obvious, that no matter what I wrote, the major emphasis had to be that the marriage bond had not existed from the beginning. So, in writing up my "case," I addressed the issues that I knew existed in both my and my former spouse's families of origin: abuse, lack of intimacy and inappropriate role models for relationships. My focus was that this type of home life could not prepare anyone for making a good choice in a marriage partner and, in fact, actually impaired both parties in advancing in growth and development of their respective persons and made them incapable of long-term commitment. During the hearing, the monsignor who was conducting the proceedings repeatedly tried to get me to say that I thought from the very beginning that the marriage wasn't going to last forever or that I wasn't committed from the very beginning. I never agreed to that because it wasn't true. Both my former spouse and I wanted a family so badly, I believe that we never entertained the thought that it would not last. We also believed that we could do anything.

After the hearing, I had to secure three witnesses who would write to different aspects of my life: someone who knew me as a child, someone who knew me when I was dating my spouse, and someone who knew me when I was married. I chose my brother, a close girlfriend, and a friend from my former neighborhood. Fortunately for me, these people love me, because the lengthy questionnaire (seventy-three questions, I think) was filled with embarrassing questions that made all three people feel very uncomfortable. The questionnaire was identical for all three of them, which is stupid because each was chosen to address a different period of my life. My brother was barely able to complete his questionnaire; he had never addressed the abuse that occurred in our family to anyone but me and his wife. My girlfriend was appalled that she would be commenting on how I managed my sex life and dating as a young person as well as how I had managed my money in my marriage. And my friend from my old neighborhood completed the form, but told me later that after the experience she would never file for an annulment because what was asked on that questionnaire was no one's business and she would not share that with anyone.

I also had to meet with a psychologist provided by the tribunal. He had to interview both me and my former spouse. (The latter did cooperate because he did not want the marriage to be annulled and he wanted his story told.) The meeting with the psychologist was probably the high point of the entire experience; he understood what I had written and we had a good conversation about my own healing and what I was doing to take care of me. He ended the interview by telling me that I was one of the most courageous people that he had ever met and reaffirmed my approaches to the former spouse and my children.

The spouse also wrote his case; I assume that he was contesting the annulment. I could have made an appointment and read what he wrote at any time; I chose not to do this because there was no point to it. Reading anything that he wrote could open me up to more pain and I did not want to battle out an annulment with him. (Anything that either spouse submits can be seen by the other party but it is viewed in the presence of a tribunal staff member and cannot be duplicated.)

The final decision was made about seven months after all the witnesses had submitted their completed questionnaires. I received a letter from the diocesan tribunal office telling me that the petition had been forwarded to Baltimore and that I would probably have the final annulment decree in about a month. When it arrived, I put it away with the divorce decree.

As a professional who is a lifetime student of human growth and development, I want to comment here that I would not do this process again. While the effort did get me to put some things in perspective, what I wrote to get the annulment was not the whole story. I have no question in my mind that my former spouse and I wanted the marriage to work and I believe that a marriage bond existed in the early years. So, if the marriage was "sacramental," what happened and how do you make sense of this in light of the church's stand on the "indissolubility" of marriage? It doesn't make sense. The "whole" truth is that I needed that marriage to become who I am today and that, had I stayed in the marriage, the staying would have been an immoral act. Since the church does not educate its leaders (priests) in life-span development and views many issues of faith and morals in black-and-white terms, there is no room for growth and development of the individuals within a marriage from the church's perspective unless, of course, somehow the two individuals can manage to grow together and support one another no matter what! This is quite a feat for mere mortals who stand before God simply trying to incorporate aspects of the divine into a truly earthly experience.

Had I written how much the marriage had actually benefited me by moving me along on my own growth trajectory and how, by ending this marriage, I finally found out who I was, there would have been no annulment. I was also unable to write that for me, at the time I married, marrying my former spouse was the "right" decision. None of these statements would have "squared" with a marriage "not existing" from the beginning. So . . . in summary, I would say that the church has miles to go on the issue of separation, divorce, and remarriage. Much of this would be rectified if we had married men and women priests!

COMMUNION WITHOUT AN ANNULMENT

After my first husband's death from cancer, and shortly after my second marriage, I became interested in the Roman Catholic faith. After attending mass for a few weeks I hooked up with the RCIA (Rite of Christian Initiation for Adults) group in my town's parish and attended class on a weekly basis for more than a year.

This RCIA group was truly inspiring. The experience for me was spiritually provoking and nourishing. Our weekly discussions of Scripture opened my mind and helped me appreciate Christ's teachings and the weekly mass. I loved every minute of it. Hanging over my head was the fact that my present husband's first marriage had never been annulled, with the hint that this may affect my being accepted into the Catholic Church. I never took these hints seriously. After all, my relationship with God has nothing to do with the failure of my husband's first marriage. I watched as the RCIA class of 1996 took their First Communion at Easter, and looked forward to being welcomed by the parish in 1997.

At the beginning of Lent I was allowed to stand before the parish and declare my intention to join the church. The next evening, after my RCIA class, I was told I could go no further in the process, and could not take First Communion until my husband's marriage was annulled.

I was devastated. I felt I had been slapped in the face. I felt humiliated because the entire parish had watched me declare my intention to join, and felt they would now question why I was not a member. I attended a couple more RCIA classes, but it was very painful for me, knowing I could not take communion. So I quit. My husband had started the annulment process out of kindness to me because he did not want to see me excluded from church. However, he does not want to annul his first marriage. He feels this marriage is valid, and loves his beautiful daughter who was very much a part of it. He has not participated in any church since he was a teenager, and watching what I was going through reinforced his lowest opinion of the church's hypocritical stance to archaic rules. My husband then made the decision NOT to go through with an annulment.

This left me stranded. Not taking communion at mass made me feel very angry. As if I was being punished because my husband's first marriage had failed. I interpreted the rules as being manipulative. I felt that in an effort to force my husband's annulment, the church was punishing me by denying me communion. I stopped going to mass.

I had attended a Protestant church for many years every Sunday, and not going to church at all did not sit well with me. I really liked to worship as a Catholic, yet this church was not letting me participate in communion.

Finally it was a couple of fellow parishioners who reached out to help me. One couple involved in the RCIA program wrote asking me how I was doing. Another couple (the wife was the sponsor in my conversion) invited me over to dinner. I poured out my frustration to them and they all suggested I start taking communion without the "official" First Communion ceremony. (After all, I'd been attending classes for some thirteen or fourteen months.) My conversion sponsor's daughter also suggested I attend a parish in her neighboring town, where the priests are known to be open-minded.

So I started at the neighboring town, which reinforced my resolve to continue worshiping as a Catholic. I picked a Sunday and started receiving communion. After a few Sundays, I felt like I was hiding something every time I took communion, as if I was lying and not a "real" Catholic. I got up the courage to go to confession, and God blesses this priest for helping me through my situation. Here is what he had to say:

Roman Catholic canon law was written as a representation of an ideal, as a vision of perfection, something that all people can strive for. However, life is neither simple nor perfect, and the church knows this. The annulment process was written in recognition of this lack of perfection. As a priest, he feels the annulment process is extremely important. When marriages dissolve there may be loose ends. An annulment gives people a chance to resolve open issues and heal spiritually before committing to another relationship. As an aside, he also told me that Protestant marriages that end in divorce must also be annulled before people take communion as Catholics—the Catholic Church respects all marriages as sacred. However, as a priest, he cannot deny communion to anyone.

I argued that in my case I had no control over my husband's decision not to get an annulment, so why couldn't I take communion anyway? He said that the church looks at people as a whole. Out of respect for my marriage relationship that includes my husband, I am not supposed to take communion.

I asked if he could make an exception. He said no, that without church law, without these ideals, there would be no church. He said that bending the rules might make him a popular priest with some members of his parish—temporarily—but that he and everyone else would ultimately lose respect for him or worse, perhaps the church.

He let me know, however, that I have a choice in this matter. I can choose to take communion. He stressed that this choice is mine and mine alone to make. He said he knew of practicing Catholics whose first marriages had failed, who had not gotten annulments, who were remarried, attended mass regularly, and felt free to take communion. But the decision is up to the individual. Each individual must decide based on his or her own conscience, life circumstances, and relationship with God and church, what is best for him or herself.

I thanked him sincerely for helping me see the other side of my circumstances; I attended Saturday mass and took communion with a clear conscience.

So, without the pomp and circumstance, without the fanfare of "official" ceremonies, I am now a Catholic, and soon will be joining my new church. For what it's worth, this is my story.

NOT PUBLIC AND PERMANENT ADULTERY

I am a divorced, annulled, and remarried Catholic—and, I should add, remarried in a civil ceremony for almost twenty-four years. We waited, but the process took so long that we decided to marry in a civil ceremony. I do not feel for one moment that my husband and I are living in a "situation of public and permanent adultery," as the *Catechism* describes it. I, too, receive the sacraments in good conscience and so does my husband. We left the Catholic Church for many years because of the Vatican's position on divorce, but returned approximately three years ago. We returned for the sake of the children and at our daughter's request. It was refreshing having a priest from our parish tell me that everyone is welcome to the communion table at his parish.

I firmly believe that Jesus, who is all-loving and forgiving, does not approve of the way the present pope is stifling God's people. We must continue to pray for the hierarchy in Rome that they begin to see the real message of the gospel, love of God and love of humanity.

WHICH MARRIAGE WAS THE REAL ONE?

In June 1941 I met a man, a lawyer, who courted me so persistently that I gave in after three weeks. I purposely got married in front of a judge, a friend of his, so that the marriage wouldn't be valid. I'd tried to break it off the day after the wedding, but he pleaded that his buddies would think impotence was the grounds for annulment. So I said I'd try to learn to love him.

I sent for my baptismal certificate and went through the procedures of having the marriage recognized by the church. Then in December came Pearl Harbor. He was a reserve officer in the Army and promptly went on active duty. Our house became a place where servicemen whom he had known in schools previously could relax out of uniform, a sort of private U.S.O. It wasn't a bad life, and I was busy doing volunteer work in hospitals, and so on.

We were divorced when the war ended, and he returned to private practice. I got a job in 1946. An old family friend was already working in my town. Though I hardly knew him, I knew his grandfather well, a friend of my father, as well as his cousins. Anyway we became good friends and, in 1949, got married. We started a family—a boy was born in 1952 and a girl in 1953.

When I tried to get our marriage OK'd, all the priests said "no way." My ex-husband refused to cooperate in seeking an annulment: the old criteria still were impotence and/or nonconsummation. So we went along for about ten years. Then I read about the solution of "brother/sister," which would legitimize our cohabitation. My husband was not happy with that solution. We were separated, got back together, separated again. He wanted a divorce. Finally, he said he wanted to marry another person. So, in 1974, I gave in. I'd always hoped we would get back together until he died in 1990.

In 1986, my first husband finally got around to filling out annulment papers so I could be married in the church with my second husband, but it was too late to restore our family life.

I sent the kids to Catholic schools, but neither is Catholic now, though they both are churchgoers —one is Anglican like her dad and husband, the other a fundamentalist like his wife.

When my second husband and I had talked about marriage, I explained to him that it wouldn't be possible to be married in the church. He was Anglican and also not allowed to marry a divorced person at that time. But his subsequent marriage was in the church. Vatican II came about ten years too late for us.

I'd never felt married to my first husband. I did feel married to my second, and God blessed us with two beautiful kids. We were husband and wife, but all the priests we spoke to said it was impossible. I'd have to leave him if I wanted to receive the sacraments. But that was wrong in my eyes. It was only when my husband developed a serious relationship with another woman that I let him go, so he could be happy. And I'm quite happy in my present life as a single person.

I can see now that I should have been stronger in my conviction that the second marriage was valid and not let myself get brainwashed into the belief that it wasn't. I get to receive communion, but I lost my second husband, who at first talked about converting but became disillusioned. I was selfish, wanting to be considered a good Catholic and having our family too. I'm not exactly bitter, but only sad.

How Important Are Legalities?

My husband and I were married in November 1942, in a Catholic church. We had two children. It was mostly a happy and prosperous union but ended in divorce in February 1982. Alcoholism took its toll. I tried in many ways to stay within my faith hoping to have another marriage. I approached the archdiocese and several parishes to find a group of separated or divorced Catholics, but the only ones in existence were for widows and widowers. I also tried to get an annulment.

After five years, I married a Jewish widower in a Protestant ceremony, with an invocation by a priest and a nun. Exactly a month later, my first husband died. I went to have a mass said for him. The priest gave me a big lecture on my present marriage, but I wasn't about to change anything because I felt 100 percent Catholic.

My second husband died after six years. Very much to my own surprise, I married again a Catholic widower who had been married for fifty-three years. We had led parallel lives since youth. We are very active in our parish church. We are living a truly Catholic family life enjoying our offspring and theirs.

I feel God is inspiring and guiding me in a life of wonder and discovery.

OBSERVATIONS ABOUT ANNULMENTS
BY A CLINICAL PSYCHOLOGIST

I am a Ph.D. clinical psychologist who has been doing psychological evaluations in preparation for annulments for the past three years. Here are some of my observations.

I see only the party who wants the annulment for an evaluation, which usually takes between about one and one-and-a-half hours for the interview. I then transcribe my notes in a psychological format. I have done no psychological testing, only an interview, although I must put a DSM IV (the psychological diagnosis coding) at the end of the evaluation. This is highly questionable to me since I have not done an in-depth evaluation. I only see this person for the evaluation. I know nothing of the previous history, only what the person chooses to tell me. I have no way of knowing whether the person is telling the truth or not. As I understand it, it is the party who wants the annulment that has to go through this evaluation process, and it is this person who gets the diagnosis, usually DSM IV, Immature Personality Disorder.

It seems that an unfair burden falls on this party. It usually takes two persons to end a marriage (except when one party is an alcoholic). Both persons may have been immature at the time of the marriage, but if these people are now adults and presumably more mature, why do we still treat them as children? As adults, they know it when their marriage is over. One can go through the annulment process and fake the whole thing. There is no way of knowing this.

Parents eventually have to let their children grow up. Why does the church continue to treat its members as children rather than adults who are capable of making their own decisions?

Some people may need an annulment to help them end their marriage. In my opinion they would be better off with therapy to help them put their former and current life into perspective. An annulment is not a healing process. That comes with individual therapy. This is something the church has difficulty coming to terms with.

DIVORCE AND THE INTERNAL FORUM SOLUTION

Tom and I met in college. He asked me to marry him in front of the statue of the Blessed Mother on the university's campus. We were married in 1956. Sixteen years later he left me and our four daughters for a woman ten years younger.

I was devastated, thought my life was over at thirty-nine, and fought depression for two years. Divorce in my family was unthinkable, and in 1972 I honestly did not know a divorced person. For two years I did everything I could think of to save my marriage, praying desperately, seeking counseling from priests, psychologists, anyone who would listen. Someone, somehow, was going to help me save my marriage. But Tom wouldn't budge and I filed for divorce. I then sought an annulment. I must have talked to ten priests, none of whom gave me any hope. Tom and I were considered mature adults at twenty-two, college graduates who knew our own minds, and there were no impediments. The fact that he betrayed our marriage with another woman, and quite possibly others throughout the years, mattered not at all. It was then that I decided I would take responsibility for my own sins, but, by golly, I wasn't going to pay for his. I began to date.

Six years later I met Mike and we were married by a Protestant minister. Even if I could have gotten an annulment, Tom would not have. He certainly believed that his first marriage was valid and his children legitimate. I continued to attend mass, but only went to communion if I was in a church where no one knew me. I did not want to give scandal.

A friend urged me to see one more priest, Fr. George. What could he possibly do for me? I had already talked to so many. That is when I learned of the annulment in the internal forum. What a relief! I finally felt cleansed!

Fr. George couldn't believe that no one had told me about the internal forum. He had been taught all about it twenty years before in the seminary, and one of my previous priest counselors had been his classmate!

Mike and I now live in Florida and I recently attended a reconciliation meeting where they urged annulment seeking and also explained the internal forum. I was relieved to know that it was still valid, despite Cardinal Ratzinger's pronouncement four years ago that it wasn't, and the pope's recent statement that remarried Catholics must live as brother and sister.

What a mess the church makes of an already tragic situation. It took me ten years to rectify mine and I had the advantage of having a Catholic college education, plus access to so many priests. So many people don't, and feel guilty, alienated, unsupported emotionally, and even excommunicated. Bravo to Sheila Rauch Kennedy, Janice Leary, Charlie Davis, and Maureen Fiedler for bringing this issue to national and ecclesiastical attention.

WHERE DID YOU FIND GOD IN ALL OF THIS?

When I was first divorced, I had to go to a neighboring diocese to attend a support group. Divorced people were not recognized in my home diocese. Any attempt to organize a church support group was discouraged. Any priest brave enough to permit these meetings was not allowed to advertise them in the diocesan newspaper.

When a new bishop came, there was a bit of a change. One summer, there was even a series of meetings for the divorced. Fr. Steve was the guest speaker at the first meeting. Even though I had heard him before, in the neighboring diocese, I attended this meeting. His gentle, compassionate presentation provided a positive start to the series.

The second meeting was on the topic of annulment. The diocesan priest who presided at this meeting was arrogant and rude. He complained about how difficult his job was, how he hated getting incomplete forms, and how we had better write at least sixty pages if we wanted serious consideration of our cases. I left this meeting feeling angry and humiliated. I decided I would not add to this man's woes by seeking an annulment. I also did not attend the rest of the series.

A few years later, I was a co-leader of a local group and I wanted to schedule a speaker to explain annulment. Unfortunately, the priest mentioned above was still in charge of the tribunal. He told me he did not have time to come to a meeting because he was working on a law degree. He also added that everyone else in his office was too busy. I am embarrassed to admit that we argued for some time until he finally agreed to send a member of his staff to this meeting. The nun who came did an excellent job in her presentation. However, there was still something unsettling about this whole process and I could not bring myself to begin it.

Eventually, there was a new director of the tribunal. This priest was very much like Fr. Steve in his approach to ministering to the divorced. He also was in residence at my parish, and I came to know him well enough to request an appointment to discuss the annulment procedure. We met for more than an hour, but I left his office knowing that I could never do this.

I went home to reflect on the source of my difficulty. Writing a report for the annulment was not a problem because writing is an integral part of my job. It was my soul, however, that seemed to be screaming, "How dare you trivialize all that you have learned about our lives! How dare you reduce it to 'This marriage was never a sacrament' or 'You never should have married him because . . . .'"

The following thoughts may seem scandalous to some, but I need to share them:

- Divorce is not a sex sin.
- Divorce is the opportunity for a conversion experience.
- Divorce can even be considered a soul lesson.

I can explain this from my own experience. Because I was forced into being the single mother of an infant and also a five-year-old, I called on God frequently. Because my life seemed beyond my control, I learned to trust God completely. I found that God had creative solutions for all my dilemmas. When I prayed for help in stretching a paycheck, I would win something or get an unexpected refund. When I prayed for the strength to get through a day after a long night with a sick child, a lengthy meeting would be canceled. When I needed home or car repairs, I trusted that God would direct me to competent and fair professionals. I truly learned to "Let go and let God." Needless to say, my relationship with God was growing more intimate and I was encouraged to seek spiritual direction. An excellent director, who had recently transferred into the area, agreed to meet with me. I was impressed with his wisdom, patience, and knowledge. For the six years we worked together, he challenged me to find God in all things.

In conclusion, I would like to make some suggestions for ministering to the divorced. Do not ask us if we ever overheard our spouse make disparaging comments. Do not ask us intimate details about our wedding night or our sex lives. Do not ask us for horror stories about growing up in dysfunctional families. If you really want to assist us in healing, ask, Where did you find God in all of this?

QUESTIONS LEFT UNANSWERED

On April 30, 1997, our diocesan newspaper the *Long Island Catholic* published an article about the annulment process to clarify some popular misconceptions. This article confused me more than ever. It said that impediments made one incapable of marriage and that alcoholism at the time of marriage is one of the grounds for annulment because of the lack of discretion of judgment.

Several of my Roman Catholic relatives are alcoholic and have married in the church. Through my association with Al-Anon for many years, I have met countless wonderful alcoholics who married in the Roman Catholic Church and have good, healthy, and holy families. I am reluctant to discuss impediments and canon law with these people because I am afraid I may be doing more harm than good.

According to the *Long Island Catholic:* "If a Tribunal issues an annulment, each of the parties who had once been married is free to marry again in the Catholic Church. Their marriage would be seen as never having existed in the sense of being a binding sacramental union. The first marriage would be a 'simulation of a marriage,' which by outward appearances would resemble a true marriage," according to the Judicial Vicar of the Long Island Diocesan Tribunal, who also said: "Within the past few decades, the church has expanded the grounds for finding lack of due discretion to include various psychological disorders, alcoholism, and lack of sufficient maturity."

I wrote to the Judicial Vicar whom the article quoted as an authority. I was concerned about what the article called these people, namely, living in a "simulation of marriage," and asked how do I deal with these situations. I received no reply from him.

Then I wrote a letter to Bishop McGann. The reply came from the Judicial Vicar of the tribunal. He wrote that he was directed by the bishop to answer for him and that he was happy to do that. My questions were not answered but he sent me a few sentences about impediments in general; the issue of alcoholism was avoided completely. He recommended the "appropriate pages of the *Catechism of the Catholic Church*" for further explanations.

With canon laws constantly changing to suit the hierarchy, I cannot in good conscience encourage my seven grandchildren, if I live long enough, if they choose to marry, to do it in the Catholic Church. The price to pay is much too high for what may later be declared only a "simulation of a sacrament." I would strongly urge them to have a civil ceremony only, because at least it would give them the assurance that the union is really legal and with certainty. "If marriage isn't sacred, what is?" That's an excellent point that Mrs. Sheila Rauch Kennedy brought out in a television interview on the news.

I would like to know if any canon law protects the faithful from those lacking discretion of judgment when it comes to the ordination of priests, consecration of bishops, and selection of popes. In other words, can these people be notified that their sacrament never existed (if it is found out that their ordination was not valid)?

An alcoholic Methodist widow I know, sober for twenty-seven years, shared with me that her late husband, a Catholic, tried to marry her in his church. The priest told them that, since she was divorced, they could be married in the Catholic Church without any problem if they made a five-hundred-dollar "donation" to the parish. They didn't make the donation and so were refused. They married in her Methodist church. She told me of someone she knows who was asked to donate a thousand dollars.

Is it official church teaching that alcoholics are a new group doomed to a life of mandatory celibacy? Must those already married break up to avoid scandalizing our church leaders? These questions sound crazy, but I hope I can find some answer.

CAN THE CHURCH UNJOIN WHAT IT DID NOT JOIN?

Following twenty and a half years of marriage, my former husband and I separated. We did this following much reflection, counseling, and with the knowledge that to stay together would be unhealthy. The very sad truth was that the marriage was over. Within six months we were officially divorced.

We were glad to be able to take the actions we did without anger or hate and proceeded to continue coparenting our growing children. Friends at our church were saddened when we shared our decision to separate but were supportive. Beyond that, the church played no role.

I sought help to work through this massive change in my life, my struggle with a sense of failure, and feelings that I'd let my children down. Life moved on; the kids continued to grow, enter and leave high school and college. Almost six years passed.

Then I was advised by my former husband that he wished to remarry in the church. The woman he wished to marry had gotten an annulment and she wanted him to get one. I would be hearing from the tribunal of the diocese.

When I received my first form to fill out I read the accompanying information carefully and realized that there was no chance I was going to believe or argue that I had been in a non-sacramental marriage that had been invalid from its earliest moments. I answered the questions on the questionnaire honestly amidst my anger at many of them. One that struck me as odd concerned whether I had any doubts about getting married on my wedding day. Well, I didn't. I was sure I wanted to marry Roger the day we married. But, prior to the wedding I had my moments of fear, doubt . . . and gave them their time. Marriage is a huge leap in faith and hope. If absolute certainty were a prerequisite for marriage, I wonder how many marriages would occur! More than likely, the couples who would choose to marry would be those who reflected the least.

I shared with the priest who represented the tribunal my belief that if validity is absent in so many unions (as indicated by the annulment statistics), probably at any given Sunday mass a large number of couples are not validly married. Those struggling to save the marriage might as well give up. They don't have the sacrament. The priest said that validity isn't an issue unless an annulment is sought. So, I guess some people have the sacrament and others don't. . . . They just don't know it. If this were true, how sad the struggle to preserve a marriage would be in the absence of the sacramental grace!

I also mentioned to the priest that I didn't understand how the church's tribunal could even rule on the validity of a marriage. We all know that the couples marry themselves. The priest is just a witness. Then how can a bystander years later become the party with decision-making power? In other words, the church doesn't marry us. How can it un-marry us?

I mentioned earlier that when my husband and I separated and then divorced, the church was totally unengaged. I felt a sense of incompleteness. Twenty years earlier, we had married each other before God, the church's representative, and all our family and friends. I wanted to un-marry before God and God's witness, too. I would have been willing to go to my priest, with or without my former spouse, and declare that sadly but truly the marriage was over; that I thanked God for being ever present, even during these final days when ending the union was the issue; and to pray with the church's support for the courage and wisdom to go on. Spiritually and humanly this would have been a hard but much more appropriate closure to the union. As it is, there has been no formal spiritual closure. Just denial, on the part of the church.

As the annulment process proceeded with witnesses making their inputs, my former husband's wedding day was approaching. A week before the pending wedding, I received a letter informing me that on two counts my marriage had been judged invalid. The letter didn't share what those two counts were. I wrote the tribunal and asked them to share this information with me. I have never heard from them. To this day I have no idea why my marriage was deemed invalid by the church.

The Catholic Church states that the annulment process is often a healing process. I can honestly say that this action by the church was extremely hurtful to me. When the annulment was granted, I wanted to think, "I'm not even good enough to have a valid marriage." All the time the joke was on me. Not exactly healing thoughts. It's now been sixteen months since my marriage was declared invalid. I don't think about it much. But as I wrote this piece, the hurt, frustration, and anger returned. It's not easy to share the story, even now.

I hope one not too distant day the Catholic Church will recover the wisdom of its first millennium in the matter of marriage. At the close of this millennium the church leaders in Rome defy logic in their legalisms. They disempower couples and even God.

MAYBE YOU DON'T BELONG TO THE CATHOLIC CHURCH

I am a divorced Catholic, remarried in the Lutheran Church. Here is a short history of my last twenty years.

My first husband and I belonged to St. Pius X Church in the 1960s, then moved to the Southeast. We were divorced in the late 1970s. I eventually moved back home and attended St. Pius again. I had been married twenty-one years, the last ten years of that marriage—alone—in marriage counseling.

During the years of my life when I was single again, I was a member of John XXIII Society, an organization for separated and divorced Catholics. This group met in various Catholic churches; one of its strongest points was the subject of, and preparation for, annulments.

Being the oldest of eight children, I had attended Catholic schools much of my life. Before I married I had taken a Pre-Cana course. Nothing had ever prepared me, however, for a painful marriage and eventually divorce.

Divorce should be enough for anyone to suffer at one time, but, being Catholic, it only opened another dark, ugly door. I knew that if I remarried, I would never seek an annulment. I have always found the procedure intimidating, blame setting, and degrading. There is no one who can convince me that a legal, sacramental marriage, with three children, can ever be annulled. I have read the annulment papers, and I wish they could be read aloud some Sunday at mass.

As a member of John XXIII chapter, I attended the national convention of divorced Catholics at Notre Dame University. I spoke out against the annulment process there, and I was encouraged by many that felt likewise. Priests did listen, and one sister did say it would probably exist another twenty years before its demise, simply because of lack of interest.

In 1987, I married a Lutheran at his church. He is as open-minded and realistic as I am, and we mutually enjoy attending both churches. I have never left my church, but I am extremely grateful that I have always been invited to receive communion in his church. I cannot do this in my church, nor, of course, can I even be buried with my church's blessing.

A few years ago, I sat in my husband's Lutheran church and watched two familiar acquaintances and former members of John XXIII chapter join the Lutheran Church. The thought crossed my mind: if this is happening in just one church, how many other divorced Catholics are leaving the Catholic Church in my parish? In this diocese? In the nation?

A couple of people have, politely, mentioned, "Maybe you don't belong to the Catholic Church." I have given much thought through the years to the question: To stay or to stray? But I am still here. I feel like an adult child who sees a loving but troubled parent. This parent—the church—will survive if she can refrain from rejecting some of her children and start embracing all of them.

Twenty-eight Years of Pain and Cruelty

It took twenty-eight years of being turned away, before I finally was granted an annulment. Remarriage was not the issue with me. All I wanted was the right to live a single life without feeling guilty. I was tired of being told that it was not my "vocation." I was tired of being in bondage to someone who freely chose to divorce me and remarry. If he is married to her (legally), how can I be married to him (canonically)? Don't they understand how unreasonable that is, and how cruel they are?

It took twenty-eight years of being turned away, before I finally was granted an annulment. This didn't give me back twenty-eight years of my life. It didn't take away twenty-eight years of listening to the church's recriminations. It didn't take away twenty-eight years of being told to live a lie. It gave the other party the chance to get his third marriage "validated" in the church. It left me feeling that this case was based on my many inadequacies, and that I am unfit for marriage, or as he used to tell me, that I am "worthless."

The reason many divorced Catholics do not seek annulments is that they believe their first marriage was sacramental. I finally realized that this teaching is erroneous. Marriage is not indissoluble. There is such a thing as a divorce. Right or wrong, there is such a thing as a divorce. It is about time for the church to recognize that there is such a thing as a divorce.

Once a Catholic, Always a Catholic

Recently we buried my sister's ashes over my mother's grave at St. Mary's Cemetery in Minneapolis. As she was dying from cancer over the past five years, I had many opportunities to talk and pray with her privately. As I listened and consoled her, I promised her I would write to share the pain, suffering, and misery she went through regarding divorce, remarriage, and annulment.

Terry married in 1965 at St. Joseph's Church. After their three children were grown and after twenty years of an unworkable marriage, they divorced. She subsequently fell in love and wished to get married. Terry has always been a very strong, devout, God-fearing Catholic. She was very active in her church, serving in a number of ministries, including as eucharistic minister, and she also taught religion classes. She wanted to do what is right and just. She went to her church to plan her wedding. She was told that she could not marry in the Catholic Church unless she had an annulment stating that she did not have a sacramental marriage the first time.

In good conscience Terry could not agree with this. She felt to do so would be hypocritical and a violation of her conscience, as she knew in her heart she had received the sacrament of marriage. She said many times over that both she and her ex-husband, Tom, were mature, practicing, unmarried Catholics who went before God of their own free will and received the sacrament of matrimony, witnessed by Tom's uncle, a Catholic priest. Three wonderful children were born of this sacramental marriage. They both truly intended to remain married the rest of their lives. Unfortunately conditions I'm not privy to caused the marriage to be unbearable and they divorced amicably.

Regarding the annulment process, she stated, "for both of us to have to fill out lengthy personal forms and have a judging tribunal who does not know either party say that we never received the sacrament of marriage in the eyes of God is truly unconscionable." She felt only she, her ex-husband, Tom, and God were able to make that judgment.

She felt abandoned by her own church and proceeded to be married in a civil ceremony. Now as a sinner she felt even more disenfranchised from the Holy Roman Catholic Church, no longer welcome at the table to share in the healing power of the bread of life. Having been very spiritual all her life she felt she needed support from an organized religion. The Catholic Church having turned its back on her, she looked elsewhere. She joined a very comforting Lutheran congregation that welcomed sinners. They were in the mercy business, not the judgment business. When she became ill, they were there to comfort and console this wonderful strong-willed woman. They were there to the very end. This completed her cycle, and I feel she has attained her eternal reward, being in heaven with God.

In conclusion, I most humbly and prayerfully ask the church to evaluate what it has done to so many of its divorced members. The shame and scandal that have happened, I feel, are immeasurable, unnecessary, and indefensible.

WHAT THE CHURCH SHOULD DO

I have read your open letter to the North American bishops calling for substantial change in the church's position regarding divorce and remarriage and couldn't be more in agreement. I would like to add a few thoughts of my own on the subject, which I believe reinforce your position.

1. The church should have nothing to do with divorce even under the guise of annulment. Only the parties of the marriage can end the union.

2. The church should treat all marriages with equal respect whether or not they are sacramental. Its proper role is to provide pastoral counseling to help reconcile troubled marriages and raise them to sacramental level where appropriate, and not to pass judgment on their legitimacy.

3. Recognize that divorce is an effect, not a cause, of the breakup of a marriage. The cause is the abuse, desertion, infidelity, non-support, and all the other numerous problems that result in divorce.

4. There is a name for these causes. It is called sin. One of the principal functions of the church is the forgiveness of sin. What sin? All sins except sin against the Holy Spirit. How often? Seven times seventy times.

5. When a couple's marriage has been damaged beyond recovery, it seems to me that the proper role of the church is to extend the hand of reconciliation to help those who have endured this trauma to reconstruct their lives, which certainly does not exclude remarriage.

6. Denying divorced couples this reconciliation and access to the sacrament goes counter to the church's mandate.

WHAT I LEARNED: MARRIAGE IS A SACRAMENT THAT IS CONFERRED
by Charles N. Davis

I was terribly saddened after reading through the letters of my fellow Catholics in response to a call for reform in the way the hierarchy of our church addresses the problem of divorce, remarriage, and annulments (printed in the *National Catholic Reporter* on July 4, 1997). Over twenty

Catholic reform groups called on our church leaders to drastically rethink the issue. The letters that were received in response to this appeal resonate with my own personal experience of divorce and remarriage.

I grew up a dutiful and faithful Catholic in the 1940s and 1950s. Before Vatican Council II, no one in my family would have questioned church authority. In the 1960s, my first my wife's health was affected by having four children in six years, despite (or because of) using Natural Family Planning. For the first time, I realized that my conscience would have to override the hierarchical condemnation of contraception.

The same need to work through the issue of conscience versus authority came when I found myself divorced after seventeen years of marriage and four children. I had to address the questions: What is a sacramental marriage? Should I get an annulment? In looking for answers, I had the good fortune of being counseled by a priest who said: "What do we celibates know about marriage?" I also attended the Separated, Divorced, and Remarried Group in my parish.

From this counseling and from listening to the experiences of those who had gone through the annulment process, I decided not to seek an annulment. I found that I would have to compromise my integrity to survive the contradictions of the annulment process. These contradictions include the following:

- The church asserts that an annulment declaring the first marriage not sacramental does not impugn the legitimacy of children. To me, a marriage is either sacramental and legitimate in the church's eyes, irrespective of the state, or it is illegitimate in God's eyes, and so are the children. I certainly wasn't going to make my kids try to believe that their parents' marriage wasn't sacramental. And I wasn't going to have them worry about their own legitimacy.

- The realization that my first marriage was sacramental but that the sacrament was not sufficient to hold the marriage together brought me up against the hierarchy's assertion that a sacramental marriage cannot die, no matter the conduct of the spouses. This may be technically true in the language of the ecclesiastical courts but it does not square with the experience of us laity, or even of many priests who minister to us. Fr. Richard G. Rento wrote in the *New Jersey Star-Ledger* (August 18, 1997): "A perfectly valid marriage can disintegrate to the point at which there is no longer a bond of love between the two partners and they become destructive to each other and to others whose lives their dead marriage touches."

- The *Catechism of the Catholic Church* (§§2384 and 1650) states: "A Catholic who remarries without an annulment is in a situation of public and permanent adultery" and is officially denied communion. Yet §1651 instructs priests to "manifest an attentive solicitude, so that they [the remarried] do not consider themselves separated from the Church." Does it make sense to deny us communion but also say we are not to consider ourselves separated from the church?

- How can anyone be sure to have received the sacrament of marriage when almost all requests for an annulment are granted? How can anyone believe they have really received the sacrament when about half the marriages end in divorce and people can obtain an annulment that states the sacrament never existed?

- It is ironic that convicted criminals can receive communion after confession while communion is denied to those who remarry and try to raise their kids in a household of two loving parents.

- The hierarchy grants annulments on the grounds of psychological immaturity at marriage. Who is not psychologically immature on their wedding day? And who says that those who have been granted an annulment for such immaturity are subsequently grown up enough to remarry?

In the light of these contradictions, it is no wonder that Archbishop Rembert Weakland of Milwaukee said that Catholics "simply do not understand the theology behind them [annulments], even after lengthy explanations of the church's practice and reasoning in this regard. They consider it to border on dishonesty and casuistry of the worst kind" (*America*, April 18, 1998).

Fr. Rento addresses the problem from a true pastoral viewpoint when he writes: "It has long seemed to me that the church unnecessarily further wounds and burdens some of its members who seek release from hopelessly failed marriages when it requires them to say that these marriages were never true sacramental unions from the start. Eager to be free and to enter new, mutually satisfying unions, they agree, when the simple truth is that, while they were once very much in love and committed to building a life-giving partnership, they recognize that love and commitment, on the part of one or both of the spouses, are irretrievably lost" (*New Jersey Star-Ledger*, August 18, 1997).

In my research on the subject I found that the hierarchy allowed divorce and remarriage in the first centuries. I believe today's hierarchy should look back to this early tradition.

Theology may even go further. The sacramentality of marriage is not bestowed just on the day vows and sexual intimacy are exchanged. Most of us laity know that marriage is a sacrament of grace that is conferred daily. To reach fulfillment, the sacrament must be nourished over the years and tested by life.

When a marriage fails, the gospel response would be to allow those who have been wounded to recover. Confession, communion, and the Last Rites are ever available to those who have stumbled and are in need of grace. I believe the sacrament of marriage should be bestowed again on those who have the courage to try again.

3

Disputed Biblical Interpretations about Marriage and Divorce

PIERRE HEGY

FOR CENTURIES (AND EVEN TODAY) the question of who can interpret Scripture has been more political than religious. The Trent council fathers were unable to come to an agreement about authorizing Bible translations. Hence the Habsburg emperors took the initiative of prohibiting translations in their territories. Until the twentieth century in Spain and Latin America, the importation of Bibles was prohibited; often the only Bibles available were Protestant translations (Gill 1998:89). There is also a long Catholic tradition of prohibiting lay preaching. Today, however, in the Catholic Church "lay persons can be admitted to preach in a church" (canon 766) but only priests and deacons can preach the homily (canon 767, 1).

There has been an outstanding increase in biblical knowledge among the Catholic laity over the last two or three decades, especially since Vatican II and the charismatic renewal. While fifty years ago theology was restricted to seminaries, now it is widely available outside the confines of religious institutions. Moreover, in the past theology was taught only by priests, but today many instructors in departments of religious studies are lay men and women. Church textbooks are no longer published in Latin; hence any educated lay person can read them.

With increased democratization of religious knowledge comes a new attitude toward religious teaching. When the church had the monopoly of theology, students often were in the position of first graders who could only acquiesce. With the democratization of religious education, church authorities are confronted with a new challenge: not only do they have to justify their teaching with primary sources; they must also engage in a constant dialogue about the interpretation of these sources. In a world where natural law is no longer recognized, church leaders can no longer simply say: "Divorce is a grave offence against the natural law" (*Catechism of the Catholic Church* §2384). Nor can they state: "The Lord Jesus insisted on the original intention of the Creator who willed that marriage be indissoluble" (*Catechism of the Catholic Church* §2382). Even giving five references is not convincing, since the first one, Matt. 5:31–32, contains an exception clause allowing divorce.

This situation confronts us, the readers, with a new challenge. While many of us may like church experts to tell us what to believe so that we may simply acquiesce, this abdication of our responsibilities is no longer reasonable. Many Catholics have internalized the belief that obedience is a great virtue; indeed, it is a great virtue, for example, for children and subordinates, but not always for adults and the educated. Hence—ideally—every reader should do his or her own research about marriage and divorce in Scripture.

This writer is a lay nonexpert. I have surveyed the scholarly literature on the topic and received feedback and comments from experts. I stand by my conclusions but learned that a great variety of interpretations are equally possible. Little of what I say is new; unfortunately much of it is buried in expert publications not easily available to busy readers. Moreover, if the reader disagrees with me, then let him or her come up with further research to enlighten us all.

The outline of this chapter is straightforward. First I will begin with the first New Testament text on divorce, namely, Paul's instructions to the married in the first letter to the Corinthians; the purpose of this section is to raise basic exegetical questions. Next we turn to the various Gospel texts on marriage and divorce. I return to Paul at the end to raise questions of social philosophy and political institutionalization, because the social ban on divorce is also a question of politics and social philosophy.

EXEGETICAL ISSUES: PAUL'S INSTRUCTIONS TO THE MARRIED

The first letter to the Corinthians, written around 50 C.E., contains instructions about divorce in case of marital breakdown. Referring to Jesus' teaching on marriage and divorce in 1 Cor. 7:10, Paul writes:

"To the unmarried
- I give this ruling (*The English Bible*)
- I have this to say (*New American Bible*)

- I give instructions (*New American Standard Bible*)
- I give this command (*New International Version*)
- I give charge (*Revised Standard Version*)
- I give command (*King James Version*)
- I enjoin (*Darly Translation*)
- I announce (*Young's Literal Translation*)

We might have expected a clear and simple teaching; instead we have a multiplicity of English translations. What is the Lord's teaching on divorce: an evangelical counsel? An ideal? A precept? A command? A law? For Burchard (1993:51–59) Jesus' teaching on divorce is a law, actually the only law in the New Testament. We might suspect that differences in translation reflect ideological and denominational differences. Thus we might expect Catholic and/or conservative translations to present the Lord's teaching as a command or law, and the Protestant and/or liberal versions as a ruling or ideal, but this is actually not always the case. Will the original Greek text help us resolve these differences? At least the Greek text should give a clear answer. Let us look at the original term used here (*parangelia*), as well as other terms used to express commands.

Orders and Moral Commands
in the New Testament

Two major terms are used in the Greek New Testament to express commands, *parangellō* (or the noun *parangelia*) as in 1 Cor. 7:10 quoted above, and *entolē*, as in John 13:34. Bullinger (1908) thus defines the two terms: "*Parangelia*: a proclamation, public notice; *espec. as a military term*, word of command; *then* any announcement or declaration *by authority*" (italics in the text). *Entolē*, on the other hand, is "an injunction, charge, precept, a single precept; *pl.* moral injunctions, prohibition." Both terms are used in the New Testament. Thus Jesus orders (*parangellō*, Matt. 15:35; Mark 8:6) the people to sit down, but he also gives instructions (*parangellō*, Matt. 10:5) to the Twelve not to take bread or money. In reference to God's commandments of the Torah, the Synoptics use *entolē*, which tends to refer to moral commands. The first term, *parangellō*, is used seven times in the Synoptics (not in John), and twelve times in Paul; *entolē*, on the other hand, is used nineteen times in the Synoptics, eighteen times in John, and fourteen times in Paul. Thus, although Paul uses both terms, he uses the first more often, as if to insist on the public and authoritative nature of his orders, in accordance with his social philosophy of organization and obedience.

The study of *entolē* reveals significant differences between the evangelists. Since the term had been used in the Septuagint in reference to the commandments of the Torah, there are likely to be differences depending on the writer's conception and role of the Torah in Christian thought. According to Limbeck in Balz and Schneider (1994:459), "Mark and Matthew use *entolē* exclusively for the commandments of the Torah. They are God's word (Mk 7:13; Mt 15:4)." Yet there are also "considerable differences" between the two. "According to Mark 12:31 the commandments to love God and neighbor are the greatest in the law and cannot be surpassed by any other" (M. Limbeck in Balz and Schneider 1994:459). This view reflects a recent evolution in Diaspora thought according to which not all commandments are of equal importance. In this perspective, Jesus' teaching on marriage cannot be a "commandment"; there is only one commandment, to love God and neighbor.

In rabbinic Judaism and Matthew, the above evolution has not taken place; "such a differentiation is impossible: The first and second commandment are equivalent (Mt 22:38)" (M. Limbeck in Balz and Schneider 1994:459). It is forbidden to remove "the least of these commandments." The Torah is absolutely valid in all of its commandments (ibid.). Divorce is condemned in reference to creation, but is upheld in case of *porneia*, a term that refers to Deut. 24:1 or Lev. 18:6–18, texts used to legitimize divorce in Judaism. We will explore the meaning of *porneia* in our discussion of Matt. 5:32, which allows divorce in case of *porneia*.

In John the intellectual horizon is completely different. "In contrast to the other NT writings, *entolē* is never used in the Johannine literature of the Mosaic Torah. Instead *entolē* stands for the commission of the Father given to the Son and for Christ's commandment to his disciples. . . . For the disciples the *entolē* of the Son consists of the commandments to "love one another as I have loved you." According to 1 John 3:23 God's *entolē* has a twofold meaning: faith in the Son, Jesus Christ, and mutual love" (M. Limbeck in Balz and Schneider 1994:459). In such a perspective, divorce is a nonissue. When speaking to the woman at the well, the Jesus of John makes a nonissue of the fact that she had been married five times—hence divorced five times—and currently was in a noncanonical relationship. In this narrative (John 4) the issue is faith and love: "Many Samaritans of that town came to believe in him because of the woman's testimony" (John 4:39). In John, faith and love are more important than the stunning record of multiple marriages after multiple divorces—a multiple adultery according to Mark 10:11.

So far our investigation of Paul's instructions to the married has been negative and frustrating. First, different Bibles give different translations, calling Paul's instructions either a ruling, an announcement, a saying, a command, or even a law. But when checking the Greek text, the situation becomes only more complex: there are two terms in Greek with a similar meaning, yet the second term refers to different traditions in different contexts. On top of that, the wording for commands in the Gospel of John is different from all others. We must realize, however, that the feeling of confusion comes from us, the readers, namely, from our expectation that all the Gospels should speak the same language and herald the same truths. Contemporary research has come to invalidate this expectation: at the beginning of Christianity there was pluralism, not monolithic uniformity, as commonly assumed. This is an important lesson for our interpretation the New Testament texts: at the beginning there was no monolithic teaching.

The Original Pluralism

The Christian origins are commonly seen as monolithic. This view is most common when all truths and biblical texts are seen as equally important, Historically this view has been fostered by the following factors, among others. First, the book of Acts describes the uniform expansion of Christianity from Jerusalem to Rome, rather than the conflicts between the followers of Paul, James, Peter, Stephen, John, etc. Second, starting with Paul, institutional preaching has emphasized "obedience of faith," rather than faith and brotherly love as in the less institutionalized Johannine churches. Finally, even today, it is commonly assumed that Jesus' Spirit of love and unity must necessarily have produced harmonious and internally consistent descriptions of Jesus' life and teaching—a view favored by institutional teaching. And until recently, very little was known about "the churches the apostles left behind."

"About 90% of critical scholarship judges that Paul did not write the Pastorals, 80% that he did not write Ephesians, and 60% that he did not write Colossians" (Brown 1984:47). There have always been doubts about the author of Hebrews. The letters of Peter were not written by Peter, those of John were not written by John. Much more troubling is the fact that the author of Acts shows no knowledge of the letters of Paul; Paul shows no knowledge of the followers of John and their emphasis on brotherly love, while John shows no knowledge of the Gospel of Mark and the Sayings of Jesus (Q source), which must have been in existence by then. There are great differences in the description of the first Christians: James (2:2) suggests that Jewish Christians were meeting in synagogues following Jewish customs; Paul's Pastoral letters describe institutionalized churches headed by bishops; Peter's letters are written to isolated Christians in the Diaspora; and John implies a secessionist group of Jewish Christians surviving at the fringes of traditional Judaism.

Scholarship today envisions a plurality of early Christian groups, each with its own leadership, governance, distinctive features, and doctrines. Thus Harry Eberts (1997) distinguishes between the churches of "apostles" under the leadership of Barnabas and Paul, who emphasized the crucified and risen Lord; circumcision was not to be imposed on Gentiles. The "disciples," on the other hand, were headed by Peter and the Twelve, worshiped in the synagogues mainly in Galilee, and followed traditional Jewish kosher customs. There were also the "brethren" or Hebrew-speaking Christians of Juda, under the leadership of James; circumcision and kosher laws were deemed important. Finally, there were the "Hellenists" from Caesarea, Alexandria, Ephesus, and so on. Eberts does not mention the followers of John as a separate group. Neither does he give preeminence to the churches of Rome and Antioch, as Raymond E. Brown and John Meier (1983) do.

The monolithic vision of the four Gospels as objective historical records of the life and teachings of Jesus is not supported by scholarship. In simple terms: "the 'historical' Jesus is beyond recovery" (Sandmel 1970:212). What we have instead are four social constructs of the good news recorded according to the diversified beliefs and needs of individual writers and local communities. We do not have the sayings of Jesus on the one hand and early interpretations on the other. The two are often fused into one living reality. With this principle in mind, let us now turn to the scriptural texts on marriage and divorce, being aware that each Gospel may reflect a different tradition, not a monolithic teaching.

NEW TESTAMENT TEXTS ON MARRIAGE AND DIVORCE

We must first distinguish between text and interpretation. As noted by Brown (1984:10), scholars of various ideologies are often "at one as to what Scripture meant but divided as to what it means." The purpose of scholarship is, among other things, to establish the historical meaning of a text; what it means today, however, is open to debate.

The distinction between text and interpretation in the New Testament is more difficult but no less vital. Thus, about marriage and divorce, we have Paul's, Mark's, Matthew's, and Luke's interpretations, but all of these point to Jesus' original logia. What are these original sayings lurking behind the interpretations of Mark and Matthew? From Mark 10:1–12 and Matt. 19:1–12, the minimum wording of Jesus' saying may be, "What God has joined together, let not a human put asunder," while from 1 Cor. 7:10–11, Luke 16:18, and Mark 10:11 the minimum saying seems to be "Whoever divorces his wife and marries another commits adultery." These two sayings alone raise a host of questions. Does God join people in marriage? If so, why are there so many unhappy marriages? Does God join in marriage only Christians (and maybe Jews)—therefore non-Christians are not joined by God? If humans cannot separate what God has united, can the churches? If churches cannot grant divorces, on what grounds can they legitimize civil divorces through annulments? Is remarriage after divorce the same as adultery? How serious a moral failure is adultery? These questions, and many more, need to be addressed; hence the need for interpretations.

The Unexplained Aphorism of Luke 16:18–19

In Luke 16:17–19 we read: "It is easier for the heavens and the earth to pass away than for a single stroke of a letter of the law to pass. Everyone who divorces his wife and marries another commits adultery. The man who marries a women divorced from her husband likewise commits adultery. Once there was a rich man who dressed in purple and linen. . . ." Here we seem to have the very words of Jesus without interpretation or explanation. At first sight, these aphorisms seem self-explanatory; hence they are favorites in ecclesiastical apologetic discourses. "Not a single letter of the law shall pass": what a strong affirmation of Jesus' upholding of the Torah! But the next saying is tantamount to abolishing the Mosaic institution of divorce. The mere juxtaposition of unexplained aphorisms—on the law, divorce, and the rich man—can lead to confusion and/or literalism.

This logion on divorce is puzzling in its brevity. How grievous is adultery and why? In Judaism adultery is a sin because it was a property crime, the wife being the property of the husband; she was part of a man's chattel (Exod. 20:17), along with his servants and livestock. Adultery, then, "is the act by which the possession of a women by her husband or fiancé is violated (Lv 20,10; Dt 22, 22 ff)" (Leon-Dufour 1977, s.v. *adultery*). Today we do not see adultery as a property crime; hence our question is: Why is adultery immoral? Adultery violates the marriage promises; but these promises are a necessary requirement for a valid Catholic marriage. Is adultery by mutual consent morally acceptable? Our moral sense rejects such a view, but it is imperative to explain why. Without a rationale, it is impossible to see how sinful adultery is.

The prohibition of adultery is one of the Ten Commandments. Scholarship has shown that the Decalogue is a mixture of social customs (honor thy mother and father), ritual prescriptions (keep holy the Sabbath, do not take the name of the Lord in vain), elementary moral prescriptions (do not steal, bear false witness, or commit adultery) and obvious minimum moral standards (do not kill a fellow Jew). But the Decalogue does not condemn divorce. Hence one might conclude that it is less important than the laws on stealing and honoring one's parents.

Is adultery as grievous as theft? We commonly distinguish between petty theft (e.g., of less than fifty dollars) and the felony of larceny (theft of greater value). Can we similarly distinguish between petty adultery and more grievous forms of adultery? Is divorce no more than petty adultery or petty theft? Empirical knowledge about adultery tends to confirm such a view: adultery is more common in unhappy marriages, and then it is often viewed with leniency. Divorce is also the usual end result of unhappy marriages; then it is also generally viewed with understanding. Shall we conclude that in many cases, divorce is no more grievous than minor adultery?

Adultery carried the death penalty in Mosaic law (Lev. 20:10); however, it was rarely carried out. Similarly in the United States, adultery may carry penalties of imprisonment and a fine, but that is a very rare occurrence today. In the United States criminal justice, the greatest crime after murder is rape (including conjugal rape), not adultery. Most people would also rank child molestation and spousal beating as more grievous than adultery among family crimes. While the Torah seems to condone or ignore rape, child molestation, and spousal abuse, it condemns under penalty of death the property crime of adultery. Such discrepancy between the values of the Torah and our own does not bode well for the scholastic claim of a universal natural law valid for all cultures and societies. Traditionally, Mosaic law was seen as universally valid. Today we tend to see it as culturally and historically conditioned, and in need of interpretation.

Finally, in Judaism, sexual relations between a husband and a nonmarried women did not constitute adultery. Luke seems to say the opposite: not only does the man "who marries a woman divorced from her husband commit adultery" but also the man "who divorces his wife and marries another (presumably nondivorced, nonmarried woman) commits adultery." The latter statement would have been puzzling to a Jewish audience. It is equally puzzling to us. In brief, if a man of whatever culture—a Muslim, a Buddhist, or a Jew—remarries after divorce, he commits adultery—such a statement is puzzling: Why would a Muslim or a Buddhist commit adultery by remarrying? Jesus' aphorism needs interpretation; this is what we find in Mark and Matthew.

Mark's Maximalism: Let No Church Annul What God Has United

Mark makes the ban on divorce universal; he also explains why. "The *woman* who divorces her husband and marries another commits adultery" (Mark 10:12). Scholars see this pericope as Mark's creation; in a Jewish context where divorce was not available to women it would have made little sense. Mark also explains that remarriage after divorce is "adultery *against her* (the wife)." What does it mean? Traditionally adultery was a tort against the husband, who could ask for redress, for example, in court. Could a divorced woman request redress against her ex-husband? No court would hear her case in ancient Judaism.

The institution of divorce is explained as a concession to human "hardness of heart." Although in secular writings the term *sklērokardia* ("hardness of heart") was used in the psychological sense, in the biblical writings it refers to Israel's "stubbornness" (another translation of the word) in not listening to God (see Balz and Schneider 1994, s.v. *sklērokardia*). In reference to divorce, the hardness of heart is to be taken not in the psychological sense, as mutual insensitivity of the spouses but in the religious sense. In institutional Christianity hardness of heart is seen as insubordination to God's law as interpreted by the church. However, if the essence of Christianity is love of God and neighbor as in the Johannine model of the church, then more is at stake here. We will return to this question in the analysis of divorce according to John.

"At the beginning it had not been like that." What is the antecedent of "it"? Is it divorce or hardness of heart? The Greek is of no help here (see Yeager 1978, 3:12). Because the text is unclear, the churches are faced with alternate policies in their effort to return to the original state: they either abolish divorce at the risk of being permissive about adultery as in *ancien régime* Catholicism, or allow divorce at the risk of opening the door to abuse. Generally speaking, the Western church opted for the first alternative and the Eastern churches the second. Moreover, Mark seems to favor the first, Matthew the second.

The absolute rejection of divorce seems based, I will argue, on a literal and maximalist interpretation of God's plan. "At the beginning of creation God made them male and female; for this reason . . . the two shall become as one. They are no longer two but one flesh" (Mark 10:6–8). In Jewish law and practice the wife had no independent status apart from that of her husband. At marriage, two became one: the female's existence as daughter ceased and she became one with her husband. The two became one physically, economically, religiously, socially, legally; they became one flesh. The conclusion seems obvious: "Let no man separate what God has united."

There is no hint here, as there is in Matthew (see Matt. 5:32 discussed below), that marriage permanence in paradise was ideal rather than real, which allows us to understand "two in one flesh" symbolically, not just literally. If we take the ban on divorce to its maximal conclusion, we arrive at the following consequences:

1. The ban on divorce applies not only to Jews but to all cultures and societies. This universal ban is best expressed in canon 1141: "A ratified and consummated marriage cannot be dissolved by any human power or for any reason other than death." All ratified and consummated marriages— those of Muslims, Jews, Buddhists, and so on—are indissoluble. Such an absolutist view is difficult to justify today.

The nonbiblical distinction between sacramental and nonsacramental marriages allows one to say that nonsacramental marriages are indissoluble but can be dissolved, for example, by Pauline and Petrine privileges,[1] while the sacramental marriages are indissoluble with "special firmness" (canon 1056). To the lay reader these distinctions appear as meaningless hair-splitting. We are supposed to distinguish between nonsacramental marriages, which are indissoluble *as marriages* but can be dissolved by Petrine privilege, and sacramental marriages, which are indissoluble *as sacraments* and cannot be dissolved. In other words, the distinction is between "dissoluble-indissoluble" marriages and "indissoluble with special firmness" sacraments. Again, not convincing.

On the other hand, if one holds the absolutist view according to which "a ratified and consummated marriage cannot be dissolved by any human power or for any reason other than death," then Paul stands as condemned when he allowed the remarriage of Christians divorced by their non-Christian spouse (1 Cor. 7:15). To rationalize the discrepancy by speaking here of a "Pauline privilege" is not convincing. It is tantamount to saying that all marriages are indissoluble . . . except when they are not, by some special privilege.

2. Divorce is more than a property crime; it is something "intrinsically evil." The notion of intrinsic evil is often taken as self-evident. But what is self-evident to the Congregation of the Doctrine of the Faith may not be so to the educated lay men and women of today. The notion of intrinsic evil is not universally accepted in moral reasoning.

3. The absolute ban on divorce seems to apply to annulments. Historically, annulments were requests for permission to remarry, or what today we call divorce. In the Middle Ages, unable to secure a divorce from church authorities, the powerful of the day raised in court the question: Are we (who secretly seek to divorce) married at all? The question could not be eluded when coming from powerful patrons, especially when great political gains and losses were at stake. The powerful patrons seeking a divorce did not need a divorce when an annulment (or the denial of a socially accepted reality of an existing marriage) was granted instead. Today, at a rate of forty thousand per year in the United States, annulments are divorces under a different name. Moreover, a civil divorce being a necessary prerequisite for an annulment, the latter can be seen as an ecclesiastical legitimation of civil divorce. In a maximalist perspective like that of Mark, such a practice seems difficult to justify.

The Social Philosophies of "Two in One Flesh"

The crux of the argument in both Mark 16:1–10 and Matt. 19:3–12 is the divine natural order: "The creator made them male and female. . . . They are no longer two but one flesh." But, I will argue, the conclusion "Let no man separate" holds only if "two in one flesh" and "what God has united" are taken literally.

"Two in one flesh" can be taken literally as in sexual intercourse. God made all animals male and female. Through intercourse, they become one, yet there is no permanent bonding between them. For humans it is different. According to Robert W. Wall (Freedman 1992, s.v. *divorce*) "marriage thereby establishes a new physical relationship ('one flesh') comparable to other familial relationships, held together by a natural (i.e., hereditary) and therefore indissoluble covenant." In marriage the bonding through sexual intercourse establishes a relationship as strong as that of blood relations. Why was this bonding supposed to be permanent? In antiquity, female premarital sex was very rare. "There is no word in the Near Eastern languages that by itself means *virgo intacta*" (Freedman 1992, s.v. *virgin*). Female premarital sexuality was made improbable by early betrothal, often before puberty, and early marriage. In the absence of premarital intercourse, the sexual intercourse between husband and wife came to be seen as characteristic of the marital state and could be said to be permanent. Such a view, however, does not take into account the male-centeredness of family life.

In ancient Israel, family wealth and name were transmitted through the males. Wives and daughters did not inherit at the death of the father. Men could have intercourse with their female servants, and their offspring would become part of his household. This family system was stable only because female adultery was prohibited under penalty of death. What would have happened if wives had taken lovers among their male servants and unmarried lads, as men did? If wives had borne children from lovers who were not their husbands, the family system based on male inheritance would have collapsed. Does "two in one flesh" create a permanent union by its very nature? Obviously not between husband and female servants, or between wife and male lovers. To state that intercourse between husband and wife creates a permanent union and that between lovers does not is precisely what needs to be proven. In moral discussions, the existence of non-marital intercourse is simply ignored or denied (e.g., by having the adulterous wife stoned), or it is implied that it should not—hence does not—take place.

If intercourse itself were to create marriage, then in ancient Judaism men would have found themselves "married" to their premarital sexual partners, and so would today most Christians in the West, where premarital sexuality is commonly practiced. Even Paul was aware of the problem when he acknowledged that through prostitution men and women become "one flesh" (1 Cor. 6:16)—as in marriage—although they are not bound. To say that in marriage sexuality creates the marital bond is tautological and ambiguous: Does marriage *or* sexuality create the marriage bond? If sexuality out of marriage does not create a marital bond, then how can sexuality in marriage be said to create by itself such a bond? Moreover, in Hebrew "flesh" is much broader than the English equivalent (see Leon-Dufour 1977, s.v. *flesh*).

Do spouses become "two in one" legally and socially through their marriage? It has been argued that they become one when they give up their individual, independent, and separate existence by creating a marriage. This view has been commonly accepted in the West for centuries. As a nineteenth-century lawyer put it: "When the contract between the parties is executed by the marriage, a relation is created between the parties which they cannot change" (quoted in Popenoe 1996:159). After entering into a marriage contract, the partners do not totally belong to themselves anymore. They have accepted objective duties and obligations which may be enforced by the courts. Such was the opinion of the U.S. Supreme Court in 1888.

Today this view is not upheld anymore. Today we hold a nearly opposite view: "The marital couple is not an independent entity with a mind and heart of its own, but an association of two individuals, each with a separate intellectual and emotional make-up," wrote the U.S. Supreme Court in *Eisenstadt v Baird* (quoted in Popenoe 1996:159–60). Today a couple is not "two in one" except symbolically. Both spouses are independent psychologically (the wife is not asked to fuse with the husband as in the past), economically (both are likely to have incomes), legally (the rights of husband and wife are equal), and socially (the term Mrs. is being replaced by Ms.). Our marriages are not arranged anymore by parents or elders, as in past Judaism. But if the couple is not "two in one" anymore because they are *not* "an independent entity with a mind and heart of its own," the rationale for the prohibition of divorce (two in one flesh) collapses, because other relationships can also be "two in one" metaphorically.

Moreover, only from a literal interpretation of "what God has united" can we conclude "let not man put (it) asunder." In marriage the couple is not literally united by God since they themselves dated, proposed, and committed. In the folklore of romantic love, however, it is often believed that there is a special Mr. Right "out there"; finding him becomes the purpose of the romantic quest. From the literal interpretation of "what God has united" one can easily conclude that romantic marriages must be made in heaven since there seems to be a divine preordination for Mr. Right to marry Mrs. Right. This could be called romantic predestination: Miss Eve was forever predestined to be united to Mr. Adam. There is, however, no trace of romantic predestination in the biblical texts: the creation of Eve seems an afterthought, coming from the realization that it is not good for a man to be alone.

By no stretch of the imagination can "what God has united" come to mean marriage as a contract consummated by postnuptial intercourse as defined in canon law. If only ratified marriages were real marriages, then the millions of arranged marriages in the East, with little or no consent (the bride was unveiled only *after* the wedding in traditional China) would all be invalid. Clearly, "what God has united" cannot be restricted to Western marriage ceremonials, as the literalist view would have it.

"What God has united" may refer to marriage itself rather than individuals. From the story of Genesis 1–2, it seems that marriage itself was meant to be permanent, even if not all marriages are permanent. "Two in one flesh," although not true anymore literally, is true symbolically in reference to the permanence of marriage. The various social institutions of marriage are not divine, as a literal interpretation would have it. Different cultures create different institutions of government, marriage, education, and so on; such a realistic view of social institutions does not contradict the biblical claim of the permanence of marriage as God's design. In summary, a *metaphorical* understanding of "two in one flesh" and "what God has created" leads one to see marriage as *permanent* (rather than indissoluble—a legalistic term) and hence leads to the conclusion "Let not man put (it) asunder." We are now confronted with a new question: Is the permanence of marriage a norm, a law, or an ideal?

Matthew 5:32: Marriage Permanence as Ideal or Norm

Matthew presents the ban on divorce twice, first as part of his collection of Jesus sayings (Q source), and later by following the order of Mark. The first presentation is part of the Sermon on the Mount and does not appear to be taken literally. "You have heard. . . . You shall not commit murder. . . . What I say to you is: everyone who grows angry with his brother shall be *liable to judgment*" (Matt. 5:21–22). Not only should followers of Jesus not commit murder; they must also curb anger that is at the root of murder. This is an ideal, maybe a nearly unachievable ideal, but it would be chimerical to take it literally and prosecute in court all those harboring anger and hold them *liable to judgment*. "You have heard the commandment, 'You shall not commit adultery.' What I say to you is: anyone who looks lustfully at a woman has already committed adultery with her in his thoughts" (Matt. 5:27–28). As anger is at the root of murder, so is lust at the root of adultery. But in our society, to eradicate lust would require that men and women dress like monks and nuns and that magazine covers only portray unattractive individuals—which may still not eradicate lust. Even if men and women were to withdraw into monasteries lust would follow them into their retreats. Then, "if your right eye is your trouble, gouge it out!" (Matt. 5:29). No monk has ever gouged his right or left eye to escape temptations, for it is obvious that the statement is not to be taken literally. Yet the following logion on divorce has been taken literally for centuries: "Everyone who divorces his wife forces her to commit adultery" (Matt. 5:32). Next comes the saying on turning the other cheek. Never to "offer resistance" and always "turn the other cheek" may be neither feasible nor desirable (except in the view of pacifists). The final saying on loving one's enemies is an achievable Christian norm, however. In summary, the Sermon on the Mount contains ideals impossible to practice (gouge your left eye), sound moral counsels of perfection (*sometimes* turn the other cheek), and clear norms for Christian life (love your enemies). How is one to distinguish ideals from norms?

The texts themselves suggest an answer: it is the moral principle itself that must be intrinsically—not extrinsically—a law, commandment, norm, or counsel. Thus it would make little sense to make the control of anger a law, and the punishment of murder a counsel, or the turning of the other cheek a norm rather than an ideal. Celibacy cannot be made a law for all, even if deemed desirable. Similarly the universal ban on divorce cannot be made a law for at least two reasons: Joseph intended to divorce Mary; and Matthew explicitly excludes cases from a universal ban on divorce. I will conclude this question after inquiring first into the actual evil of divorce.

Matthew 19:3: The Unjust Dismissal of Wives

The Greek text speaks not of divorce but of "dismissal" (*apolyō*). There is nothing intrinsically evil in dismissing servants or wife; it may even be necessary in exceptional circumstances (e.g., Joseph and Mary). The issue here is unjust dismissal, as suggested by the very question: "May a man dismiss his wife *for any reason whatever?*" The very question whether men can dismiss their wives for *any* reason while the latter can dismiss their husbands for *no* reason reflects a highly unjust social system.

The view of ancient Judaism was this: "Married women are outsiders in the household of their husbands and sons, while daughters are prepared from birth to leave their father's household and transfer loyalty to a husband's house and lineage" (Freedman 1992, s.v. *women*). Such practices are still commonly followed in the Far East. Because daughters do not inherit from their father, they are homeless in their own home. Their real and permanent home will be their husband's through an arranged marriage. Thus, the dismissal of wives can be compared to the dismissal of orphans from their adopted homes: they have nowhere to go.

For divorcées, there was never an "honorable discharge." All dismissals were public humiliations as failures. Childlessness, always seen as the fault of the woman, was the ultimate disgrace, being seen as personal failure as well as divine disfavor (Gen. 30:23; 2 Sam. 6:20). In the case of barrenness, the wife could be divorced or expelled from what is now her home at the husband's death (Freedman 1992, s.v. *women*). In either case she was sentenced to poverty, being able to claim neither inheritance nor support from sons in her old age. A wife could also be dismissed for trivial failures in household tasks, in which case her situation was worse than that of a servant who might find employment elsewhere. When a dismissed housewife was publicly branded as a domestic failure, her prospects for remarriage were dim. Moreover, in all cases of dismissal, the wife was not allowed to respond to the accusations: by status she had no rights. If dismissed, she would lose income, access to her children, and the right to an honorable name.

Priests were permitted to marry neither prostitutes nor divorcées (Lev. 21:7); priests could only marry virgins (Lev. 21:14). By equating divorcées with prostitutes, Scripture assigns them an equal rank. There are, however, famous and honorable prostitutes like Tamar (Gen. 38) and Rahab (Josh. 2; 6). The latter is seen by Matthew (Matt. 1:5) as the progenitrix of great men. Moreover, Samson's relationship with a prostitute (Judg. 16:1) is presented as dishonorable to neither. Throughout the biblical literature, there is no famous and honorable divorcée. Hence they seem to have ranked lowest of all, lower than servants and maybe prostitutes. Such a status was the mere creation of the male practice of wife dismissal. Freed slaves could request to stay with their master because of poverty (Exod. 21:5–6; Deut. 15:16–17; see Meyers 1987, s.v. *servant*). Divorced women did not have such rights. One does not have to be a prophet in Israel to realize the great social injustice of such a situation; however, the Pharisees did not see it, because their frame of mind was legalistic and self-centered.

Could dismissal be temporary? Until the husband's remarriage one could entertain the possibility of negotiations, compromise, and an eventual reunion. The remarriage of the husband made the humiliation of the dismissed wife final and without recourse. Hence, "Whoever dismisses his wife and marries another commits adultery *against her*" (Mark 10:11). It is hard to see why divorce by itself would be intrinsically evil, but it easy to see that the unjust dismissal of wives and their definite status as social outcasts through the ex-husband's remarriage are crimes "against her" that cry for divine vengeance.

In ancient Judaism, the dismissal of wives was clearly unjust. There was nothing unjust in divorce by mutual consent in the Roman society in which Paul lived and wrote. The dismissal of wives has disappeared from our legal codes. Hence, the ban on divorce based on the unjust dismissal of wives does not seem to apply to our times.

Matthew and the Exception Clause of Porneia

Matthew 5:32 and 19:9 condemn the dismissal of wives "except in the case of *porneia*." What is the meaning of this exception? "Everything about these exceptive clauses is contested" (Freedman 1992, s.v. *divorce*). Is this logion from Jesus himself? The answer would shed little light since it is the text itself that is unclear; hence interpretation is unavoidable. Yet in the absence of clarity of the text, all interpretations are nothing but interpretations.

The maximalist interpretation contests the very notion of exception. Although in Greek and English the word "except" is meant to be an exception, the maximalist position, although literal in its interpretation, tends to deny it. Thus, for Daniel Harrington, the exception clause refers to "a marriage contracted within the degree of kinship forbidden by Lev. 18:6–18," namely, the incestuous unions with parent or sibling (1963:78). Since such "marriages" do not exist today, Matthew's exception clause becomes irrelevant and can be dismissed.

Edward Mally's interpretation in the Catholic *Jerome Biblical Commentary* comes to the same conclusion. *Porneia* according to him refers to "premarital sexual intercourse on the part of a woman engaged in a Jewish betrothal." Since the husband "had been deceived into believing that his wife was a virgin . . . [he] was obliged by Jewish customary law to sue for an annulment of the marriage contract." Today both betrothal and its customary laws have disappeared, hence Matthew's exception clause is obsolete. However, if premarital sexuality were grounds for divorce not only in Judaism but in Christianity as well, not only for men but also for women, then most marriages today would be open to the challenge of divorce, a consequence which the author could not foresee when he wrote in the 1960s.

In the New Testament, the meaning of *porneia* is not clear; in most instances the term refers to sexual immorality generally, but in other instances it has a specific meaning which remains unclear; in non-Catholic translations, it is often translated as "adultery." In reference to Matthew's statement on divorce, if adultery were the specific ground for divorce in that text, then why did he not use the word adultery (*moicheia*)? Historically, however, adultery has been the only real question about divorce: Should not the "innocent party" be allowed to remarry? This question was endlessly raised in the first centuries of Christianity. Historically, *porneia* has been understood as adultery in the Greek-speaking East, and has been translated as such by the Reformers in the West. Adultery seems to be the only exception that is a real exception. Moreover, in recent times the vagueness of the term *porneia* has allowed churches to grant divorces for many reasons besides adultery. As the Catholic Church has come to use its nonbiblical notion of marriage invalidity to include a vast array of annulments, so the Protestants have come to use the vagueness of *porneia* to include a vast array of grounds for divorce. Thus, the Catholic translation of the exception clause could read: "except in cases of marriage invalidity" for which annulments are readily available. The historical battle for the interpretation of *porneia* has become obsolete: the Orthodox and Protestants have stretched the grounds for divorce, while the Catholic Church has stretched the limits for annulments. It is the stretching of these limits that seems deceitful, when it is claimed that annulments are not divorces.

Paul on Marriage as Companionship
(1 Corinthians 7:15)

Paul has written more on marriage and divorce than the rest of New Testament authors. His position is most challenging because we find revolutionary insights buried in a conservative social philosophy. Let us begin with the former.

"If the unbelieving wishes to separate, let him do so. The believing husband or wife is not bound in such case. God has called you to live in peace." Does "not bound" mean free to remarry? "Since the 4th century, Christian tradition . . . has concluded from this passage that the Christian convert is free to contract another marriage" (Kugelman in Brown et al. 1968:264). Hence what we have here is a clear case of separation and remarriage.

"If any brother has a wife who is an unbeliever but is willing to live with him, he should not divorce her. And if any woman has a husband who is an unbeliever but is willing to live with her, she should not divorce him." Is "should not" a prohibition or a moral recommendation? Some, for example, like Tertullian and Jerome, made it a prohibition; others such as "Cyril of Alexandria, Augustine, Ambrosiaster, Pelagius, and almost all medieval commentators, including Thomas Aquinas, regarded it only as a counsel" (Kugelman in Brown et al. 1968:263). Why such a liberal view? Paul himself introduced his recommendation with "I know of nothing the Lord has said" (1 Cor. 7:12); hence, he enjoyed freedom of action. If we side with the interpretation of the majority of the medieval commentators, then we have another case of separation and remarriage.

What is the rationale of Paul's suggestion? One reasonable answer is found in Paul's own words: "God has called you to live in peace." Paul's understanding of marriage was that of his time, that of a practical arrangement for the continuation of the family name (procreation). In antiquity love and sex were separate, and so were the spheres of men and women; moreover, the women's sphere was under the ultimate authority of their husbands. In such an arrangement, however, conflict was manageable: each spouse could retreat into his or her own sphere. In such an arrangement, there was no room for two different religions, because servants, slaves, and wives adopted the religion of the master; hence a household with two different religions was quite unmanageable because the role of religion was pervasive in family life. In such a case, as in many other cases of marital conflict, the issue becomes whether the spouses should stay together for the sake of the household (for the sake of the children, as we say), or separate for the sake of peace. The conflict centers on the issue of marriage as an institution for procreation versus marriage as companionship.

Since Augustine, Catholic theology has single-mindedly emphasized procreation as the primary end of marriage, but from Gen. 2:18 ("It is not good for man to be alone; I will provide a partner") companionship seems equally or more important. Which of the two is more important? In the case of marital conflict, the question of the primacy of marriage as institution for the sake of procreation versus marriage as companionship can be raised. Over the centuries, the Catholic West has single-mindedly emphasized the primacy of procreation at the expense of companionship. In reference to "mixed" marriages, Paul clearly did the reverse. Why did he not extend such a principle to all marriages? The answer lies in his traditional and conservative conception of marriage.

Paul's Social Philosophy of Marriage and Celibacy

History tells us that in antiquity procreation and love were separate. The purpose of marriage was procreation, not love. Men could find the enjoyment of sex with prostitutes, female servants and slaves, and not too rarely, homosexual relationships. Such practices prevailed even among Christians: Corinthian men frequented prostitutes with the attitude "Everything is lawful for me" (1 Cor. 6:12). Paul's repeated warnings against sexual license (1 Cor. 6:15ff.; 10:8; 2 Cor. 12:21; Col. 3:5; Rom. 13:14; Gal. 5:16–19) seem to refer to real practices. He even mentions a case of incest, "a kind not even found among the pagans" (1 Cor. 5:1).

In his teaching on marriage Paul reinforces the separation of love and sexuality, at least indirectly. "To avoid immorality, every man should have his own wife and every women her own husband. The husband should fulfill his conjugal obligations toward his wife, the wife hers towards the husband" (1 Cor. 7:2–3). Marriage is seen as legal sex in order to avoid immorality. There is not a word here about companionship as asserted by Kugelman (in Brown et al. 1968:263): "Since marriage is a remedy for concupiscence, those single persons who cannot control themselves should marry. 'It is better to marry than to be continually on fire' with sexual desire."

If marriage is for the weak, for those who cannot control themselves, it is not much of a charism. Moreover, Paul sees intercourse as a "debt," part of an implicit contract: "In the marriage contract the spouses hand over their bodies to each other so that each has the right or power over the partner's body, and neither has power over his (her) own" (Kugelman in Brown et al. 1968:263). In view of such a conception of marriage, celibacy indeed seems better—especially if the *parousia* (end of the world) is near, as Paul believed.

What is marriage according to Paul? "A wife does not belong to herself but to her husband; equally, a husband does not belong to himself but to his wife." Here the Jewish conception of marriage as property becomes mutual.

In ancient Judaism, only wives were property. From his principle that in Christ men and women are equal, Paul takes marriage to be an association of equals, but marriage itself still remains mutual property for sexuality, not really for companionship. This view of marriage has become part of Catholicism ever since as a mutual contract for procreation. In his commentary Kugelman reminds us that "in the marriage contract the spouses hand over their bodies to each other" (see also Osiek 1977).

If such is marriage, is not "a man better off having no relations with a woman?" (1 Cor. 7:1—this statement has been seen as a question since Origen). In reference to the *theological* question of the charism of marriage versus the charism of celibacy, Paul gives *empirical* answers which research can show to be questionable. "The unmarried man is busy with the Lord's affairs, concerned with pleasing the Lord; but the married man is busy with the world's demands" (1 Cor. 7:32). This is not the case in the United States: here young men spend their leisure time socializing and/or drinking, not on the Lord's affairs. As to Corinth, Paul says that the men frequented prostitutes and did not attend to the affairs of the Lord.

"The unmarried woman is concerned with the things of the Lord, in pursuit of holiness in body and spirit. The married woman, on the other hand, has the cares of this world" (1 Cor. 7:34). Is this more than wishful thinking? In the United States, women (as indicated by women's magazines) show great concern for physical appearance but little pursuit of holiness in body and spirit. Paul's statements can also be understood as statements of possibilities rather than facts: the unmarried men and women can—are able, have the time, and so on—to dedicate themselves to the Lord. From these practical reasons it is often concluded that celibacy is preferable, especially for clergymen. But from "having the time" it does not follow that one will take the time. Often those who have most time (e.g., students on vacation) are the least productive. One may investigate scientifically whether celibate priests spend more time in the pursuit of holiness than married priests and/or clergymen. From available evidence, the general answer is negative. From a sample of Canadian priests and pastors in twenty-two denominations, Don Swenson (1998:43) concludes: "There are no significant differences in dimensions of religiosity and parochial commitments between celibate priests and married clergy."

Finally, in Paul's opinion unmarried women are "happier" (1 Cor. 7:40—another translation is "more blessed"). This statement, too, is open to verification. According to U.S. survey data, married women are happier than unmarried women (Bernard 1972:54–55). This makes sense: in Western societies women are socialized to raise a family; getting married for many women is their most important wish. More generally speaking, the scale of happiness is as follows: married men are most happy, unmarried men rank second; next come married women; finally, at the bottom, unmarried women. If this is so, men should marry, but women should not. This sociological excursus makes us realize that Paul has switched from the theological discussion of the charisms of marriage and celibacy to an empirical discussion about who does what and who is most happy. This switching happened because of the conservative social philosophy of his time, which he did not transcend. It is to these issues of social philosophy that we must turn, after a brief look at divorce in the Gospel of John.

Divorce according to the Gospel of John

Compared to the Synoptics, the Gospel of John seems strange. There is no infancy narrative, no temptation in the desert, no baptism of Jesus by John, no mention of baptism by Jesus himself, no ministry in Capernaum, no Sermon on the Mount, no Beatitudes, no sayings on divorce, no Transfiguration. Instead, in John, we have long monologues, which seem late reconstructions. How is this possible? Two opposite explanations are possible: either John had no knowledge whatsoever of the letters of Paul, the three Gospels, and the various collections of Jesus sayings, or, at the other extreme, knowing them all, he wanted not to repeat them but to supplement them. I opt for the latter interpretation.

In the confrontation between Jesus and the Pharisees, the latter are told: "because of *your* hardness of heart Moses let you divorce your wives" (Matt. 19:8). Here it is the Pharisees and all those asking to divorce *for any reason whatever* who are accused of hardness of heart. It would be an illegitimate extension of the text to attribute it to all divorced individuals past and future. Matthew describes at least one couple that would not fit. Joseph is described as "upright" and unwilling to create the public humiliation of a public "dismissal" (divorce) (Matt. 1:19). In Matthew we seem to have a *second exception clause* besides *porneia* allowing for divorce—*when the main motivation is not religious hardness of heart*. It is likely that this exception clause would apply to most Catholic failed marriages of today. As in recent times marriage has become companionship rather than institution, most marriages fail because of relationship breakdown rather than the turning away from God. Hence, the ban on divorce because of religious hardness of heart does not apply to most divorces today.

Enter the five-times-married woman of John 4, currently living in a common-law marriage. Her husbands may all have died of natural causes; hence she may never have divorced. Did she manifest religious stubbornness? Quite to the contrary, she showed faith, and many Samaritans found faith through her (John 4:39–41). Our conclusion would be the same had she been divorced five times. The view that salvation may come through prostitutes and sinners is part of the romantic heritage of Christianity: it is easy to accept it as long as it happened a long time ago, not in our own real world. The challenge of John 4:28 is that having six husbands is a nonissue in comparison to the importance of faith. The story of multiple husbands would be of great journalistic and canonical interest. Canon law, however, is to serve the gospel, not the other way around.

To the five-times-married woman, the Jesus of John offers some quite revolutionary thoughts: "The hour is coming, and is already here, when authentic worshipers will worship the Father in Spirit and truth" and not in Jerusalem (John 4:23). The Torah will pass; it was made by humans. Marriages are social institutions. The children shall not pay the mistakes of their matchmakers. What a human being has united, a human being can put asunder.

For most Christians (including Catholics), divorce has become a nonissue. Should divorce be an issue, then by their divorce rate Christians would rank lowest among all religions. According to the Gospel of John, divorce, in comparison to faith, is a nonissue. On this point the Fourth Gospel supplements the first three. Yet the first three Gospels also supplement the Fourth: divorce is, indeed, a global issue; it is a global issue that urgently requires that we deal with it at the global level. Obsolete laws will not do.

The contrast between John and Paul is quite striking. How can two Christian leaders come to such different conclusions in reference to marriage and divorce? The answer seems to lie in the differences in assumptions and social philosophies. But is "Wives, be subject to your husbands as to the Lord" (Eph. 5:22) part of revelation? Or is it a cultural interpretation of it? Is gender inequality ("no woman can have authority over a man" [1 Tim. 2:12]) part of revelation? Are cultural assumptions and social philosophies part of revelations?

CULTURAL ASSUMPTIONS AND INSTITUTIONALIZATION

The critique of cultural assumptions is often the crux of biblical hermeneutics. By stating that there is a hierarchy of truths, Vatican II has opened the door to a rational critique of tradition. Not all truths, not all biblical, ecumenical, or papal documents are equally insightful. In reference to the New Testament itself, is it Jesus who is "the Way, the truth, and the life" (John 14:6), not Paul, Peter, or James. If there was sexism and authoritarianism in the early church, none or very little can be found in the Jesus of the Synoptics. As to social philosophy, what is conspicuous in the Synoptics is precisely the absence of it or even the avoidance of it.

The Relative Absence of Social Philosophy
in the Synoptics

Jesus announced the kingdom of heaven in parables and metaphors whose interpretation is open-ended; like poems, they offer little basis for abstract philosophical theories. Yet, when this kingdom was institutionalized, hierarchy and a social philosophy were inevitable. Even among the Twelve the issue of hierarchy arose. "An argument arose among them as to which of them was the greatest" (Luke 9:46). The answer, "Whoever does not receive the kingdom of God like a child shall not enter it" (Luke 18:17), refuses to address the issue of social structure. Another answer, "Whoever would be great among you must be your servant" (Matt. 20:26), is no more useful in creating a concrete social hierarchy.

Legitimation can clearly be seen in the case of Peter. Among the Twelve he is always mentioned first, yet he is given no official position or title. Speaking anachronistically, we may ask: Was he made the first *pontifex maximus* (pope)? Or the first *episkopos* (bishop)? Jesus' answer is vague and elusive: "Upon this rock I will build my church"(Matt. 16:18). Yet this elusive text can be used (and has been used) to legitimize papal authority. This is a central issue of Christianity: while Jesus spoke about the kingdom of heaven in general and metaphorically, his followers had to institutionalize it into positions of power and authority, institutional programs, and moral codes. None of these, however, can often be traced back directly to Jesus.

The absence—or rather the avoidance—of social philosophy is most prominent about the role of women, to the chagrin of both conservatives and feminists. This absence might have been socially embarrassing in the formal setting of a banquet when a women, supposedly a "sinner" or prostitute, began "to wet his feet with her tears, and wiped them with the hair of her head, and kissed his feet . . ." (Luke 7:38). Taking place at a formal dinner, this embarrassing situation called for a clarification about the proper role of women. Similarly, when a woman (but not her lover) was caught in the act of adultery, the situation called for a clarification about the proper conduct of women, but none came. Rather than make statements about social philosophies, Jesus promoted universal respect for all, men and women, rich and poor, sinners and nonsinners, as if it were only through respect that future philosophies of equality could emerge centuries later.

Not to take sides is not always possible, especially about controversial issues. It was promptly noted that Jesus' disciples did not fast and on a Sabbath plucked heads of grain (Luke 6:1). Moreover, Jesus was found not to wash before dinner (Luke 11:38). Are these transgressions just petty crimes, or are they examples of subversiveness, a major crime in most societies? On several occasions Jesus was tested for subversiveness. "Is it lawful for us to give tribute to Caesar or not?" (Luke 20:22). The question called for a philosophy of collaboration with the enemy (paying tribute), or one of national rebellion against a foreign power (not paying). As is well known, Jesus avoided the question with an elusive "Render to Caesar what belongs to Caesar."

From the above—and numerous other examples that could be given—it seems that the Jesus of the Synoptics avoided taking sides about controversial issues of social philosophy as if the latter were not the essence of his teaching. But institutionalization is impossible without social philosophy. Thus, "Whoever would be great among you must be your servant" (Matt. 20:26) will be institutionalized differently in a hierarchical and a democratic church. Jesus' teaching, however, is on the importance of service, not the importance of hierarchy or democracy. Although no society can survive very long without a social organization and an implicit ideology, these will come in due time with the first generation of Christians, that is, when the unstructured mass of followers became institutionalized into local synagogues/churches, and later, a universal church. These social philosophies, however, are not part of revelation, neither the philosophy of Paul, to be considered next, nor that of John, to be seen later.

Paul's Social Philosophy

The texts known as the Deuteronomistic History (see Noth 1972, 1981; Fretheim 1981, 1983; Nelson 1981) contain a social philosophy of submission and punishment: success for those who follow the law (literally) and punishment for those individuals and nations that do not. This implicit philosophy is conveyed by terms such as fear, favor, glory, guilt, love, pleasing, power, punish, sacrifices, shame, vengeance, wrath, and so on. Yahweh is described in terms of love (term used 427 times), but also of glory and power (434 occurrences in the New International Version; these numbers are merely indicative and change slightly from translation to translation). Because Yahweh is also a God of wrath (194 times), his power and glory often outshine his love. Fear of the Lord (330 times) is a prominent theme of the wisdom literature. One must "please the Lord" with sacrifices and obedience, or face guilt (104 times), shame (141 times) and punishment. This broad philosophy is eminently social, since fear, guilt, and shame are the prominent tools of social control. Moreover, when the interpretation of the Law became a quasi monopoly of the religious elite, the Law itself became a tool for national unity, uniformity, and control. To what extent Paul has internalized this moral philosophy is debatable, but what is not debatable is that his emerging communities needed a social structure and a social philosophy. To a certain extent, the structures and philosophy Paul suggested have become part of Christianity itself.

In the Pauline corpus (excluding the letter to the Hebrews) the authors (Paul's followers have written some of the letters attributed to him) write about God's power (*dynamis, exousia, archē*) and glory (*doxa*) sixty-two and sixty-six times respectively, while the three Synoptics use these terms only thirty-seven and twenty-four times respectively, according to Bullinger's Greek Concordance. When power and glory are attributed to Jesus in the Synoptics and Paul, there is a difference of great institutional significance between the two: in the former the power of Jesus, for example, to heal and cure, is the power of the historical Jesus, while in Paul it is the power of the resurrected Christ, the new cosmic Adam. In the Gospels the power of the incarnated Jesus was not co-opted by individuals (e.g., the sons of Zebedee) or groups (e.g., the three, the twelve, or the seventy). Paul's language of divine power, however, is open to appropriation by would-be power groups; then the power of God is used for institutional submission. Paul comes close to such a practice when he writes: "Those who will not obey the gospel of our Lord Jesus shall suffer the punishment of eternal ruin, cut off from the presence of the Lord and from the glory of his might" (2 Thess. 1:9).

The language of power and glory can be used to legitimize social structures. Thus the church itself may come to define itself in terms of power and glory; then the power and glory of God are seen in the power and glory of the church. Paul comes close to such legitimation when he writes lovingly about Titus and his co-workers, adding that they are "an honor to Christ" (2 Cor. 8:23). If a pope were to call a cardinal (e.g., Ratzinger) "an honor to Christ," it would clearly be religious legitimation. The language of power and glory is also used to legitimize gender roles: "man is the image and glory of God, but a women is the glory of man" (1 Cor. 11:7). The language of power came to blossom centuries later when the priesthood itself came to be defined canonically in terms of power, the power of jurisdiction and the power of order.

Paul's great innovation is his emphasis on obedience. The word "obedience" is used only fourteen times in the whole Bible (New International Version), but the Greek word for obedience (*hypakoē*) is used eleven times in Paul's letters, most prominently in the letter to the Romans; to obey (*hypakouō*) is used five times in the Synoptics and sixteen times in Paul. "By one man's disobedience many were made sinners, so by one man's obedience many will be made righteous" (Rom. 5:19). According to Gerhard Schneider (in Balz and Schneider 1994, s.v. *hypakouō*), "For Paul, faith is essentially a matter of obedience, just as the lack of faith is understood as disobedience toward God and his message." The contrast between the two is made an absolute dichotomy in the letter to the Romans: "For humankind there is, according to Rom 6:16, only the either-or of slavery under sin or slavery under obedience (of faith)" (ibid.). Thus in Paul, disobedience becomes *the* cardinal sin, and obedience *the* cardinal virtue. In contrast to faith that is an inward disposition, obedience involves an external manifestation of submission; it is "giving in to the orders or instructions of one in authority or control (an obedient child)" (Webster, s.v. *obedient*). As an external manifestation, obedience can be enforced and even coerced, as in childhood or the military. Obedience as external compliance is a cardinal virtue in most societies, especially authoritarian ones, as it is a cardinal virtue of childhood. In Kohlberg's scheme of moral development, however, obedience to an outside authority best describes conventional morality. In postconventional morality, the locus of authority for moral action is the self, not an outside power.

As a religious leader, Paul wants "to *win obedience* from the Gentiles" (Rom. 15:18). He praises the Romans not for their faith but for their obedience: "*your obedience* is well known to all" (Rom. 16:19). Since a strong social organization requires the external submission of all, the role of faith itself is transformed: faith must be subsumed by obedience. What is important is "to bring about *the obedience of faith* for the sake of his name among all nations" (Rom. 1:5); there the glory of God is manifested in the "obedience of faith." This theme is repeated in 2 Cor. 9:13: "You will glorify God by your obedience in acknowledging the gospel of Christ." Moreover, for Paul, God's plan disclosed by the prophets is "to bring about *the obedience of faith*" (Rom. 16:26).

As an external manifestation, obedience can be coerced, for instance, by threats and fear. In the Deuteronomistic philosophy, "fear of God" is the beginning of virtue, as was the fear of hell in traditional Catholic preaching. So it is, to a certain extent—in Paul, for example, when he acknowledges his intent to "*compel* every human thought to *surrender* in obedience to Christ, and we are prepared to *punish all rebellion* when once you have put yourself in our hands" (2 Cor. 10:6). He wants to "compel" and "punish"; he requires "surrender" from those who "have put (themselves) in (his) hands." In the same letter Paul praises the Corinthians not only for their obedience to Titus, Paul's co-worker, but also for their "*fear and trembling*" when receiving him (2 Cor. 7:15).

This social philosophy of obedience would not be complete without the darker sides of the Deuteronomistic philosophy. Indeed Paul writes about wrath, vengeance, and shame several times more often than the Synoptics. The then prevalent culture of glory and shame is used for social control, for example, by casting shame on those who disobey. "If any one refuses to obey what we say in this letter, note that man, and have nothing to do with him, that he may be ashamed" (2 Thess. 3:14). This is a clear threat of shunning, or excommunication, a typically Christian tool for social unity and control. The threat of divine vengeance is also clearly spelled out: God will *"inflict vengeance* upon those who do not know God and upon those who do not obey the gospel of our Lord Jesus. They shall suffer the punishment of eternal ruin, cut off from the presence of the Lord and from the glory of his might" (2 Thess. 1: 8–9). Paul had already reminded his Roman readers: *"Vengeance is mine,* I will repay, says the Lord" (Rom. 12:19). Paul writes about "wrath" ten times in the letter to the Romans. If the Christians are "storing wrath for (themselves) on the day of wrath when God's righteous judgment will be revealed" (Rom. 2:5), what will happen to the heathens? The greatest wrath and fury are heaped on those who disobey: "for those who are factious and do not obey the truth but obey wickedness, there will be *wrath and fury"* (Rom. 2:8). By using fear of eternal judgment to bring about the "obedience of faith," Paul is using the Deuteronomistic philosophy of religious obedience and control.

One must admit that these darker sides (e.g., authoritarianism, sexism, political sacralization) are very much in the background in Paul's writing, yet they are there, ready to be used and abused. What is debatable is whether these darker sides are preferable to those found in other early Christian communities, e.g., the apparent total lack of social structures and constant in-fighting of the Johannine communities, as we will see below.

On Love and Obedience in Paul

Love seems even more important than obedience: Paul writes about *agapē* fifty-five times (only twice in the Synoptics), and about *phileō* and *agapaō* (to love) twenty-nine times (thirty-two in the Synoptics; forty-seven times in John). His emphasis on love is constant and pervasive. It is justified theologically: "There are three things that last forever: faith, hope and love, but the greatest of them all is love" (1 Cor. 13:3). Love will never end, but knowledge and prophecies will. Hence he might have said: "*at^2 the beginning there was love; at the end of times there will be only love." This view, however, is not pursued. We did *not* read in Rom. 5:19: "*By *one man's self-ishness many were made sinners, so by one man's total love,* many will be made righteous." Nor do we read in Rom. 13:1–2: "*there is *no love but from God*; consequently, anyone who refuses God's love has no part in God's kingdom." In Rom. 13 we have a sacralization of religious secular institutions: "existing authorities are instituted by God; consequently anyone who rebels against authority is resisting a divine institution." How could the Roman Empire based on conquest, plunder, and slavery be called "an existing institution instituted by God"? One possible answer is that for Paul obedience is love and love is obedience; hence praiseworthy obedience may sacralize unjust social institutions. Yet if there is conflict between love and obedience, the latter will have precedence: "If anyone has no love for the Lord, let him be accursed"(1 Cor. 16:22). Love is in obedience; it is the obedience of love; and let those who do not conform be accursed.

The citizens of Rome, head of the mightiest empire of the world of that time, must have been pleased to read—Paul endeavored to please them— "Every person must submit to the supreme authorities" (Rom. 13:1). One generation later, a writer, presumably from Rome, using the name of Peter, emphasized the need for Christians to be socially accepted. The persecution of Nero did not deter him from writing: "Be obedient to every human institution, whether to the emperor as sovereign or to the governors. . . . Such obedience is the will of God"(1 Pet. 2:13). This writer was a pragmatist who saw the benefits of social integration, not a social philosopher. For the first Christians, persecutions and the death of Peter and Paul were less threatening than internal dissent. Writing again presumably from Rome, the third successor of Peter wrote: "Love knows of no division, promotes no discord. . . . Those of you, then, who were at the root of these disorders, pray now make your submission to the clergy" (1 Clement 49.5; 57.1). His final wish and prayer are for universal obedience: "Make us to be obedient both to thine own almighty and glorious Name, and to all who have the rule and governance over us upon earth" (1 Clement 60.4–61.1; quoted from Early Christian Writings). It is no coincidence that civil obedience was also a cardinal virtue of the Roman Empire, which rested on obedience to the law and public order.

On numerous occasions Paul writes about brotherly love. "Love one another with brotherly affection" (Rom. 12:10). All the commandments "are summed up in this sentence: You shall love your neighbor as yourself" (Rom. 13:9). This theme is repeated in Gal. 5:14: "The whole law can be summed up in a single commandment: love your neighbor as yourself." What is strange is that Paul writes as if he were expressing his own or a commonly held opinion. In the three Synoptics (e.g., Matt. 22:34), however, a lawyer asked the question, "Which is the greatest commandment?" as if the answer were not obvious. In Mark (12:32) the lawyer is impressed by the sagacity of Jesus' reply ("love your neighbor as yourself"—the same words as in Paul). Paul seems to have no knowledge of this; the sayings of Jesus had, indeed, not yet been recorded. There is no reference to Jesus' "new commandment: love one another" (John 13:34). John's Gospel will only be written about a generation later.

What is spousal love in the Pauline corpus? "Husbands love your wives as Christ also loved the church" (Eph. 5:25; this was probably written by a follower of Paul). In Rom. 5:19 we learned that Christ's love for the church was "obedience"; hence, spousal love is likely to be found in subordination. For wives, this duty is clearly spelled out: "Wives be subject to your husbands as to the Lord; for the man is the head of the woman, just as Christ is the head of the church" (Eph. 5:22). Aristotle believed that friendship is possible only among equals. How can there be friendship when the difference between husband and wife is as great as that between Christ and the church? How much spousal friendship can there be when the wife is made the source of all evil: "It was not Adam who was deceived; it was the woman who, yielding to deception, fell into sin" (1 Tim. 3:13—written by a follower of Paul)?

On Love and Secessionism in John

The Gospel of John stands in sharp contrast to both the Synoptics and Paul's ecclesiology. The eschatological kingdom of heaven is not mentioned. There are no parables. There is no reference to the institutionalization of baptism and the Eucharist, the two basic non-Jewish practices of the early Christian Jews. The term "apostle" is not used. There is no sending out of the Twelve. There is no imagery of working in the Lord's vineyard and bringing in the harvest. The beloved disciple is the role model for discipleship, which emphasizes individual relationship with Jesus as Christ. The Paraclete will dwell in the believers, without an institutional dimension mentioned here. Love is the ultimate sign of discipleship (John 13:35). Mutual love is a "new commandment"; but it is thus truncated from its Jewish sources: there is no reference to the Torah as in Matt. 22:37–39. John's fundamental metaphor of community is that of the vine and the branches (John 15:5), which is as individualistic as it is egalitarian. It contrasts sharply to the Pauline metaphor of head and body, which introduces a hierarchy among members.

There is a fundamental structure that shapes the Johannine communities, that of an opposition between the in-group (the disciples) and the out-group ("the Jews" first, all secessionists later). The Johannine community is warm and close—as are those communities that are persecuted, isolated, and/or in conflict with their environment. It is this antagonism that keeps them close. When the antagonism comes to an end, the community is likely to disband.

The time has come when "the real worshippers will worship the Father in spirit and truth"—not in Jerusalem (John 4:23). Thus the stage is set for a general confrontation between "the disciples of Moses" (John 9:29) and the disciples of Jesus. Yet the verdict is already written on the wall: "anyone who acknowledges Jesus as Messiah should be banned from the synagogue" (John 9:23). The Johannine Christians were close because they were persecuted. Within years, the conflict with outsiders (the Jews) turned into a conflict against insiders, false prophets (1 John 4:4) and Antichrists (1 John 2:18–19). This conflict also became ideological, against those "liberals" who "go too far" in doctrine (2 John 9), and those "Gnostics" who do not acknowledge "that Jesus has come in the flesh" (2 John 7). Finally, in the book of Revelation, which may have emerged from a Johannine community, there are strong images of tears and laughter, fear and joy, which are open to easy manipulation. In sharp contrast to the darker side of institutional religion in Paul, coercion here is internal, based on the disciple's own fears. The disciples' hopes, too, are personal and individual: "Yes, I am coming soon, and bringing my recompense with me, to requite everyone according to his deeds" (Rev. 22:12). In contrast to Paul, 1 Peter, and *1 Clement,* no obedience is due to the beastly Roman emperor (Rev. 13). The book ends with a dichotomous vision of insiders in clean robes and outsiders who are "dogs, sorcerers and fornicators, murderers and idolaters" (Rev. 22:14–15). Johannine love does not seem to apply to outsiders. (For this section, see Brown 1984, chap. 6).

From a sociological point of view, both authoritarian hierarchical societies and decentralized chaotic love communities have their limitations. What is at stake here, however, is that a hierarchical society is likely to impose social and moral codes, for example, on marriage and divorce, while a decentralized one will not. Hence, if moral codes and regulations about divorce are a by-product of the need to regulate society, they may have little universal intrinsic value. In other words, the regulation of marriage and divorce is very much a matter of politics.

CONCLUSION: THE POLITICS OF
MARRIAGE AND DIVORCE

As indicated in 1 Cor. 7, Paul felt equally free to give commands, recommendations, and suggestions. "To those married, I give this command (though it is not mine; it is the Lord's): a wife must not separate from her husband." As the translation of *New American Bible* suggests, this is Paul's own command. As explained in the *Anchor Bible Dictionary* (s.v. *divorce*) "the parenthesis qualifies Jesus' prohibition as an afterthought because of its pastoral utility rather than a normative principle." Any leader must be able to make decisions on his/her own, for the good of the community. And such decisions are political, that is, pertaining to the common good.

The regulation of marriage and the prohibition of divorce through laws, whether civil or canonical, are political acts that must be judged by their political value (the common good) rather than just their orthodoxy. Divorce has been a political issue throughout Western history. "In 778 the Ninth Synod of Carthage, convoked by Charlemagne, prohibited the remarriage of any person who had been repudiated by his or her spouse." Charlemagne made this decision a state law throughout his Christian empire. "For three hundred years, after Augustine had enunciated the absolute indissolubility of marriage, the church had hesitated on the question, but now a secular law upheld it for all Christians. The church itself continued to hesitate . . ." (Phillips 1988:24). In the East, marriage and divorce remained a secular political issue for over a millennium. It was a political decision of the American Catholic bishops to brandish excommunication against those who divorced and remarried outside the church, as it was a political decision to abolish such a measure as recently as 1977. Similarly, it was a political decision to maintain in the 1983 Code of Canon Law the prohibition against such persons receiving communion in the Catholic Church.

Laws must be judged by their political benefits for the common good. Whatever the benefits of the canonical prohibition of divorce when Catholicism was a social power in Western societies in the Middle Ages and the *ancien régime*, it may now have outlived its usefulness. Today the vast majority of Catholics disregard it, seeing it as obsolete or unjust. Many divorces are clearly not inspired by "hardness of heart." The church recognizes such a claim and generously grants annulments. But it is the very generosity of annulments that proves the obsolescence of the canonical ban on divorce: Why, in an age of priest shortages, dedicate vast resources in personnel and money to tribunals that essentially legitimate secular divorce decisions?

In summary, Jesus preached precepts that can be understood as ideals, norms, or commands. Jesus did not bring canon law nor any part of it. By definition, laws are human-made and must be judged by their usefulness. The current situation of marriage and divorce in the West clearly requires a rethinking of our marriage laws, both secular and religious.

In the next chapter, E. Schillebeeckx will probe further the ideological and anthropological dimensions of the institution of marriage.

Notes

1. It is common to refer to Paul's ruling on divorce as the "Pauline privilege." The popes have also reserved to themselves the right to dissolve marriages in certain cases; this is known as the "Petrine privilege." The latter is discussed in chapter 6.

2. It is customary in discourse analysis to print counterfactual (hypothetical) statements with an asterisk before the text.

WORKS CITED

Balz, Horst, and Gernard Schneider
    1994   *Exegetical Dictionary of the New Testament.* 3 volumes. Grand Rapids: Eerdmans.

Bernard, Jessie
1972   *The Future of Marriage.* New York: Bantam Books.
Brown, Raymond E.
1984   *The Churches the Apostles Left Behind.* New York: Paulist Press.
Brown, Raymond E., and John Meier
1983   *Antioch and Rome.* New York: Paulist Press.
Brown, Raymond E., Joseph A. Fitzmyer, and Roland E. Murphy, eds.
1968   *The Jerome Bible Commentary.* Englewood Cliffs, N.J.: Prentice Hall.
Bullinger, Ethelbert W
1908   *A Critical Lexicon and Concordance to the English and Greek New Testament.* London: Longman, Green.
Burchard, Christoph
1993   "Jesus of Nazareth." In *Christian Beginnings,* edited by Jürgen Becker. Word and Community from Jesus to Post-Apostolic Times. Louisville, Ky.: Westminster/John Knox Press.
Early Christian Writings
1968, 1976   Translated by Maxwell Staniforth. Harmondsworth, England: Penguin Books.

Eberts, Harry W.
1997   "Plurality and Ethnicity in Early Christian Mission." *Sociology of Religion* 58, no. 4.
Espenshade, Thomas
1984   *Investing in Children: New Estimates of Parental Expenditures.* Washington, DC: The Urban Institute Press.
Freedman, David Noel, ed.
1992   *The Anchor Bible Dictionary.* 6 volumes. New York: Doubleday.
Fretheim, Terence
1981   *The Exile and Biblical Narrative: The Formation of the Deuteronomistic and Priestly Works.* Chico, Calif.: Scholars Press.
1983   *The Deuteronomic History.* Nashville: Abingdon Press.
Gill, Anthony
1998   *Rendering unto Caesar.* Chicago: University of Chicago Press.
Harrington, Daniel J.
1963   *The Gospel According to Matthew.* Collegeville Bible Commentary. Collegeville, Minn.: Liturgical Press.
Kohlberg, Lawrence
1981   *The Philosophy of Moral Development.* San Francisco: Harper & Row.

Leon-Dufour, Xavier
  1967, 1977   *Dictionary of Biblical Theology.* New York: Seabury
                      Press.
Mally, Edward J.
  1968   "The Gospel According to Mark." In Brown et al.
                      1968.
Meyers, Allen C., ed.
  1987   *The Eerdmans Bible Commentary.* Grand Rapids:
                      Eerdmans.
Nelson, Richard D.
  1981   *The Double Redaction of the Deuteronomistic History.*
                      Sheffield: JSOT Press.
Noth, Martin
  1972   *A History of Pentateuchal Traditions.* Englewood
                      Cliffs, N.J.: Prentice Hall.
  1981   *The Deuteronomistic History.* Journal for the Study of
                      Old Testament, Supplement Series 15. Sheffield: JSOT
                      Press.
Osiek, Carolyn
  1977   "First Corinthians 7 and Family Questions." *The Bible
                      Today* (September).
  1997   *Families in the New Testament World: Households and
                      House Churches.* Louisville, Ky.: Westminster John
                      Knox Press.
Phillips, Roderick
  1988   *Putting Asunder: A History of Divorce in Western Soci-
                      ety.* Cambridge: Cambridge University Press.
Popenoe, David
  1996   *Promises to Keep.* Boston, Mass.: Rowman & Little-
                      field.
Sandmel, Samuel
  1970   *The Genius of Paul: A Study of History.* New York:
                      Shocken Books.
Swenson, Don
  1998   "Religious Differences between Married and Celibate
                      Clergy: Does Celibacy make a Difference?" *Sociology
                      of Religion 59*, no. 1.
Yeager, Randolph O.
  1976–1985   *The Renaissance New Testament.* 18 vols. Bowling
                      Green, Ky.: Renaissance Press.

4

Christian Marriage and the Reality of Complete Marital Breakdown

EDWARD SCHILLEBEECKX

Whoever divorces his wife and marries another makes himself guilty of adultery against her. (Mark 10:11, a saying of Jesus himself, according to historical-critical scholarship)

THE CHURCH'S INTERPRETATIONS OF JESUS' WORDS

NEITHER JESUS NOR THE NEW TESTAMENT spoke as though monogamy was a requirement in marriage. It is true that in Jesus' time monogamy was the rule for social and economic reasons, but polygamy was not necessarily excluded. But it is also true that Jesus spoke about marriage (both monogamous and polygamous) in a radical sense, and each time it had to do with the wife being divorced. Mark 10:11 is an example of this.

In the patriarchal view of marriage, which remained normative among the Jews in Jesus' time despite other changes in Jewish culture, a husband could violate the marriage of another man but he could not violate his own marriage. His wife was his property by right; therefore he as the owner could not act unjustly against her. On the other hand, a wife, as the husband's property, could for that reason violate her own marriage and sin against her husband. In Mark 10:11, Jesus protests against this discrimina-

Originally published in Dutch as "Het christelijk huwelijk en de menselijke realiteit van volkomen," in *Annalen van het Thijmgenoorschap* (1970).

tion and proclaims the reciprocity of the bond of marriage. He defends the weak and powerless party by stating that the husband can violate his own marriage; that is, he can sin against his wife. Jesus asserts in a radical way the reciprocity of mutual fidelity in marriage.

Implied here is a fundamental inspiration of far-reaching importance that can be found concretely expressed in various ways throughout the New Testament. Paul formulates a new vision of indissoluble marriage as "a command of the Lord" (1 Cor. 7:10–11): neither partner may divorce the other. If divorce nevertheless happens, then in Paul's mind there are only two possibilities: either reconciliation or remaining unmarried. This interpretation of Jesus' fundamental inspiration is perfectly clear. Nevertheless, this text is directly followed by an exception (see below), from which it is evident that this "command of the Lord" is difficult to translate into legal categories or the unforgiving words of formal justice.

One problem that must be faced is that the New Testament, which says that marriage is indissoluble, never tells us what marriage is. Marriage is a cultural phenomenon; it cannot be derived from some a priori "human nature" that is established once and for all. What it means to be a husband and wife in marriage is subject to historical development. It is likewise determined by economic, social, and psychological factors. Conditioned by these factors, human beings again and again seek their own humanity, which is being held out to them as a new task in ever-changing circumstances. Thus, in human history, large-scale developments occur that produce a continually greater achievement of humanity—a humanity which, interpreted religiously by the believer, can be rightly named the "will of God" at that moment.

A consequence of this creative acquisition of humanity is that human beings cannot in good conscience reverse that course. Lest they be regarded as unworthy, they can no longer abandon what humanity has consciously achieved. Nevertheless, beyond this point of development, the direction always remains open toward still greater actualizations of humanity in other situations. In this way, the developing ethos of marriage never reaches a conclusive stage. By maintaining and transforming from within that which has already been achieved, it stands open to the future, and in the future, other forms of human marital experience can appear, on the condition that the humanity already achieved is not abandoned (even if it appears in an entirely new form).

Both the development of marriage as a social phenomenon in the human race as a whole and the twists and turns within the church's tradition regarding the indissolubility of marriage clearly demonstrate that social values determine what is considered a truly indissoluble marriage at any given point in time. I want to illustrate this with seven facts. My starting point is that in the past marriage was fundamentally considered a social institution with intrinsic, pre-given rules, by which people remained bound for life once they had consciously and freely entered into it. In other words, even when this institutional view of marriage, and the later interpretation of it as a "natural given," held sway (and thus before talking about the modern view of marriage), an entire gamut of possibilities was already evident.

1. In Jewish society, the exclusive purpose of marriage was the preservation, continued fertility, and strength of the extended family. Therefore, a legally valid and completed marriage was not one that was sexually consummated but one that was sealed with at least one child. In fact, a marriage that had remained childless for ten years could for that reason be dissolved.

This view, by the way, is not a thing of the past. Living in a preindustrial agrarian world, African bishops are confronted with the same social structure. During the Second Vatican Council, various African bishops asked me whether it would not be meaningful for Africa to regard the birth of a child as the consummation of marriage, so that a marriage that was childless for years could be dissolved. Socially and economically a childless marriage in many parts of Africa appears really meaningless, and childless couples do in fact separate from each other. The "complete breakdown" in this case is therefore social in nature, which is characteristic of a patriarchal view of marriage.

2. After mentioning Jesus' radical teaching (1 Cor. 7:10–11), Paul nevertheless gives his own interpretation of what a complete marriage breakdown is. Concretely, a marriage can break down on the basis of changed religious convictions (1 Cor. 7:12-16). In antiquity, social and religious beliefs formed an integral whole, so consider what would happen if one of the partners of a non-Christian marriage became a Christian.

Normally this must have referred to the conversion of the husband, for the wife normally followed what the husband did and could take the initiative herself only with difficulty. Given this patriarchal view of marriage, a wife's conversion would in and of itself be an intrinsic challenge to the marital arrangement. On the other hand, could Paul perhaps have had the conversion of a wife in mind?

If the conversion of one of the married partners to Christianity is not accepted by the other party (so that the foundation is laid for the breakdown of the marriage), then Paul finds that the demand for indissolubility is not in force. Marriage should not be slavery, he says; in such a case the believer may let the unwilling party go: "God has called us to peace" (1 Cor. 7:15). It is clear that complete marriage breakdown here serves as the real Pauline principle of interpretation, for if the nonbelieving partner wants to continue the marriage harmoniously with the new Christian, then the believer may not divorce him or her (7:12).

In what has come to be called the Pauline privilege (as canon law treats this), this vision of Paul is completely lost, and an entirely different view comes to the fore. In Catholic canon law, a "natural marriage" may be dissolved for the sake of a "Christian marriage," even if the nonbelieving party does not want this. This passage from Paul, however, shows his general intention: for the sake of the gospel, there are situations in which a Christian must be able to give up everything, even his or her spouse. It is nevertheless foreign to Paul's reasoning to conclude in light of this that a "natural marriage" is dissoluble for the sake of a "Christian marriage." In Paul's thought, the real issue is marital breakdown.

Let me add in passing that the Pauline privilege in its canonical interpretation serves to weaken all of the arguments that moral theology presents for indissolubility based purely on the "nature" of marriage. As a result, the sacramentality of marriage, interpreted ontologically as a representation of the indissoluble covenant with God, is the sole remaining premise supporting the indissolubility of marriage. In other words, this view of marriage removes any human foundation for marriage, which those who argue this way seem to forget.

Paul says nothing about remarriage in this case. Apparently, he judges the possibility of remarriage after such a breakdown according to the principles that he gives further on in his letter. In view of the proximity of the Lord's return, it is preferable not to marry, but it is better to marry than to burn with lust (1 Cor. 7:17–40).

3. In spite of some remaining uncertainties recognized by Catholic exegetes,[1] it is becoming more and more clear, on the basis of Matt. 5:32 and 19:9 in connection with Deut. 24:1, that it is very likely that some early Christian communities in Palestine understood there to be exceptions to the norm of indissolubility. A marriage that was broken because of some type of immorality (*porneia*) was regarded as no longer in existence, and in such cases remarriage was allowable. The precise nature of the behavior regarded as *porneia* is difficult to determine.[2] One possibility is that a marriage that was validly contracted according to Hellenistic marriage laws and customs (and which were acceptable to Hellenistic Christians) could be considered as *porneia* (and therefore invalid) according to Jewish laws and customs. Modern exegetes are in agreement that the concepts of legal separation and "separation from bed and board" are not to be found in ancient cultures. *Porneia*, however, can imply more than a marriage that was not recognized as legally valid, and so Matthew may also have had something like marital infidelity in mind when he used that term.

Our search for insight from historical facts yields at least this. In the

Christian message or gospel, the indissolubility of marriage was and remains an inviolable principle. However, what concretely is considered an indissoluble marriage is culturally determined, and about this the New Testament does not pass judgment.

4. In the twelfth century, Pope Alexander III, a canon lawyer, decided that indissolubility did not apply simply to any juridically valid marriage, but only to a marriage that was also sexually consummated (*ratum et consummatum*). This interpretation at first meant that if sexual consummation had not yet taken place, the contracted marriage could still be dissolved because one of the partners "desired" (was forced, very likely) to enter the cloister. Later this interpretation was broadened so that any legally valid but nonconsummated marriage (*ratum tantum*) could be dissolved. Thus there came into existence the notion that legally valid marriages could be both dissoluble and indissoluble.

In comparison with what was said in the Bible, this was a completely new interpretation that nevertheless left untouched the Christian ideal of marriage as such. The question now was: What is a true marriage that can be said to be indissoluble? Alexander III was attempting to forge a compromise between two competing schools of thought. The theologians of Paris viewed the mutual agreement of the partners as essential to forming a marriage, but the canonists of Bologna considered sexual intercourse as the essential ingredient. One consequence of the pope's decision was that it made official the semiofficial criterion that had been used for some time to determine the legal validity of a marriage. According to this criterion, sexual intercourse in a marital relationship made a marriage valid and consummated, even if the marriage had taken place in secret (*matrimonium clandestinum*), and even though clandestine marriages were forbidden by law. This situation prevailed until the Council of Trent.

5. Since the existence or nonexistence of clandestine marriages was difficult to prove in court, when such marriages failed, permission was often given for a second marriage. With respect to this practice, therefore, the Catholic bishops at Trent wanted to impose a little more order. They took the decisive step of decreeing that, henceforward, a wedding ceremony before witnesses was required not only for the marriage to be in accordance with church law but also for the validity of the marriage. With this change, a juridical and institutional element entered into the essence of marriage in the Catholic Church.

Let me state clearly that it was not the intention of the bishops at Trent to turn marriage into a purely ecclesiastical matter. In medieval Christendom, the so-called family wedding, which was a civil affair performed in accordance with secular customs, was a ceremony performed at the doors of the church and followed by liturgical rituals (a blessing or a mass). The secular elements were parts of a whole, and the whole took on a religious character. Moreover, initially at Trent it was not thought that a priest should be the witness for marriage. Some council fathers even claimed that a government official was the proper witness. In their mind, it was a matter of making marriages public, not making them ecclesiastical. In the sixteenth century, all of this was closely intertwined, and many bishops felt there would be more certainty about a marriage's publicness if a priest was in charge of the official registration. Only later, with the advent of civil weddings in the contemporary sense, did publicness as established by Trent come to imply a church wedding in contrast to a modern secular wedding.

6. Very recently in church history—since 1924, to be exact—all sorts of provisions can be found in canon law that can be classified under the so-called Petrine privilege. These provisions derive from the presumed privilege of the successor of Peter to dissolve even an ecclesially contracted and sexually consummated marriage in certain cases. This papal privilege is based on a idea called the "vicarious power of Christ."[3] The explicit justification of this idea comes from the view, developed over the course of time, that a nonsacramental marriage is not indissoluble in and of itself, and so, for the sake of a sacramental marriage (which is interpreted as the marriage of two baptized people), it can be dissolved. In this view, then, baptism becomes a ground for divorce.

We will pass over the obvious mistakes and injustices to which this canonical legislation can give and in fact has given rise.[4] We will also say nothing about the erroneous view that the pope with his supreme power can dissolve such marriages without first determining whether or not a real marital bond exists. Rather, if we pay attention to the original requests for dispensations in such cases, we see that the starting point was almost always a marriage that had completely broken down and had done so because of religious convictions, even if the non-Catholic party was opposed to the divorce.

Although in these cases, marital breakdown and the primacy of the human and personal union were often interpreted in a very church-centered way, it is evident that the idea of complete marital breakdown with the possibility of remarriage is not foreign to the canonical legislation of the Catholic Church. The church thus reflects Paul's inspiration, even though it does so legalistically and on the basis of a dubious theology. There have been cases where, on the basis of Catholic jurisprudence, a so-called canonically *ratum et consummatum* marriage has been dissolved. Practically speaking, then, church law today does not treat the basic principle of Alexander III (which is fundamental in the whole code of canon law) as set in stone.

7. As the seventh fact, I would point to the judicial practice of many papal and episcopal marriage tribunals. Here also the human reality of complete marriage breakdown appears to function as a possibility for a second marriage, whether by cunning or formal circumventions.* What is very often the case is that one partner from a broken marriage reports to an episcopal or papal marriage tribunal. After one or many pastoral conversations, a judgment is formed that the marriage is indeed broken, repair appears humanly impossible, and the fact that these people are turning to church officials is a sign of their Christian commitment. If a church dissolution of marriage is found desirable, the search for a possible way out begins. Can one find a formal juridical reason for the marriage to be declared invalid? Even with a good conscience, one can often find something juridical that can help at least some of these broken marriages.

It can hardly be denied that in judicial practice the fact of marital breakdown plays a fundamental role, yet juridically it does not function as a ground for the dissolution of marriage. This practice has helped many people, but in essence it is unhealthy, unfair, and legalistic. For this reason, in the last few years some episcopal tribunals have searched for new pastoral practices. The question is as follows. Has not complete marital breakdown already been long accepted in ecclesiastical practice as open to the possibility of a "second chance" in a second marriage? This question takes into account that marital breakdown in Rome and diocesan churches is in fact a fundamental reason for looking for loopholes in the juridical net (for the happiness and harmony of the people involved), in order to declare the marriage invalid for reasons that may in fact be irrelevant in the present case. I am expressing myself intentionally in these terms because I do not want to speak in a Christian perspective about grounds for divorce, as will become evident from the argument below.

The question therefore becomes: How can the reality of marital breakdown itself be thought of in a Christian way, so that there is no longer need for juridical circumventions such as the ones described above?

The Ethos of Marriage and Christian Love

The writings of the Old and New Testaments revealed no new institution and no new ethos with regard to marriage (at least directly). Rather, they revealed a new God—Yahweh, the Father of Jesus the Christ—to a people

---

*This article was written prior to the recent practice of extending the grounds for annulment to various forms of psychological incapacity. Schillebeeckx is speaking here about a time when the grounds for annulment were still rather narrowly interpreted.

whose marriage ethos had been developed on a rather patriarchal foundation.[5] For Christians, the socially defined institution of marriage was lived "in the Lord." Those who accepted the God proclaimed by Jesus entered into customary marriage structures with all their traditional religious experience, convictions, and mental expectations. At the beginning of Jewish history, however, these structures were polygamous and were accepted as such. Moreover, the transition from polygamy to monogamy (which in any event was never absolute) was not caused by religious factors, but was the result of social and economic factors that made it impossible for most men to have more than one wife.

Moreover, marriage was lived out from the Old Testament to the New Testament—and in all of church history until a few centuries ago—on two different levels. On the one hand, there was the patriarchal social institution and the marriage ethos that was based on it, according to which the wife was completely subordinate to the husband. At this level, marriage was an institution for the perpetuation of the clan, the extended family, and (from a broader perspective) the human race. On the other hand, there was the Old and New Testament's message of love, lived in the light of the covenant of God with his people, interpreted christologically by Paul as the covenant of Christ with his church. This love, which "in Christ" knows no distinction between husband and wife or between master and slave, nevertheless left the social structures of the times as they were, even in marriage. In and through Christian love, the wife was "sister" and equal, but by social custom she remained in marriage completely subordinate to the husband and not an equal. Thus the total subordination of the wife to the husband was not abolished, but it was taken up into the Christian spirit of love, which rounded off the sharp edges of social discrimination.

Social and patriarchal relationships remained unchallenged, and sometimes this established order was considered the eternal will of God. Relationships were nevertheless drawn into a more personalist sphere. New life was breathed into the existing institution, and this newness would break open the old patriarchal institution of marriage as soon as social and economic structures would make it possible. We can only deplore the fact that the Christian message of love, which rightly demanded reciprocity, did not have the revolutionary power to break more directly through the injustices of marriage in a patriarchal social order. Obviously Christian love is not directly in a position to do this; it could only be realized through an analysis of social structures themselves.

Existing marriage relationships with their particular ethos acquired, especially in the Middle Ages, an ideological foundation. "Natural physiology" (based on physical differences between men and women) came to be valued as an ethical norm that was unknown in the Old Testament. Nevertheless, the two levels described above continued unchanged until the end of the Enlightenment and the beginning of romanticism, when a tendency toward secularism and its characteristically rationalistic assumptions emerged. Marriage was conditioned as well by completely new economic and social situations, and by the I–Thou philosophy that was developed in this period by Fichte and others. Moreover, during this same period (especially in romanticism) sexuality was thought of for the first time in the West as the bodily expression of interpersonal love, which in principle overcame anthropological dualism.[6] Interpersonal mutual love, embodied in sexuality, began to be valued as the very essence of marriage.

In the past, charity (Latin *caritas*; Greek *agapē*), friendship, and mutual affection provided only the Christian environment in which the essence of marriage (i.e., the patriarchal and "natural" institution of marriage) was to be lived out. Since then, however, there has been a very sensitive reversal in human experience. From the past perspective, a marriage without love was socially livable. From the new perspective—which also takes into account the completely new socioeconomic structures that have changed marriage from within—marriage without love and marital breakdown become very significant issues.

From this survey of historical developments, it appears that the meaning, requirements, and limits of the indissolubility of marriage have differed at different times according to the actual meaning of marriage in a given society, and according to its concrete function in the surrounding social system. If the social institution of marriage is the realization of an ever higher and new humanity within developing socioeconomic situations (which implies that what has been achieved may not be abandoned), then, with regard to the type of marriage that has acquired validity in the Western world in the last two centuries, one must say the following.

If marriage is seen and lived as a total, reciprocal, and permanent commitment of two persons to each other in care and love, then indissolubility is not a quality that is bound to result from the social institution, but it is a task that needs to be accomplished from within. Compared with the earlier view, this view attests to a more mature and more elevated level of culture as well as an enlarged sense of humanity. Indissolubility, therefore, does not seem to be a property that comes from an institution; rather, it is dependent on the personal conviction and decision that one wants to have a certain type of relationship with one's marriage partner. If one therefore views marriage as an interpersonal relationship, then one must say (in the light of this human achievement) that monogamous and faithful marriage is indeed "the highest possibility"[7] of this social institution.[8] In such a marriage, two people commit themselves in mutual love to each other for life. Nevertheless, they do not consider their love to be the last word, but they keep themselves open to the responsible possibility of a child in the future. New forms of marriage may yet come into existence, but their value will have to be judged according to their fundamental human worth.

THE HUMAN ETHOS OF MARRIAGE

If one does not think of marriage as a social institution or as determined by nature but simply as a human reality, then one can ask what, in light of humanity's present achievement, are the essential elements of marriage? Human marriage occurs in many different dimensions that together make it humanly valid. Let us examine three dimensions here.

The Interpersonal Dimension

As already stated, one can no longer abandon in good conscience a human value that has been acquired through centuries of history, for such a decision will be regarded as unworthy by those who live according to that value. And in contemporary culture, the fundamental ethical value in married life is the interpersonal marital relationship.

A marriage of mutual love, care, and commitment is one in which, by giving oneself away to the other, one receives back and actualizes oneself in a new way.[9] Indissolubility in this human context is dependent on the conviction of the two partners that they intend to create a marriage that is an unbreakable bond between them. Such a marriage intrinsically excludes the possibility of separation because the interpersonal relationship grows into such a bond that the two partners are existentially incapable of doing anything except remaining together in love.

Indissolubility is thus a task to be accomplished despite many difficulties. It does not rest on an extrinsic will of God or on a previously established institution, according to which two people who are going to marry find themselves obligated by a commandment of indissolubility imposed from outside, as it were. A tension is therefore created in this contemporary vision of marriage when the question is asked: What is a marriage if the interpersonal relationship is completely broken?

The interpersonal marital relationship, however, is not the sole and sufficient ethical norm for the "human validity" of marriage. For this relationship also encompasses another dimension.

The Social Dimension

Martin Buber, the twentieth-century philosopher who devoted a great deal of attention to the I–Thou relationship, insists that such a relationship is possible only if a greater "we" surrounds it. Human existence, including the interpersonal marital relationship, has an inescapable social dimension that is essentially and intrinsically determined by customs and laws. Moreover, this determination is historical; that is to say, concrete norms are not deduced from some previously given and fixed human nature, but they are the fruit of a culture-creating community that is always searching for new ways to be human in the midst of ever-evolving socioeconomic situations. Human law on the subject of marriage has its own history.

If this is the case, the interpersonal community of marriage has an intrinsic relationship to a legal order. However intimate and personal a marriage is, it is not purely a private matter. The specific nature of this personal relationship is something that involves the larger community. For one thing, the other members of the community are by definition excluded from the personal relationship between the two married people. At the same time, however, the surrounding community needs to respect the marriage relationship; otherwise the community makes the relationship simply impossible. In one way or another, the law-creating community has to recognize the marriage bond if it wants two people to be able to function as a married couple in society.

Marriage therefore inescapably has an institutional element; it belongs essentially to the concrete humanity of marriage, precisely as an exclusive interpersonal relationship. Both the publicness of marriage and the legal system in which an interpersonal marital relationship is recognized as legally valid (thus involving the society) flow from this starting point.

In other words, the ethical norm of interpersonal love in marriage, understood from a concrete human perspective, is always surrounded by a legal system and a social norm. Moreover, the latter is not an extrinsic addition to a self-sufficient interpersonal relationship but must be present if there is to be such a thing as marital love in an actual human situation.

So we come to the following conclusion. The constitution, unity, and indissolubility of modern marriage cannot be exclusively based on the interpersonal relationship as a self-sufficient reality. *The existential "yes" of the two partners, insofar as that affirmation is socially accepted (that is, assented to and ordered by the community), is constitutive of marriage as a human reality.* Thus the legal system protects the inner task of making the interpersonal relationship indissoluble. This very fact, however, creates another possibility for tension, for what is to be done if a socially recognized and legally valid marriage becomes completely broken as an interpersonal relationship?

The Religious and Christian Dimension

As a theologian, I have intentionally remained silent until now about the Christian meaning and sacramentality of marriage. Human marriage, lived in faith according to its various cultural forms, is considered a sacrament in the Catholic tradition. The interpersonal relationship that contemporary couples experience as the essence of marriage in today's society is, when it is lived in Christian faith and hope, radically reoriented toward a love that has Christ's unconditional self-surrender as a model for living. This loving relationship necessarily entails forgiveness and reconciliation when it brings together two persons who are good but imperfect people—*simul justus et peccator,* in the classic phrase of Martin Luther. Such believers derive the energy to reorient their marital love radically from their deep Christian convictions and also from their liturgical celebrations of God's covenant in Christ. For in a sacrament such as the Eucharist, faith expresses itself in language that expresses believers' acceptance of God's supremely free love, giving thanks for the power of the living Lord that bears them up and asking for that power from the Christ who is indissolubly united with the church. Christian faith and its sacraments, which are symbolic expressions of faith, reveal a conviction that human history at its deepest level stands under the sign of Jesus' resurrection from the dead.

The sacramentality of marital love is not some sort of automatic, ontological quality that is never experienced, nor is it simply the knowledge that this love is, in the church's view, a reflection of the faithful covenant love between God and humanity, or between Christ and his church. Rather, the sacramentality lies in the depth and authenticity of marital love itself, to which married Christians are called by baptism and which they live out in faith. Such an experienced bond between two people, such a loving reciprocal commitment in all aspects of daily life represents at one and the same time the meaning of human marriage in contemporary culture and the meaning of Christian salvation—which is community-building, caring, redeeming, healing, and forgiving love. This is the reason why the Catholic Church calls marriage a sacrament.

Marriage is therefore indissoluble not because it is a sacramental sign, but it is a sacrament because and to the extent that it realizes within itself the intention of the partners to grow into an unbreakable union of fidelity with each other. It is the existential reality of intentional faith, not the simple fact of being baptized, that transforms marriage into a living sacrament.

Many Protestant churches do not recognize marriage as a sacrament, as Catholics do. Personally, I believe that they nonetheless have substantially the same vision of Christian marriage as the one presented above, despite their resistance (understandable for historical reasons) to the technical word "sacrament." When we get to the heart of the matter, I do not see any reason for a confessional conflict over this point.

The Christian dimension of marriage reveals itself in two ways. On the one hand, one can consider the interpersonal marital relationship itself. Lived out in Christian faith and Christian hope, it is radically transformed into a human love that finds in Jesus' forfeiture of his own life for others a model to which it orients and raises itself. Such an ideal, the gospel itself, cannot be captured in law or legislation—not even in church law. For a person who lives according to this ideal of life, asking about the grounds for divorce is irrelevant and meaningless. The question, "For which reasons is it permissible for a Christian to divorce?" is as legalistic as the old answer, that a "legally valid and sexually consummated marriage" should remain indissoluble, whatever its actual status as a relationship. This Christian vision implies, in my opinion, that no power in the world (neither church nor state) can or should dissolve a truly vital marriage bond between two persons, all canonical "Pauline and Petrine privileges" notwithstanding.

On the other hand, personal faith is not a private affair but has a social dimension because religious faith is always attained in and through a witnessing community. This anthropological fact is the foundation of the ecclesial nature of Christian faith; the Bible itself is an ecclesial witness of early Christianity. This implies that the church has a prophetic, pastoral, and proclamatory task with regard to the Christian standard of marriage as a human social reality. It does not imply, however, that the church ought to set certain conditions for the validity of marriage. Any ordinary human marriage is socially recognized and legally valid, even for baptized persons who live out their marriage in a Christian spirit. The fact that the Catholic Church has set conditions for the validity of marriage is the result of a particular development in Western history; it does not follow inevitably or essentially from its view of the sacraments. The church's policy can therefore be changed, as is clear from what happened in church history prior to the Council of Trent.[10] From a doctrinal perspective, then, there is no reason why the church could not consider so-called civil marriages of Christians as valid (and thus sacramental) marriages. The religious meaning for believers of such marriages could always be liturgically celebrated and affirmed afterwards in the church.

The fact that Christian marriage can be proclaimed by the church and pastorally judged by Christian standards also implies that the church has a role to play with regard to the complete breakdown of a marriage. If, in spite of everything, a Christian marriage is broken, believers have every right to expect from their church a response that is faithful to the gospel and therefore always good news, in a truly Christian sense.

With this as a background, it now becomes possible to speak meaningfully about what is possible for Christians, when a marriage between Christians really runs aground in spite of everything and is irrevocably broken.

CHRISTIAN POSSIBILITIES AFTER MARITAL BREAKDOWN

Human Invalidity

In the present state of human development, marriage as a lifelong commitment to care for one another "for better or for worse" (as the Anglican marriage liturgy realistically expresses it) requires (a) a profound human decision (*actus graviter humanus*), which is conditioned by the maturity and emotional state of the individuals involved, and (b) their moral capacity to build the lifelong relationship that modern marriage demands, for better or for worse, not only generally, but as a concrete relationship between this man and this woman.

Measured by these human standards, many marriages that are valid according to the present norms of canon law are humanly invalid, to coin a phrase, for they do not reach the level of humanity that is required for a true marriage in contemporary culture. This would be the case, for example, when young people are forced through "shotgun weddings" because they have been sexually active with each other, when unwed mothers feel compelled to marry for social or economic reasons, or when teenagers marry in order to get away from their parents. Regardless of their status as civil marriages, such marriages are not the sort that can be considered indissoluble from a Christian perspective. Many cases of marital breakdown are therefore not a problem theologically, even though in such cases there can be severe human problems, for which society is often more guilty than the individuals involved.

Furthermore, the reciprocal yes of an interpersonal relationship is not a single event that takes place at a privileged moment, even if mutual self-giving is the high point of a wedding at the beginning of marriage. The giving of consent is an evolving event that begins before the marriage, knows a moment of solemn affirmation in the socially recognized joining called a wedding, and continues to evolve throughout the life of the couple. The question can therefore be asked: At what point does marriage become consummated, so that the canonical standard of indissolubility can be said to apply to it?

The importance that canon law attaches to the first act of sexual intercourse after the wedding does not make much sense today. Humanly speaking, this first "marital act" may be a failure and therefore irrelevant to the construction of the marriage. It is even possible that in this act is planted the first seed of an eventual marital breakdown. If we can rely on sociological statistics, the length of time spent living together does not seem to play a decisive role in determining whether a marriage is consummated in the sense that two people are completely married to one another. In some cases, the marriage may be consummated in this sense even before sexual intercourse has taken place. In other cases, it may be impossible to say that two people are fully married to each other in a human sense even after they have slept together for a relatively long time.

It turns out that the traditional concept of consummation is not very helpful for thinking about indissolubility from a human point of view. What might be more helpful these days to the anthropologist and theologian alike would be research into the factors that lead to divorce and the factors that lead to a lasting marriage. There is good reason for thinking that only a successful married life has a right to be called "consummated." Furthermore, it seems that the medieval distinction between a marriage that is *ratum tantum* (there has been an exchange of marriage vows but the couple has not yet slept together) and a marriage that is *ratum et consummatum* (there has been an exchange of vows and an act of intercourse) is irrelevant today, even though it is still found in canon law, especially when premarital sex is included in the picture.

The real problem that we ultimately have to deal with is this. Many marriages start out well and appear to be happy for a long time; one can therefore presume that they are humanly valid. Yet in a given marriage there may be a lot of friction beneath the surface while the couple try to stay together "for the sake of the children." Finally, in spite of good will and repeated attempts to repair the relationship—let us say that there is an escalation of conflict—the situation becomes unbearable, and the marriage completely breaks down. Does Paul's prescription still hold, namely, that the partners must either be reconciled (which in this case is impossible) or remain unmarried? Or are there other ways to interpret New Testament prescriptions of this sort?

The Breakdown of a Humanly Valid Marriage

Before addressing the hermeneutical issues, which are most important for theology, I want to face the pastoral issues implied by these questions. In Christian pastoral practice, it often happens that a hermeneutical problem (that is, the problem of how to interpret a biblical passage) implicitly gets solved in the process of living through it. The Christian feeling or sensitivity that arises within caring praxis can, often as not, be an impetus for theoretical hermeneutics, suggesting a justifiable reinterpretation of a biblical passage that may on the surface seem to say something quite different.

Praxis opens one's eyes when it comes to scriptural interpretation, and orthopraxis appears to be a valid hermeneutical principle. To put it another way, pastoral practice often contains a criterion of truth that can be generalized and applied to other cases.

The Pastoral Approach of Oikonomia

What can the church offer to divorced believers who do not want to forgo the possibility of remarrying?

First of all, in the present, it can help them to recognize honestly that their first attempt at marriage has failed. Implicit in this recognition is the Christian conviction that when true marital union is achieved, it is indissoluble, and so this recognition is a sincere affirmation of the ultimate meaning of marriage even in the face of this marriage's brokenness. Moreover, Christians need to live through this experience of brokenness in faith, and the church should have a "ministry of reconciliation" (2 Cor. 5:18) to help them in their need.

Second, the church ought to help divorced believers move into the future. It should not be inquiring about the past or trying to find out who is guilty of causing the divorce. Instead, it should be addressing the future of the two believers, and in that process the past will naturally have to be taken into account.

Sociology tells us that in today's society, divorce and remarriage appear to be two steps in a single social process. After a marriage breaks down, all sorts of social and personal factors come into play to pressure divorced individuals into remarrying. As a result, most divorced people do in fact remarry. This state of affairs confronts us with a new question that, like the previous one, demands a Christian answer.

The question is whether remarriage is justifiable for Christians, and, more to the point, can Catholics justifiably remarry?

As P. Huizing has pointed out, indissolubility cannot mean that a first marriage continues to exist as a prohibition against a second marriage. Such a prohibition would leave indissolubility without any actual meaning; for it says nothing, realistically speaking, about the first marriage in question. If that marriage has in fact completely broken down, then humanly speaking there is no more marriage; there is no longer anything to which "indissolubility" or "dissolubility" can be applied. Instead, there is only the reality of a radical failure, regardless of how one might assign guilt for it; there is the reality of an irrecoverably lost marriage.

Faced with this situation, a Christian can appeal to what Eastern theology calls *oikonomia* (an untranslatable Greek word that can perhaps best be understood as taking everything into account). The Eastern Church is sensitive about not tarnishing the ideal of marriage; it affirms that the intrinsic aim of marriage is an interpersonal relationship, but it also believes that Christians, as Paul says in this context, "are called by God to freedom" (1 Cor. 7:15).

Now, the practice of Christian churches, especially those whose ecclesial nature is generally recognized, is for Catholics a source of theological information (*locus theologicus*) that can no longer be ignored. These churches, acting with an *oikonomia* that recognizes human failings, do not juridically veto people's desire to remarry, which they regard as a private decision of the two people concerned. This is clearly a pastoral interpretation of a practical problem for which there are models in the New Testament, although in a different cultural context than our own.

If we want to be honest, we have to admit that the practice of *oikonomia* has come into existence in the Catholic Church, although for the time being it has to remain underground because it conflicts with the code of canon law. This practice calls into question the legalism of the code, which attempts to safeguard the gospel but does so by translating it into strict legal language that can overstate the proper meaning of the evangelical ideal. We need to reflect on this new practice and on the growing appreciation among Catholics (though not in official circles) for a general Christian consensus with regard to a pastoral practice of recognizing and respecting divorced people's desire to remarry. In this spreading pastoral practice, there is a measure of truth coming to light, albeit indirectly.

Before we go into this, we should see what sociology has to say about what happens to divorced people who remarry. People in pastoral practice are not blind, and they have some sense of what happens in these new marriages. But to be better informed, we ought to take into account some of the new sociological data on this phenomenon, and there are even some emerging sociological theories about them.[11]

Some studies have been done in the United States, where the divorce rate is even higher than here [in the Netherlands], which makes the results rather surprising. On the one hand, divorce in second marriages occurs twice as frequently as in first marriages. On the other hand, two-thirds of these "second chances" succeed and become happy, unbreakable marriages. W. Douma rightly asserts that if 83 percent of the married population remain in a first marriage without divorcing, this means that all together 92 percent "achieve a stable marriage, partly with the help of divorce."

Statistics like these seem to contradict the dire prediction that a new interpretation of *oikonomia* would open the floodgates to divorce. Such warnings also fail to recognize that most people deeply desire to live in an intact marriage. For this reason, we could say that allowing the mechanism of divorce into a social system that values marriage as an indissoluble interpersonal relationship actually affirms the ideal of marriage, from a purely sociological point of view, rather than tarnishes it. Allowing for the possibility of divorce reveals how a certain percentage of first marriages may be humanly invalid because they are based on a fundamental mistake or some other reason. It also shows that the desire to create to an indissoluble bond is still present in more than 90 percent of the married population.

From this we can conclude that the proposed pastoral practice would not promote the general collapse of married life, as some authorities fear and assert without evidence. In the long run, a pastoral practice that takes human brokenness into consideration will increase the value of indissolubility.

Supported by this knowledge and informed by pastoral practice, we can now attempt to arrive at a more credible interpretation of the biblical message.

Hermeneutical Awareness

In earlier times, even in a patriarchal culture, a marriage could break down. In one way or another, such breakdowns were ruptures in the social structure, and they resulted in the abandonment of one party by another. Emotionally unhappy marriages, however, did not break down because people were under psychological, social, and economic pressure to stay married. Emotional estrangement remained unnoticed and played scarcely a role in the social evaluation of marriage as an institution, however painful the situation might have been for the people concerned. Yet even in ancient times, marriage at its core was a matter of being in love or enduring its painful absence. But the breakdown of marriage as an interpersonal marital relationship is really a modern phenomenon.

It was not until the Enlightenment in post-Renaissance Europe that marriage began to be valued as an interpersonal relationship. Hence it was only in modern society that there appeared a brand-new problem for which there is no direct answer in the Bible or the ancient traditions of the church, namely, the experience of an unbearable, totally broken marriage. With the coming of industrialization and specialization in the workplace, and in general the growing division between living and working, marriage lost its previous economic role as a social unit that provided goods and services. When this economic function of marriage was lost, however, marriage transformed itself into an interpersonal relationship.[12] The breakdown of marriage in the modern sense therefore confronts us with the creative task of discovering a new way to be human.

Seen in this light, one can think of Jesus' demand for Christian reciprocity in marital love as something of a time bomb, planted under the patriarchal rules of marriage in an agrarian society, that would explode as soon as the social and economic circumstances supporting the old style of marriage were radically altered. In continuity with ideals that had already begun to appear in the Old Testament, Jesus brought to the social situation of his time a broader demand for reciprocal love. When it began to be lived out, this reciprocal love in the long run caused the old structures to crumble, and at the same time they began to be analyzed and questioned. Thus, when marriage began to be lived and thought about as an interpersonal relationship in the industrial era, this and other historical factors led to the social phenomenon of widespread marital breakdown, posing a set of questions that were unknown in New Testament times.

This brings us face to face with the historicity of the essence of marriage, and the complex hermeneutical problem that goes with this awareness. So, what are our principles of interpretation? The contemporary context of experience and understanding, with its restructured relationships, is different from what it used to be. How can we translate and bring to life the early Christian message about the un-Christian nature of a complete break between a married man and woman, considering that the New Testament message presumes a very different social milieu? It is definitely true that human beings should not dissolve what God has joined, but what exactly has God joined? What we need to find out is whether and how a criterion of truth is implied in the pastoral practice of *oikonomia*.

Time and time again, I am impressed by the expertise and erudition that enable biblical exegetes, using the various analytical methods of form criticism and redaction criticism, to dig through the successive layers of textual development and sift through a tangle of reinterpretations by the early church, in order to reach the words that were spoken by Jesus himself. I am convinced of the theological relevance of this type of painstaking investigation. For, among other things, it means that the Scriptures themselves, which are a norm and rule of faith for Christians, are in fact the product of a complex history of interpretation.

When one thinks about this, it becomes apparent that the Scriptures themselves suggest a new model for interpreting the Scriptures. The biblical text itself, because of the way it came to be written, prohibits any sort of literalism or fundamentalism that tries to use the text theologically without taking into account its social and historical context.

One must also remember that the Bible, as the canon of faith for believers, is essentially a book of the church. If one says that Scripture alone is the basis of Christianity, one needs to realize that the church as a whole is the interpreter of Scripture. Only by way of the church's interpretation does Jesus' message come to us in the Scriptures. Therefore an element of church history with its characteristic diversity is part of what we call the Christian message. And it is ultimately the diversity of the early church's testimony about Jesus that is the concrete norm for Christian life.

We can certainly admire exegetical reconstructions of biblical texts, but we also have to be cautious about exegesis as a methodology. For the historical reconstruction of a biblical text and its interpretation, we always have to put our trust in the scientific expertise of the exegete. As it happens, one exegete may consider Mark 10:11 to be an authentic saying of Jesus, while another on the contrary considers Mark 10:9 to be authentic. When I go to the Bible for guidance, am I putting my trust in the word of Jesus or actually in the skill of exegetes, among whom I may have to choose? This dilemma highlights the fact that the conclusions of exegetes are scientifically responsible hypotheses and that other hypotheses are always possible, even if the others may be less probable.

This is not the place to deal with the broader issue of the relationship between exegesis and doctrine. Right now, we need only to see that the Bible presents us believers with a variety of interpretations made by early Christian communities. From these our faith draws inspiration, in the belief that through the early church's multicolored prism the good news of Jesus sheds light on our life. The authority of Jesus, which for Christians is unassailable, nevertheless comes to us through the vicissitudes of a historical church that is guided by the Spirit of God.

The point here is not that exegetes come to different conclusions about the Bible. Even if exegetes were able to reach unanimity about the most important issues through greater precision in their methodology, this scientific progress would not advance doctrinal reflection one step further. Exegetical conclusions (whether unanimous or not) only help us get back to the faith of the first Christians and to their expressions of faith. But why did these early witnesses preserve some words of Jesus and not the many other things that Jesus must have said? From the very beginning, then, the writing of the Scriptures was based on decisions influenced by faith. The faith of those who talked about Jesus, and afterwards the faith of those who wrote about Jesus, was and remains a believer's interpretation of Jesus and their experiences with him. In other words, it is a faith response to an event.

Now, our own interpretation of the Scriptures is obviously conditioned by our own presuppositions about the world, human life, history, and so on. At the same time, however, God's unconditional revelation in Jesus unavoidably comes to us through the interpretative response of human beings who had their own presuppositions about the world, human life, and history, and much of their vision of reality was different from ours. Nor can that vision ever be our own.

"Biblical theology" is thus a very thorny issue. Looked at from the perspective of pure exegesis, the problem seems quite insoluble. Something else besides exegesis must be involved here. For even if we can identify some of the sayings of Jesus as historically authentic, and even if we can put together some essentials about the man called Jesus of Nazareth, a fundamental hermeneutical question would still remain: What normative value do these findings have for us today?

Before this question can be answered, however, there are two things that need to be determined. First, to what extent can a single historical event have a decisive meaning for all human beings, including people today? And second, what is truly universal in that historical event, in contrast to what is purely historical and contingent? Note that these are questions that are of particular importance to believers. If one accepts these critical questions, moreover, one accepts the idea that philosophical reflection, whether it is done explicitly or implicitly, is going to be found in any expression of faith, including the theology that is found in the Bible. Even more importantly, one accepts that the revelation of God in Jesus of Nazareth is truly historical, and that it is permeated with historicity. These implications reveal that Christian faith itself is marked by historicity and relativity because there is no single philosophy that is perennially true, as was once believed.

This means that the authoritative teachings of Jesus do not come to us separated from what the first Christians believed about Jesus and his teachings. Therefore, any theology or other expression of faith is fundamentally an attempt to find in our own lives an adequate response to the first-century record of faith, understood as God's revelation in Jesus.[13]

There is an enormous creative potential for faith here. Because each Christian response is bound by its own historical limitations, it is never an exhaustive expression of faith but is always partial and inadequate. This holds even for the faith response that we find in the Bible, which is normative for us. But if this is the case, then the door is open to the possibility of creative faith responses in new situations. At the same time, the biblical expression of faith, which Christians accept as normative, remains a human response to God's loving revelation that was formulated at a certain point in time within a given philosophical and cultural framework. This is true even though we as believers regard the Scriptures as a human response that surpasses all others in the past at the same time that it reveals an expectant hope for the future.

Because of their historical limitations, therefore, we cannot take biblical statements literally, as though they were the unconditioned words of God that could be accepted without critical interpretation. What the Bible gives us is normative models for both a critically thoughtful response to revelation and a Christian orthopraxis, or a Christian way of living at both the personal and societal level, in which the good news is best expressed in our own situation.

The prophetic and radical self-giving love of Jesus, which his disciples strive to interpret and reinterpret in their own lives as marriage evolves through history, is the Christian ideal for proclamation. This ideal, however, cannot be satisfactorily translated into legislation that says, for instance, that neither of the partners of a broken marriage has permission to remarry. The notion of "having permission" simply does not fit the prophetic ideal of radical love. Likewise, looking for "grounds for divorce" can perhaps be justified in civil law, but it falls outside the Christian perspective on marriage. For this reason we can say that the Catholic Church, even more than other churches, rightly proclaims the authentic Christian teaching on marriage (for it too is a *locus theologicus!*), even though it does so in an inappropriate and legalistic way.

When we are confronted with a broken human reality, we should not be asking legalistic questions about whether Jesus' radical demands should be met in this situation before making exceptions. Questions of that sort fail to appreciate the deeply significant pressure that the Christian ideal of marriage can exert on the lived experience of marriage, the way that a social utopia can influence modern society, or the way that the paradoxes of the Sermon on the Mount can affect the way people try to live. By the same token, policies of Eastern churches, which respect the desire to remarry because of the principle of *oikonomia,* should be regarded not as an abandonment of the Christian ideal but as a blessing (in the utopian sense of the Sermon on the Mount) for persons who would otherwise want to remain faithful and refuse to remarry despite the failure of their marriage, the way that someone might refuse to remarry out of faithfulness to a deceased loved one. For in a monogamous marriage, remarriage is the definite break with a previous love.

The Catholic Church insists on marital fidelity, not in the prophetic manner of the Sermon on the Mount but in a legal manner that neglects the love of humanity that lies at the very heart of Christianity as good news. Authentic Christianity can never inspire legalism, however, whether it is the legalism of the Catholic Church attempting to legislate the Christian meaning of indissolubility, or the legalism of other Christian churches looking for juridical grounds for divorce. Yet in spite of such legalism, the churches testify to the human and Christian reality of marriage, each in its own way.

The Institutionalization of Divorce

At issue here is divorce after the complete breakdown of a marriage. If we proceed from the understanding that marriage as it is defined and valued at the present stage of human development (which is not yet the kingdom of God) is a mutual self-giving that is acknowledged and accepted by society, then the possibility of a second marriage is also of concern to society. In this respect, there is a reciprocal relationship between marriage and society, for something that needs acceptance by society to come into existence needs acknowledgment by society to be juridically dissolved. Just as marriage on the grounds of mutual love requires legal ordering, so also does divorce on the grounds of a broken marriage. Being the negative side of contemporary marriage, divorce as people experience it today is a new social phenomenon that calls for new legal structures. Some recognition by society of the complete breakdown of a marriage is therefore necessary, but how this recognition is institutionalized need not concern us here. Suffice it to say that it can be done in a variety of ways.

The notion of a complete breakdown raises a problem when people speak of a one-sided breakdown of marriage in certain cases. At first glance this seems to be a contradiction in terms, but what is meant here is that although the marriage is completely broken, one of the partners does not want to divorce. There can be many reasons for this, some of which may be unjust or unfair—such as threats from the former partner, financial considerations, or the pressure of public opinion. From a theological standpoint, we can disregard cases like these. But we do have to face the problem that arises when one of the partners rejects divorce out of human and Christian fidelity to his or her former life companion.

In my opinion, it may be appropriate to question the desire for this sort of faithfulness from a Christian perspective, when the "faithful party" rejects divorce after a marital breakdown. In and of itself, such fidelity and continued care for the other are worthy of honor, but after an actual separation, this type of attitude has no meaningful object. It may well be that, in such a situation, one person's commitment to the other and loving concern for true happiness free the partner to pursue his or her personal happiness. One thus agrees to the divorce, which from a human perspective is already a fact. Paradoxically, in the brokenness of the human situation, refusing to divorce can actually contradict the deepest purpose of an interpersonal relationship of caring for a life partner. In such cases, one can meaningfully practice fidelity to the former partner only by letting him or her go free and, if one can cope with it, by remaining unmarried on account of that fidelity.

Ecclesiastical Affirmation of Second Marriages?
A final problem—one especially for the institutional church—has far-reaching implications for faithful Christians who want to remarry after the breakdown of their marriage.

Should the church, in order to protect its ideal of the indissolubility of marriage, refuse to celebrate liturgically a second marriage even though it recognizes the second civil marriage as valid and therefore also sacramental? From a purely doctrinal perspective, such a policy would be possible because a church wedding is not an intrinsic requirement for the sacrament of marriage. By adopting a policy such as this, the church would respect people's desire to validly remarry, while on the other hand it would keep a certain distance by refusing a liturgical celebration of the marriage because of the first marriage's failure to live up to the Christian ideal. Such a position would thus embody two authentically Christian values.

A proposal of this sort certainly makes sense, but it raises questions nonetheless. A recognized second marriage would be a marriage of baptized persons, the sacramentality of which could not be denied, especially if the church recognizes the civil marriages of other believers as valid. Why then should the church deny the evangelical sanction of a sacramental liturgy to what it recognizes as a new sacramental mandate?

In my opinion, the question of whether or not a second marriage should be liturgically celebrated ought to be answered ecumenically. That is, the solution to this problem ought to be reached through consultation among Christian churches that have a diversity of values, which would not exclude a church wedding in the canonical sense in the Catholic Church. Such an ecumenical dialogue among the various churches could make the Christian message more believable in today's world, where marriage is often regarded as a relationship of mutual convenience. Moreover, if the idea of a church wedding for second marriages were accepted, then I think that the possibility of a separate wedding liturgy ought to be considered. Such a liturgy would not remind people of their previous failure; they have been through enough already. Instead, it would express the conviction that even in the brokenness of the human condition, God's mercy does not leave humanity in the lurch; it is always possible to be a Christian in process. The liturgy could also express the idea that the basic intention behind the first marriage, which admittedly went awry, can be fulfilled in the second marriage, as sociological data seem to indicate.

In today's secularized world, even in what appear to be completely secularized relationships, the building of a marriage bond through a life of caring for one other despite the odds could almost be considered a type of religion. A marriage relationship of mutual self-giving is the intimate place where, even in the absence of formal religion, some absolute self-surrender takes place, which is the reason why marriage has been viewed as a natural sacrament. God's revelation in the Old and New Testaments finds no better concepts, no more sublime images, and no more powerful words to communicate the meaning of God's covenant of grace than what human experience discovers in the lives of married people who are lovingly faithful to each other.

Let me conclude by suggesting that the pastoral practice based on *oikonomia,* although it is a benevolent and scripturally justifiable approach to remarriage, cannot be the last and most important word on this subject. I believe that a person who does not want to remarry because of wanting to remain faithful to a separated partner, yet who has freed the former partner to pursue his or her own happiness,[14] may be pursuing an even higher gospel value. Such a loving commitment to the welfare of the other would be just as much a sign of the Christian ideal of marriage as is a marital relationship of mutual self-giving, proclaiming that ideal in a way that can be seen by all.[15]

Translated by Daniel Thompson

Notes

1. See, among others, A. Dubarle, "Mariage et divorce dans l'Evangile," *L'Orient Syrien* 9 (1964): 61–73; see also the critique of J. Dauvillier, "L'indissolubilité du mariage dans la Nouvelle Loi," *L'Orient Syrien* 9 (1964): 265–89.

2. Literature on this topic can be found in R. Schnackenburg, "Die Ehe nach dem Neuen Testament," in H. Greeven et al., *Theologie der Ehe* (Regensburg/ Göttingen, 1969), 16–18.

3. V. Steiniger, *Auflösbarkeit unauflöslicher Ehen* (Graz-Keulen, 1968), especially 94–100.

4. The injustices and absurd consequences of the current codex are analyzed by Steiniger (*Auglösbarkeit*).

5. See my book *Het Huwelijk: Aardse werkelijkheid en heilsmysterie,* vol. 1 (Bilthoven, 1963), 28–37, 109–14.

6. I will set this out more fully in the second volume of *Het Huwelijk.* For now, we can make the observation that thinking about marriage as an interpersonal relationship began in middle-class (bourgeois) society during the eighteenth century and the beginning of the nineteenth. During that same period, sexuality began to be suppressed in the West, and not before. (See the enlightening study of J. van Ussel, *Geschiedenis van het seksuele probleem* [Meppel, 1968]). Moreover, the analysis of the male–female relationship in the romantic I–Thou philosophy was very essentialistic, in that it spoke about eternal characteristics of masculinity and femininity and developed on this foundation a theory of the complementarity of the sexes. At that point in time it was not yet clear that these characteristics are very culturally determined.

7. See H. Ringeling, "Die biblische Begründung der Monogamie," *Zeitschrift für evangelische Ethik* (March 1966): 100.

8. This does not mean, for example, that we in Western Europe can consider the African practice of polygamy (which is based on very different cultural values) as immoral. This creates all sorts of problems for missionary activity and evangelization. We must bear in mind that industrialization and urbanization will set in motion social forces that will naturally break through typically African marriage practices. See E. Hillman, "Hernieuwde bezinning op polygamie," *Concilium* 4, no. 3 (1968): 148–66.

9. Within this interpersonal relationship, the issues of sex and children must also be considered. In considering divorce, however, it seems less necessary to consider the question of children, although children naturally play a role in the problem of

divorce. On the other hand, a broken marriage that continues for the sake of the children is also a great problem, because children are often victims in that situation. At this point, however, I am setting aside this very important question.

10. See *Het Huwelijk,* 160–262.

11. W. Douma, "Een sociologische kijk op echtscheiding," in M. Nevejan et al., *Echtscheiding* (Bussum, 1969), 11–46 (with literature).

12. See, among others, "Het moderne huwelijkstype een genadekans," in *Het Huwelijk,* 13–22, especially 14–17.

13. See "Het 'rechte geloof,' zijn onzekerheden en zijn criteria," *Tijdschrift voor Theologie* 9 (1969): 136–40.

14. In this category might also be considered those who do not remarry, not because of fidelity to their lost beloved but because Catholic canon law tells them they may not remarry and therefore they do not do so. In both cases it is not so much a matter of the pure fact of not remarrying, but a matter of how this is lived out.

15. This article is a condensation of a chapter from the not yet published second part of my book *Het Huwelijk.* [Editor's note: Both volumes of *Het Huwelijk* were published in English as *Marriage: Human Reality and Saving Mystery* (New York, 1965). This chapter, however, either was left out of the English translation of that work or was deleted from the original before it was published.]

5

The Indissolubility of Marriage in Orthodox Law and Practice

ARCHBISHOP PETER L'HUILLIER

IN OUR SOCIETY, which bears more or less a Christian imprint, the idea, which in the past was widely accepted and according to which marriage does not normally end before the death of one of the spouses, has been seriously shaken. The principle of a lifelong association is far from evident for many of our contemporaries. Until the middle of this century, divorce, except in a few restricted situations, was an exception to the rules dictated by the predominant morality. Today even Christian couples who marry with the initial intention of forming a permanent union break up and consecrate their rupture in a divorce. Besides, almost everywhere civil legislation has reflected this evolution of custom; it has in a certain fashion made divorce banal. One could not suffer the illusion that this is only a passing phenomenon, since several factors which come into play in the creation of this new tendency are far from being a simple accident. This situation has already been the object of prolonged studies,[1] and it does not fall within the limits of the present paper to digress into these problems of sociology. We realize we must take them into consideration to the extent that they influence ecclesiastical practice and offer food for thought on the perennial nature of canonical doctrines. Let us begin with a few remarks, which we shall later develop.

(1) Certain passages in the New Testament deal with the question that interests us. Yet the hermeneutic problems they raise are delicate; they are limited to the explanation of Matthew's "clause of exception." It must be realized that these texts do not offer a ready-made answer to the questions asked by theologians and canonists.

(2) Neither in the East nor in the West did the early church develop a systematic matrimonial law. If this fact is not taken into consideration, the testimonies from that age run a great risk of being situated in a false perspective.

(3) During the late Middle Ages, a certain system began to develop. Although the Byzantine East and the Romano-Germanic West were still in ecclesiastical communion, nevertheless for historical reasons this development took place separately.

Let us examine these three points individually.

1. It is an incontrovertible fact that Jesus took a stand against divorce. This is clearly confirmed by St. Paul around 55/57 and later in the Synoptic Gospels.[2] Considering that Jesus exercised his public ministry in the non-Hellenized world of Palestinian Judaism, we may deduce that he viewed divorce concretely as it was practiced in this milieu, that is to say, the repudiation of a woman by her husband. This remains true, even if at times the wife had the possibility of inciting her husband to initiate the procedure.[3] It may be noted as well that all the Synoptic passages dealing with divorce are dominated by the idea that divorce leads to adultery.[4] Without entering the debates on "interim ethics," it therefore appears to our mind that these passages do not really contradict the *logia* on family ties related to the coming of the kingdom.[5]

Here we do not have to go into the problems of the transmission of the sources used in the New Testament. In any event, the attempts to reestablish the *ipsissima verba* of Jesus on divorce belong to the realm of pure hypothesis. The intention of St. Paul and the Synoptics is to adapt the Lord's teaching to the times and places to which their writings are destined.[6] Paul and Mark have in mind the legislation of Rome; they state precisely that the woman must not divorce.[7] St. Paul is aware as well that the Lord's commandment does not cover all the possible causes of separation, and he finds himself called to give his own opinion, as is clear from the expression he uses: *"legō egō, ouk ho Kyrios."*[8] In this occurrence arises the question of what will later be termed the "Pauline privilege."

Luke reports in precise form the Lord's teaching.[9] This is not, however, an occasion for deducing from this editorial brevity that Luke's text reproduces exactly the very words of Jesus, Matthew is addressing Judeo-Christian communities. In his presentation of the teachings of Jesus, he makes use of two sources: one is the collection of *logia* conventionally designated by the letter Q; the other is the one which forms the basis of the Gospel of Mark. This is why the teaching on divorce is found twice in this Gospel. In both passages, the restrictive clause appears *parektou logou porneias* (5:32) and *mē epi porneia* (19:9).[10] The formulation that is proper to Matthew's account in 19:2–12 shows that this evangelist places the debate between Jesus and the Pharisees in the framework of the controversies of tannaitic Judaism over the meaning and the application of Deut. 24:1 (*'erwat dābār*, literally a "nudity of thing"). In the Septuagint version, this is rendered by *aschēmon pragma* ("something shameful"). Given the context of the episode related in chapter 19, there is no reason to seek for the word *porneia* any other meaning than "misconduct."[11] Matthew, it seems, wishes to avoid attributing to Jesus any teaching that would be seen as morally shocking, namely, that a husband must not repudiate his unfaithful wife. To carry on with conjugal life in such conditions was regarded as sharing in the defilement of this woman.[12] Can it be concluded that Matthew is presenting the teaching of Jesus on divorce as a straightforward alignment with the position of the school of Shammaï? This is only true with regard to the sole reason accepted for divorce, but in Jewish law, the writ of repudiation (*get*) was intended to let it be known that the wife was free to remarry,[13] which is contrary to the commandment of Jesus. Moreover, it cannot be inferred from the interpolated clauses in Matthew that there is a right of remarriage for the former spouse. The grammatical construction of 5:32 and 19:9 suggests that the clause of exception applies to divorce itself and does not imply the impossibility of a subsequent remarriage.[14] Otherwise it would be difficult to understand the apostle's reflection, "if such is the condition of the husband with a wife, it is better not to marry" (19:10). The global interpretation of the two passages from Matthew on divorce followed by a remarriage is in conformity with the whole of the doctrine expressed elsewhere in the New Testament.

2. To what extent was this norm applied in the early church? In examining the Christian literature of the first two centuries, the impression emerges that a strict application was prevalent.[15] Just the same, as Charles Munier observes about the entire pre-Nicene period, testimonies on the subject of divorce and subsequent remarriage are very few; their formulation is laconic and almost exclusively marked with apologetic or parenetic considerations.[16] We do not know, either, how the ecclesiastical authorities exercised their control in the conclusion and eventual dissolution of marriage. In any case, from a legal point of view, the procedures were entirely beyond their competency.[17] Did the church really consider to be married, people who no longer had the *jus conubii* but nonetheless lived in a monogamous and stable union? A clearly formulated answer to this question cannot be expected from the sources of Christian antiquity. One can say at most, without bringing into question the civil law, that the ecclesiastical authorities did not regard such unions as blameworthy.[18]

It seems beyond dispute that during the first centuries, cases of divorce followed by remarriage were infrequent among Christians. The stand taken by our Lord in this regard certainly played a dissuasive role; but one must also take into consideration the strong ascetic tendency influencing Christianity at that time.[19] Although the greater church was quick to distance itself from the excesses of the Encratites, it remained nonetheless true that continence appeared to be the ideal in life. The remarriage of widowed spouses, while tolerated, did not merit any esteem.[20]

3. Given these conditions one may imagine how the remarriage of divorced spouses was considered. In spite of this, certain cases did occur. In 246 the fact was noticed and discussed by Origen. Mentioning in this regard the permission granted by certain bishops, Origen asserts that this concession is contrary to Scripture, although he does observe that the church leaders did not act without reason (ou mēn pantē alogōs). They showed an attitude of condescension in order to avoid greater evils.[21] With regard to this well-known and now oft-quoted passage, we should like to draw attention to several points.

(1) The formulation of Origen suggests that these incidents are not entirely isolated since they concern several bishops.

(2) In the cases in question, permission was previously sought from the ecclesiastical authorities; in other words, the divorced parties did not simply take recourse to civil procedures.

(3) The bishops were of the opinion that the problem fell within their spiritual competency.

(4) Origen's text only makes allusion to the remarriage of the wife. Although the argument e silentio must be treated prudently, it is not unreasonable to suppose that the opposite case also arose.[22]

(5) The bishops did not take lightly the New Testament teaching, except they thought that in this question as well as in other ethical demands expressed by the Lord, adjustments inspired by pastoral considerations were sometimes necessary.

From this perspective, the hesitations of the legislators are understood as the jus scriptum emerged. This appears for example in the drafting of canon 11 decreed by the Council of Arles in 314: "For those who discover their wives in the offence of adultery and who otherwise are still young and faithful, to whom remarriage has been forbidden, it has been decided to advise them to the extent that it is possible not to remarry as long as their wife, even an adulterous one, remains living."[23] In two letters addressed to St. Amphilochus of Iconium, St. Basil answers different questions that the former had asked. In this framework, St. Basil explains the custom (synētheia) of the Metropolitan Church of Caesarea on the remarriage of husbands abandoned by their wives. It is evident that in this case the church tolerates remarriage.[24] Great ingenuity is required to diminish the weight of this testimony. Indeed St. Basil uses the term *syggnōstos,* which means "worthy of pardon," to characterize the husband who remarries. With regard to the expression "pardon will be granted to him to receive communion in the Church," its full significance is seen when one recalls that refusal of communion was the only recourse available to the church to penalize those who entered a marriage that the church did not sanction. Toward the middle of the sixth century, these answers were added to the canonical corpus of the Byzantine Church. They thus acquired the status of official ecclesiastical norms.[25]

4. The early church did not seek to undermine the existing social order, which includes the institution of marriage. However, the church made efforts to ensure respect by the married faithful for the principles of moral decency. In addition, as the clergy began to appear as a class definitely distinct from the laity, they were subject to strict matrimonial regulation.[26] By way of contrast, certain canons relating to marriage that were decreed in the fourth and fifth centuries seem to indicate that the ecclesiastical authorities were not to control marriage of the laity.[27]

In fact, the written canon law of the fourth and fifth centuries adds almost nothing to our subject. Apostolic canon 48 declares briefly: "If a layman, after having left his own wife marries another or if he marries a divorced wife, he shall be excommunicated."[28] This canon prescribes for the guilty a penance whose length is not specified. We shall see further on how this text was interpreted in the East during the Middle Ages. In any event, the author of the collection has no illusions about the reality of the situation, as is evident from the wording of canon 18, which mentions as an irregularity of ordination marriage with a divorced woman (*ekbeblēmenēn*).[29]

5. The numerical increase of the church as a consequence of its gradual establishment as the religion of the empire inevitably led to greater difficulty for the hierarchy in exerting control over the individual lives of the faithful. This phenomenon must have been especially acute with regard to marriage, since the church was not legally involved either in the formation or the eventual dissolution of marriage contracts. A rule decreed at the Council of Carthage in 407 appears very significant in this respect. It stipulates: "It seemed well, according to evangelical and apostolic discipline, that neither the husband abandoned by his wife nor the wife abandoned by her husband should remarry another; either they remain as they are or they reconcile. If they ignore this prohibition, they shall be subjected to penance. In this matter it must be requested that an imperial law be passed."

Patristic literature of this epoch offers very few practical indications on indissolubility or on conditional solubility of marriage. This literature belongs for the most part, as far as it concerns the subject of marriage, to the parenetic genre. From time to time allusions to the difference between Christian exigencies and the laxity of Roman law are found.[31] On the subject of remarriage for the divorced, other than the above-mentioned passage of St. Basil, there is a very clear testimony from St. Epiphanios.[32]

The idea by which the matrimonial bond subsisted in spite of a justified divorce, that is, one founded on Matthew's clause of exception, is formally contradictory to the general position of the Eastern fathers. It would be tedious to mention all the explicit testimonies to this effect. Let it suffice to mention St. John Chrysostom, who confirms that through adultery marriage is dissolved and that after fornication, the husband ceases to be the husband.[33] As for St. Cyril of Alexandria, he expressly states: "It is not a writ of divorce that dissolves marriage before God, but bad actions."

In the West at the same epoch, St. Augustine put forth a theory of the intangibility of the marriage bond for Christian spouses. For the bishop of Hippo, this characteristic derives from the *sacramentum,* that is, the irrevocable engagement pronounced by the spouses before God.[35] Was St. Augustine convinced in his innermost thoughts of the solidity of these arguments? One cannot be entirely sure, for in his *Retractations* he admits that the question is obscure and difficult.[36] The views expressed by St. Augustine had no effect on canonical practice in the West before being used by the scholastic theologians and the canonists of the Middle Ages. These views remained entirely unknown in the Greek East. We mention them briefly now, because they form the basis of later developments in Western law of the notion of the persistence of the marital bond.

6. The restrained tolerance of remarriage after divorce such as is shown from examples in the early church must be understood in the light of a general attitude. It is certain that the church fathers saw complete abstinence as the perfect state. But the church, as opposed to certain Encratite sects, fully accepted the legitimacy of the first marriage. On the other hand, as we have already shown, second marriages were seen as a concession to the weakness of the human condition. The church showed her disapproval by imposing penance on the bigamous.[37] She forbade priests to partake in nuptial festivities.[38] In this perspective, the early canonical texts do not distinguish whether penance imposed on the bigamous was only for the remarriage of widowed spouses or also for the divorced. The latter possibility seems the more likely.[39]

The problem of remarriage after divorce remained complicated for a long time by the absence of doctrine on what constituted a valid marriage in the eyes of the church. It must be noted that Roman law offered little assistance in this area; even its terminology was obscure. Outside the case where the *matrimonium* was considered *justum,* this term may designate a variety of unions.[40] Furthermore, the canonical legitimacy of marriage did not depend on the fulfillment of religious rites. In these conditions a practical consideration arose. Was it necessary to consider as bigamous the one who had entered a first marriage before baptism and a second one after having become a Christian? Divergent opinions on this question emerged toward the end of the fourth century and during the fifth.[41] The controversy was void in the East because apostolic canon 17, accepted as normative in the East, only takes into consideration marriage contracted after baptism.[42] It must be noted in this debate that the question of the validity per se of the first marriage was not directly raised; the divergence in the positions concerned qualification for ordination.

7. The affirmation which states that "it is through civil law that divorce entered the Church"[43] gives rise to serious reserves. The displacement toward the East of the center of gravity of the empire did not cause radical change in Roman law, at least up until the eighth century. Christian emperors, invested in theory with unlimited legislative power, had nonetheless to take into account the institutional continuity of *Romanitas.* It is within the framework of the Roman law that, starting in the reign of Constantine, the emperors attempted to render divorce more difficult.[44] This indicates that civil legislation must be seen as a series of attempts to breathe a few Christian principles into a judicial system that hardly lent itself to this. The most flagrant disagreement was over the nature of consent in marriage. Since the end of the Republican era, Roman law, reflecting a widely prevalent feeling, founded marriage on the mutual consent of the spouses. Consent was necessary not only to form marriage but also to maintain it. If the *affectio maritalis,* or the will to be husband and wife, disappeared, the marriage was dissolved.[45] Needless to say, the church could not accept this theory even if many Christians seemed to. This is why the church found it more and more difficult to have divorce by mutual consent eliminated from civil law.

In his legislative work, the emperor Justinian deals in several instances with divorce. One can discern a chronological evolution to his thinking, First he appears quite liberal, as is evident from the numerous divorce cases still accepted in 535 in *Novellae* 17.[46] The publication in 542 of *Novellae* 117 marks a turning toward greater strictness.[47] This law is important to the extent that it constitutes the basic element of the future Byzantine nomocanonic synthesis. The idea which motivated the emperor was that divorce must be the exclusive result of reasonable causes, expressly stated in law. These causes were enumerated. In addition it is precisely stated that divorce *ex consensu (apo synaineseōs)* was no longer admissible.[48] This latter stipulation was so directly contrary to the prevailing customs that it was not of much effect. Nevertheless, Justinian reiterated this prohibition in 556.[49] Ten years later, his successor, Justin II, alleging that in all likelihood the law was too difficult to enforce, rescinded it purely and simply.[50] This return of the legislation to the *statu quo ante* did not modify at all the Byzantine Church's position on divorce, as is proven by canon 87, promulgated in 691 by the Council in Trullo. This canon merely repeats the dispositions found in answers 9, 35, and 77 of St. Basil. It may be summarized thus: "The wife who abandons her husband without a valid reason and joins with another man is an adulteress, and her husband is not to re-enter marital union with her. As for the husband, if he remarries, he is worthy of pardon. On the contrary, the man who abandons his wife and takes another is guilty of adultery, which necessitates a penance of seven years."[51] This canon has two particularities: contrary to certain decisions adopted at the same council, it does not give specific reasons for its publication; it does not refer to abuses to be corrected. Whereas other canons from this council, which deal with irregular marriages,[52] require the dissolution of these unions, this is not the case in canon 87. It may be supposed that the council fathers in Trullo wanted to stress the church teaching on the causes of divorce.

8. Divorce by mutual consent was finally eliminated from Byzantine civil law with the publication of the *Eclogue* in 741.[53] This code not only strictly limits the causes of divorce but also recalls that the principle of indissolubility *(adialytou)* has been established by God. If this norm is not entirely reflected in the legislation, it is because the legislator must take into account unfortunate factual reality. The restriction of admissible causes for divorce and especially the suppression of divorce by mutual consent seem to indicate the growing influence of Christian ideas on marriage in Byzantine society. In general, the *Eclogue* shows a weakening of the ideas conveyed from Roman law.

As the *Eclogue* was published by the iconoclast emperors Leo III and Constantine V, it was eventually criticized and held as null and without force. Nevertheless, some of its dispositions, especially those relating to marriage, were adopted in later legislation.

9. As we have already seen, one does not find in the Eastern patristic tradition the idea that the marriage bond persists after divorce. The doctrine of absolute indissolubility cannot be found in Byzantine law.[54] It is necessary to recall that in the West during the Middle Ages, not only did the application of the principle of indissolubility encounter difficulties, but as well the determination of its conditions was the result of a long and com-

plicated process. In the East, there had not been an interruption in the continuity of the existence of the Roman state. That is why it did not enter the minds of Greek canonists in the Middle Ages to question the competence of the imperial authority in the area of matrimonial legislation, where Christian influence made itself more and more felt. This can be seen in the *Basilika*, the great judicial compilations undertaken on the threshold of the tenth century. In this work, passages of the *corpus juris civilis* that are incompatible with the views of the church on marriage are omitted.[55] It is during this epoch in Byzantium, that the concordance of civil law and church law relative to marriage was taken for granted. Starting from this supposition, Byzantine canonists from that time on made use of notions borrowed from Roman law and revised in a Christian perspective. It is for this reason that in the twelfth century, Zonaras, Aristenos, and Balsamon underline the fact that marriage can only be dissolved for reasons expressly stipulated in the law. Zonaras and Balsamon confirm that this requirement had previously existed.[56] Although Aristenos does not explicitly state this theory, it underlies his paraphrase of apostolic canon 48: "Let him who divorces his wife unless for reasons foreseen by the law (*tōn nenomothētemenōn aitiōn*) and marries another, be excommunicated."[57] Reasons for the dissolution of marriage are divided into two categories: those which result from an offense, and those which do not imply culpability. The first are founded not only on adultery but also on serious assaults against marriage as a *consortium omnis vitae*. The second are founded on impotence preceding marriage, insanity, the desire of both spouses to enter religious life, and a solid presumption of the death of the husband during wartime.[58]

We may presume that on the whole the system operated correctly. It is certain that during the Byzantine Middle Ages the divorce rate was lower than during late antiquity. This is partially the result of the fact that divorce involved a judicial procedure and was only accorded on the basis of definite causes. Violation of these principles was likely to raise a strong reaction from the church, as is shown by the case of the emperor Constantine VI toward the end of the eighth century.[59] The decisions relating to divorce found in the work of Demetrios Chomatenos, archbishop of Ohrid in the thirteenth century, show that the dissolution of marriage was not a subject taken lightly.[60] That is why, when Pope Eugene IV at the end of the Council of Florence asked the Greek bishops to abolish divorce, the answer was given in good faith that marriages in the East were only dissolved with valid reasons.[61]

10. The nomocanonic synthesis on marriage which developed progressively in the East in the course of the Middle Ages represents an important phenomenon, since it forms the basis of matrimonial law for all the Ortho-

dox churches. However, this statement needs qualification. The Byzantine juridic model fitted into a well-determined social-political framework and as such was not susceptible to an integral transposition outside of this context. The Byzantines furthermore had not imposed a systematic treatment on the formation and dissolution of marriage. Jurists and canonists quote certain maxims formulated in Roman jurisprudence and collected in the *Digest*. Two of these maxims are frequently quoted. The first is from Modestine: "Marriage is a union of man and woman, a lifelong association (*consortium omnis vitae*).[62] The second is from Ulpian: "It is consent and not cohabitation which makes marriage."[63] It is also worthwhile taking into account the commentaries on the canons.[64]

On the whole and without question, Byzantine legislation tended to limit divorce. This is evident from the principle of establishing a list indicating the causes of divorce. Nor must it be forgotten that besides the strictly ecclesiastical sanctions *(epitimia)*, civil law punished the party proven guilty.[65] This attitude was founded on the interpretation of Sacred Scriptures,[66] and, as we have seen, on a Christian understanding of the Roman definition of marriage as a *consortium omnis vitae*.

Whatever the case, the Byzantine position on determined causes of divorce entails a few weak spots from the point of view of canon law teaching. First of all, certain causes for divorce considered as evident proof of misconduct of the wife simply reflect the ideas and the customs of a given epoch.[67] But especially the idea of strictly determined and numerically limited causes, in order to be entirely credible, presupposes immutability. Yet this was not the case. In order to grasp this, one has only to compare the two almost contemporary lists of Matthew Blastares and Constantin Armenopoulos.[68] This led the way to later extensions which eventually undermined the principle.[69]

We stated at the beginning of this study, that Byzantine marriage law developed independently from Western influences. As a result, one does not find in the East controversy on the role of the *copula carnalis* in the forming of the marriage bond. In general, Byzantine canonists did not really elaborate a theory of nullity *ab initio*. This is partially a result of the fact that there did not exist a system establishing a precise distinction between kinds of impedimenta according to their gravity. At the very most, certain canons relating to irregular unions stipulate that these unions must be dissolved. This is why Byzantine and post-Byzantine canonists include in the category of divorce what in the West would be considered cases of nullity or simply separation, which have no influence on the continuation of the marriage.[70] In this regard, we must note that in the West up to the sixteenth century, the term *divortium* was often used to designate all cases of separation.[71]

During the thirteenth century, the Orthodox churches accepted the sevenfold sacraments, including marriage.[72] This acceptance was achieved all the more easily since for a long time in the East, the benediction of the priest was considered necessary for a legitimate marriage.[73] The inclusion of marriage in the list of the seven sacraments had little ensuing effect on ecclesiastical practice.

11. After the fall of Constantinople in 1453, Orthodox Christians of the Ottoman Empire remained under previous matrimonial legislation. Ecclesiastical authorities retained full jurisdiction in this matter. Given the existent social conditions, divorces were not frequent. Metrophanes Critopoulos in his *Confession of Faith* (1625) presents an interesting portrait of the marriage customs of this time. He affirms categorically that the couple remains indissolubly joined. Marriage can under no circumstances be broken, unless for reasons of misconduct according to the Gospel.[74]

In the *Pedalion,* a collection of canons compiled at the end of the eighteenth century, St. Nicodemus the Hagiorite expressed strict views on the causes of divorce. Outside of adultery, the only valid motives retained for dissolution *ex delicto* were the attempt against the life of the spouse, or heresy. He mentions other causes, but these were based on impediments at the time of marriage. Moreover, he only allowed remarriage with reserve, and this strictly for the party found to be innocent.[75] This position must be noted, since the *Pedalion* was published with the approval of the ecumenical patriarch and still remains a highly esteemed work, especially within the Greek church. However, in this matter the *Pedalion* had only limited effects on practice.

In Russia, Byzantine matrimonial law was never completely established. In the sixteenth and seventeenth centuries, even cases of divorce by mutual consent are found. But during the Synodal period (1720–1917), legislation and jurisprudence appear even stricter than previously. The causes are reduced to seven including *bona gratia* divorces: (1) adultery, (2) dual culpability in breaking of a previous marriage, (3) impotence, (4) banishment to Siberia, (5) prolonged disappearance, (6) apostasy, (7) entering religious life by both spouses. In all events, the Holy Synod had the right to dissolve marriages that did not fit the above-mentioned categories. In addition, the emperor enjoyed the same privilege.[76] The Council of Moscow (1917–1918) extended this list considerably.[77]

Toward the middle of the nineteenth century, one observes here and there within the Orthodox churches a tendency toward a certain laxity on divorce and remarriage. This phenomenon resulted from several factors. It is certainly not a question of an abrupt change appearing within all of the Orthodox churches. The phenomenon is related to the slow but inexorable penetration of secular ideas into the Christian East, leading toward the erosion of what are suitably called "traditional values." There is no doubt that at least in the first instance, the absence of a doctrine of absolute indissolubility played a certain role. Indeed canonists continued to reiterate that indissolubility remained the norm;[78] but the legislation of several local churches—and even more so local practice—reflects this principle.[79]

12. The political and social mutations of the twentieth century affected the whole Orthodox world either immediately or gradually. The changes in church–state relations had this effect on matrimonial law. At the same time, there took place an evolution in customs affecting the institution of marriage. There is no need to analyze here a problem of which the factors have been amply analyzed in recent times. On the other hand, we will try to establish what the attitude of the Orthodox churches is under these circumstances. There is, in fact, not an abundant literature on this question. There is nothing comparable to the mid-nineteenth-century study by Joseph Zhishman, a monumental treatise on marriage law, which has not been recently republished.[80] If the Orthodox have not given their attention to this problem, it is because they did not have to face the same doctrinal situation as the Roman Catholics. Does this mean that the only question facing Orthodoxy would be of relevance at the practical level? In other words, is it merely a question of a simple dilemma between the strict application of the rules and a *laissez-faire* attitude? The question is certainly more complex than that. The strict application of the rules supposes the existence of precise and universally accepted ecclesiastical legislation. If, as we have seen, Byzantine nomocanonic law could not be entirely separated from its political social context, this is all the more true in our times.

In Byzantine nomocanonic law and in those systems which derive from it, the dissolution of marriages, except for cases of *divortium bona gratia,* is pronounced as a sanction of a duly recognized offense. In this perspective, officially there is no room for recognizing a psychological mistake, vitiating the consent. Marriage is considered valid if the required objective conditions have been fulfilled. Willing consent is one of the constituent elements of marriage. It is expressed by the participation of the future spouses in the rites of the office of betrothal and is confirmed with the nuptial blessing.[81] If, as we have already said, the concept of annulment has remained for the most part foreign to the Eastern tradition, this is not surprising. For annulment was the result of the elaboration of sacramental theology and canon law in the West during the second millennium.[82] As a result, in Orthodox churches a marriage can be ended, during the lifetime of either of the spouses, only through a procedure of dissolution.

13. The moral evolution that has caused an increase in marriage break-downs has severely tested canon law. Indeed, in a few well-determined cases, the law permits the dissolution of marriage. But the system was conceived and worked out for a long time under conditions that are vastly different from those that presently exist. The external stability of marriage is no longer ensured by a well-structured family, nor by social constraints. Moreover, apart from some exceptions, ecclesiastical authorities are no longer involved in the legal procedures of dissolving marriages.[83] Today, as long as one of the spouses decides, or perhaps both, that the marriage is an irreparable failure, divorce is taken into consideration. It is to be noted that in many cases the misunderstanding does not arise from any of the offenses listed in the law, and that a negative conclusion is drawn after attempts at reconciliation have been made. Whatever the case may be, according to canon law, not only is there not a motive for dissolution, but even more disturbing, these cases appear to belong to the category of divorce by mutual consent, which is rejected by the church. In all events, the decisions of canon law do not weigh very heavily in the choices made by spouses, especially when divorce is granted almost everywhere through a relatively simple civil procedure. Let us remember that according to the actual tendencies of civil law, opposition to the divorce by one of the parties does not constitute an insurmountable judicial obstacle. Separation followed by a certain lapse of time can be legally transformed into a divorce.[84]

Clearly the church deplores divorce, and it is the role of pastors to dissuade couples as much as possible from recourse to divorce. But once the conjugal union has been broken and this rupture has been legally ratified, it is difficult to pretend that the marriage continues to subsist in the abstract. Such an affirmation does not even withstand a serious philosophical analysis of the notion of bond, as was recently shown by Ladislas Orsy.[85] It is to be noted that as long as a second marriage is not foreseen, only a few divorced people begin the procedure for dissolution with diocesan authorities. Such behavior might be explained in the light of history: the Orthodox East was spared the conflicts between church and state over the jurisdiction of marriage that occurred almost without interruption in the West from the sixteenth century onward. This is why in the East there was no doctrine elaborated to strictly define the respective powers of church and state.

Because of the separation of church and state, one is not wholly correct to say that the Orthodox ecclesiastical authorities pronounce divorce. They officially certify that a marriage has been broken, both in fact and in law.[86] Consequently, on this point the ecclesiastical procedure is quite simple. It consists in identifying the applicant, the religious status of the previous marriage, and legal proof of the civil divorce. The fact that the same document that recognizes the dissolution of the previous marriage may not mention permission to remarry should not lead to confusion. It is a question here of something entirely different. However, to the extent that the problem of the canonical ability of divorced people to enter a new marriage arises, there exists a connection between the two questions. Moreover, it is in this perspective that the declarations of Jesus on repudiation are situated. It is on this practical level that the fundamental distinction between complete divorce and separation, *manente vinculo* according to Latin canon law, makes its effect felt.[87] It must be pointed out, however, that for the Orthodox church divorce and remarriage are not intrinsically related, because divorce does not *ipso facto* confer the right to remarriage. This point is made evident from current practice, according to which permission for a new marriage normally must be announced by the competent ecclesiastical authority. This permission can only be granted after examination of a documented request specifying a concrete plan for remarriage.

14. In the church's view, remarriage does not enjoy the same consideration as the first marriage. If there is a certain disfavor toward the remarriage of widowed people, there is even more so in the case of the divorced. It is true that where there is separation of church and state, ecclesiastical authorities have no legal power to oppose a civil divorce. What is the position of the Orthodox church in these circumstances? At a purely theoretical level, theologians do not give a unanimous answer, which does not, however, have a consequence on practice. It is a fact that during the first centuries of Christianity, second marriages were never sanctioned with a religious blessing. But during the High Middle Ages, the idea developed in the popular conscience that the priest's blessing was a necessary condition for the validity of Christian marriage, and this idea was eventually ratified by the nomocanonic legislation.[88] As a consequence, today, Orthodox adherents who have not had a religious marriage are considered to be in an irregular situation with regard to the church and cannot receive the sacraments.

When diocesan officials are faced with applications for remarriage by divorced parties, they must take various factors into account. The application is relatively simple if it originates from the party who is declared innocent in the previous marriage breakdown, especially if the case involves one of the permitted causes of divorce. However, most often things are not this simple, for the effective breaking of the previous marriage is not always the result of an offense, in the proper sense of the word. Moreover, if on first sight many separations seem to fall in the category of divorce by mutual consent, which is condemned by the church, this is in fact not the case. The members of a dissolved couple had initially entered a marriage that they considered to be a permanent union. Whatever the case may be, one must not suppose that the indulgence of the Orthodox churches is without limit.

Religious remarriage may be refused, for example, in the case where the applicant appears to be unquestionably guilty, with no attenuating circumstances, for the breaking of the first marriage. Besides, whether after widowhood or divorce, third marriages are only conditionally tolerated, and fourth marriages are completely excluded.[89] That remarriage of divorced people is only tolerated is made clear by the imposition of a period of penance during a specified length of time preceding the religious ceremony.

One may be of the impression that the gap between the church's professed doctrine and actual practice is somewhat old-fashioned. From a strict point of view, this can often be true. However, reality is more complex: In the first place, Orthodox churches must proclaim the holiness and the unity of marriage between Christians; in the second place, the church does not think that, in the domain of marriage as in many others, it is necessary to exclude compassion systematically, as long as this pastoral tendency does not lead to official laxity.

Would it be preferable for the Orthodox churches to update its laws and practices on divorce and remarriage? This may appear on first sight to have some advantages at the practical level. We must note, however, that this problem is not on the agenda for the meetings of world Orthodoxy, and to our knowledge no suggestion has been made in this regard. Perhaps it is preferable, despite the inconveniences involved, not to weaken he principles, while leaving a certain margin of pastoral flexibility. After all, this attitude is inspired by early Church practice before nomocanonic law was fixed. In any case, it would be utopic to expect to find a solution in this domain that would be entirely satisfactory.

Notes

1. Jean Gaudemet, *Le mariage en Occident* (Paris: Ed. du Cerf, 1987), especially 431–64.

2. 1 Cor. 7:10–11; Matt. 5:31–32; 19:3–9; Mark 10:2–12; Luke 16:18.

3. Leonard Swidler, *Women in Judaism* (Metuchen, N.J.: Scarecrow Press, 1976), 155; Samuel Sandmel, *Judaism and Christian Beginnings* (New York: Oxford University Press, 1978), 195–96.

4. E. P. Sanders, *Jesus and Judaism* (Philadelphia: Fortress Press, 1985), 256.

5. Luke 14:26 and 28:29.

6. Charles Munier, *L'Eglise dans l'Empire romain* (Paris: Ed. Cujas, 1979), 38–40.

7. 1 Cor. 7:10–11; Mark 10:12.

8. 1 Cor. 7:12.

9. Luke 16:18.

10. Kurt Aland, *The Greek New Testament*, 3rd ed. (New York: United Bible Societies, 1975), 15, 75.

11. See recent bibliography in Gaudemet, *Le mariage en Occident,* 43–44.

12. Jer. 3:1. The prophet expresses this idea as obvious.

13. Swidler, *Women,* 195.

14. Robert H. Gundry, *Matthew: A Commentary on His Literary and Theological Art* (Grand Rapids: Eerdmans, 1982), 90–91, 380–81.

15. Chanoine Nicolas Jung, *Evolution de l'indissolubilité, remariage religieux des divorcé* (Paris: P. Lethielleux, 1975), 41–47.

16. Charles Munier, "Le témoinage d'Origène en matière de remariage après séparation," *Revue de droit canonique* 28, no. 1 (1978): 17.

17. On the formation and dissolution of marriage in Roman law, see Percy Ellwood Corbett, *The Roman Law of Marriage* (Oxford: Clarendon Press, 1930; reprinted by Scientia, Allen, 1979), 68–106, 218–48.

18. Decision of Pope Callistus (217–222), unfavorably quoted by Hippolytus (*Philos.* 9.2 [GCS 26:250]). Canons 40 and 53 of St. Basil (V. N. Benesevic, *Syntagma XIV titulorum* [St. Petersburg, 1906], 491, 497).

19. Robin Lane Fox, *Pagans and Christians* (New York: Alfred A. Knopf, 1987), 336–74.

20. Athenagoras calls such a one with scornful irony "a decent adulterer" (*euprepes . . . moicheia*). Other testimonies from the second and third centuries are mentioned by Henry Chadwick, *Alexandrian Christianity* (Philadelphia: Westminster Press, 1954), 37–38.

21. *Comm. in Matth.* 14.23 (GCS 10:340–41). See the excellent analysis of this passage by Munier ("Le témoinage," 15–19).

22. Jung, *Evolution de l'indissolubilité,* 27; Theodore Mackin, *Divorce and Remarriage* (New York/Ramsey, N.J.: Paulist Press, 1984), 132. This author quotes the work of Giovanni Cereti, *Divorzio, nuove nozze e penitenza nella chiesa primitiva* (Bologna: Edizione Dehoniane, 1977), 214–15.

23. J. Gaudemet, *Concile gaulois de IVe siècle,* S. Chr. 241 (Paris: Ed. du Cerf, 1977), Latin text pp. 50 and 52, French trans. pp. 51 and 53. For criticism of the text, see p. 52 n. 1. The author explains why he does not agree with the correction proposed by P. Nautin. For the canon of the Council of Arles of 314 on remarriage after divorce, see *Recherches de sciences religieuses* 61 (1973): 353–62.

24. Canons 9 and 35 (Benesevic, 472–74, 490).

25. For the circumstances of this inclusion, see E. Honigmann, *Le Syntagma XIV titulorum,* Subsidia Hagiographica 35 (1961), 52.

26. For the development of the distinction between clergy and laity, see Alexandre Faivre, *Les laïcs aux origines de l'Église* (Paris: Le Centurion, 1984). Also see Pierre Van Beneden, *Aux origines d'une terminologie sacramentelle: Ordo, ordinare, ordinatio dans la littérature chrétienne avant 313,* Spicilegium Sacrum Lovaniense (Louvain, 1974).

27. See, for example, canon apost. 18, St. Basil, canon 27 (Benesevic, 65, 487).

28. Benesevic, 72.

29. Ibid., 65.

30. Registri Eccl. Carth. Excerpta, 102, edited by Charles Munier, *Concilia Africae, Corpus Christianorum,* Ser. Lat., p. 218. This series of African canons was introduced into Byazntine ecclesiastical legislation in the sixth century.

31. St. Gregory Nazianzus, Letter 144 (*PG* 37:248); St. Jerome, Letter 77.3 (*PL* 22:691).

32. *Haer.* 59 (GCS 31:368–69). For the reasons of accepting the text established by K. Holl, see our article "L'attitude de l'Église orthodoxe vis-à-vis du remariage des divorcés," *Revue de droit canonique* 29 (1979): 53 n. 34.

33. *Hom.* 19 on 1 Corinthians (*PG* 61:154–55).

34. *Comm. on Mt.* (*PG* 72:380).

35. *De Nuptiis et Concupic.* 1.10, 11 (*PL* 44:420) and *De Bono Coniug.* 10 (*PL* 44:381). For a synthesis of Augustine's passages on this subject, see Mackin, *Divorce*, 194–220.

36. *Retractationes* 1.19 (*PL* 32:616): "latebrosissima quaestio": 2.57 (*PL* 32:653): "quaestionem difficillimam."

37. Laodicea, canon 1; St. Basil, canon 4 (Benesevic, 267, 467–68).

38. Canon 7 (Benesevic, 239).

39. Gaudemet thinks that canon 1 of Laodicea applies to marriage after divorce (*Le mariage en Occident*, 76).

40. Corbett, *Roman Law*, 102–3.

41. Paul-Henri Lafontaine, *Les Conditions positives de l'accession aux Ordres dans la première législation ecclésiastique (300–492)* (Ottawa: Edit. de l'Université d'Ottawa, 1963), 179–81.

42. Benesevic, 65. On the receiving of "Apostolic Canons" in the sixth century, see Honigmann, *Le Syntagma XIV titulorum*, Subsidia Hagiographica 35 (1961): 52.

43. Jean Dauvillier and Carlo De Clercq, *Le mariage en droit canonique oriental* (Paris: Sirey, 1936), 85. Cf. P. Adnès, *Le mariage* (Paris: Desclée, 1963), 66.

44. Corbett, *Roman Law*, 244–48.

45. D. 35, 1, 15 i.f.: "Nuptias enim non concubitus, sed consensus facit" (Ulpien) C.J.C.I. (Berlin: P. Kreuger, 1954), 540. Cf. D. 50, 17, 30 (ibid., 921). On divorce "a diversitate mentium," see D. 24, 2, 2 (Gaius) (ibid., 355).

On this conception of marriage and its eventual dissolution, see Barry Nicholas, *An Introduction of Roman Law* (Oxford: Clarendon Press, 1969; reprint, 1982), 80–90.

46. Novellae, C.J.C. 3, R. Schoell and G. Kroll (Berlin, 1959), 146–86.

47. Ibid., cap. 8, 9, pp. 557–60.

48. Ibid., cap. 10, pp. 560–61.

49 Nov. 134, cap. 11, ibid., p. 686.

50. No. 2, J. Zepos and P. Zepos, *Jus Graecoromanum* I (Athens, 1931), 3–5.

51. Benesevic, 195.

52. Canons 3 and 72 (Benesevic, 144–47, 188–89).

53. Ludwig Burgmann, *Ecloga* (Frankfurt am Main: Löwenklau-Gesellschaft, 1983), 2.9.1–4, pp. 180–82. For the date of publication of this code, see pp. 10–12.

54. This remark applies as well to Eastern churches that were not located in the sphere of Byzantine ecclesiastical influence; see Dauvillier and De Clercq, *Le mariage en droit canonique oriental*, 96–122.

55. H. J. Scheltema and N. Van Der Wall, *Basilicorum Libri LX*, J. B. Wolters, vol. 4 (Groningen, 1962), 1.28, tit. 7, pp. 1357–71.

56. Rhallis-Poltis, *Syntagma ton . . . Kanonon*, t. 2 (Athens, 1852), 506–10.

57. Ibid., 65.

58. Matthew Blastares, *Syntagma* (ibid., t. 6 [Athens, 1859], Gamma 14, pp. 175–79). Constantin Armenopoulos, *Hexabiblos* (text and commentaries by C. G. Pitsakes, "Dodone" [Athens, 1971], bk. 4, chap. 15, pp. 270–76). We make reference to Blastares and Armenopoulos because their compilations from the fourteenth century provide a synthesis of Byzantine legislation on this subject.

59. J. M. Hussey, *The Orthodox Church in the Byzantine Empire* (Oxford: Clarendon Press, 1986), 51.

60. J.-B. Pitra, Analecta sacra et classica spicilegio Solesmensi parata 6 (Paris/Rome, 1891), passim.

61. Concilium Florent., docum. et scripta, ser. B, Acta Graeca, pars 2 (J. Gill), Pont. 1st Orient. (Rome, 1953), 471.

62. D. 23, 2, 1 (op. cit., p. 330); D. 50, 17, 30 (p. 921).

63. See, for example, Novellae 111 and 112 of Emperor Leon VI (P. Noailles and A. Dain, "Les Novelles de Leon VI le Sage," *Les Belles Lettres* [Paris, 1944], 360–73).

64. See, for example, Balsamon's commentary on canon 87 of the Council in Trullo (Rhallis and Potlis, *Syntagma ton . . . Kanonon*, t. 2, pp. 507–10).

65. Nomocanon in IV titles, 13, 4 (ibid., 1, pp. 294–96).

66. Gen. 2:18–24; Matt. 5:31–32; 19:1–9. The Byzantine preference for the text of Matthew is not based on ideological motives, but can be explained quite simply: the passages from the Gospel of Matthew contained a precision—the clause of exception—not found elsewhere. Indeed there was no doubt that this precision came directly from Jesus.

67. For example, the visiting of baths and spectacles. See M. Blastares, Rhallis and Potlis, 6, p. 176. On the life of reclusion for women in Byzantium, see L. Bréhier, *La civilisation byzantine* (Paris: Albin Michel, 1950), 10–14.

68. See n. 58 above.

69. Conc. in Trullo, canons 3 and 72 (Benesevic, 144–47, 188–89).

70. For example, by mutual agreement the two members of the couple choose monastic life (Justinian, *Nov.* 22.5, op. cit., p. 150).

71. R. Naz, "Divorce," *Dictionnaire de Droit Canonique* (Paris, 1930), vol. 4, col. 1315.

72. M. Jugie, *Theologia dogm. Christ. Orient,* vol. 3 (Paris: Letouzey et Ané, 1930), 15–25.

73. See our article "Novella 89 of Leo the Wise on Marriage: An Insight into Its Theoretical and Practical Impact," *The Greek Orthodox Theological Review* (Brookline, Mass.) 32, no. 2 (1987): 155–64.

74. John N. Karmiris, *Dogmatica et symbolica monumenta orthodoxae catholicae Ecclesiae* (Athens, 1953), 2:542–43.

75. Note on apostolic canon 48, *Pedalion,* 6th ed. (Athens: Aster, 1957), 58–62.

76. N. Souvorov, *Outchebnik Tzerkovnago Prava*, 4th ed. (Moscow, 1912), 387–90.

77. Decrees of April 20 and September 1918; see Jugie, *Theologia dogm. Christ. Orient*, vol. 3, pp. 464–65.

78. See, for example, the commentaries on apostolic canon 87 of the Council in Trullo by Nicodemus [Milasch], Pravila Pravoslavnoï Tzerkvi, T. 1 (St. Petersburg, 1911), 121–22, 577–81.

79. M. Theotokas, *Nomologia tou Oikoumenikou Patriarchelou* (Constantinople, 1897), 249–95.

Concerning the legislation decreed by the Council of Moscow, Aliran N. Smirensky writes: "It is interesting to note that the Acts of the Moscow Sobor of 1917 devoted only fifteen lines to the definition of marriage as indissoluble, and has this statement of principle followed by seven pages of instructions on how to dissolve this 'indissoluble' union," in "The Evolution of the Present Rite of Matrimony and Parallel Canonical Developments," *St Vladimir's Seminary Quarterly* (Crestwood, New York) 8, no. 1 (1964): 45.

80. Dr. Jos. Zhishman, *Das Eherecht der orientalischen Kirche* (Vienna, 1864), 97–124, 729–805.

81. See our above-mentioned article "Novella 89 of Leo the Wise."

82. Gaudemet, *Le mariage en Occident*, 195–96.

83. For the juridical situation of modern Greece, see Sp. Troianos, *Paradoseis ekklesiastikou dikaiou*, 6th ed. (Athens/Comotini: Ant. N. Sakkoulas, 1984), 356–57.

84. Gaudemet, *Le mariage en Occident*, 455–60.

85. Ladislas Orsy, *Marriage in Canon Law* (Wilmington, Del.: Michael Glazier, 1986), 271–72.

86. Nistol'naïa Kniga Sviachtchenosloujitelia, Mosk. Patriarkhiia, t. 4 (Moscow, 1983), 300.

87. Canons 1151–55, Codex Juris Canonici (Vatican City: Libr. Editr. Vaticana, 1983), 201.

88. See our article "Novella 89 . . . ," 161–62.

89. See the canonical specifications mentioned in the "Tome of Union" (July 1920). The critical text was edited by L. G. Westerrink, *Nicholas I Patriarch of Constantinople, Miscellaneous Writings*, Dumbarton Oaks Texts 6 (Washington, D.C.: Dumbarton Oaks, 1981), 58–69.

6

Catholic Marriage and Marital Dissolution in Medieval and Modern Times

Joseph Martos

M ANY PEOPLE HAVE THE IMPRESSION that the Catholic Church's under-standing of marriage is clear and consistent: marriage is a sacrament, the marriage contract is indissoluble, children are essential, birth control is wrong, divorce and remarriage are forbidden, and so on. In recent years, however, Catholics themselves have begun to challenge aspects of this tra-ditional understanding even though their church has not officially changed its teaching. In the United States, for example, Catholics now divorce at about the same rate as other churchgoing Americans; they limit the size of their families; and when they remarry, they do so for the most part without going through the process of annulment, which their church insists they must complete before entering another marriage.[1]

The Catholic theology of marriage has been stable and consistent for as long as anyone can remember, and the contrast between historical stability and recent change heightens the impression that—depending on one's point of view—Catholic discipline and morality are deteriorating, or that Catholi-cism is finally coming to grips with the realities of contemporary marriage. Both of these impressions rest on a belief, however, that what has been char-acteristic of the past four centuries is equally characteristic of earlier centuries. Yet this is not the case. Edward Schillebeeckx in the 1960s docu-mented how it took twelve centuries for marriage among Christians to evolve from a civil to a religious institution.[2] Theodore Mackin in the 1980s described the evolution of Christian marriage in even greater detail and demonstrated that what many today take as *the* Catholic theology of mar-riage (and its attendant regulations in canon law) did not fully solidify until the sixteenth century.[3] It is very plausible that, if Catholicism had not felt a need to counter Protestant attacks with a solid and consistent doctrine, the Catholic theology of marriage might have continued to evolve as it had in the past. It is also arguable that, given the pressures that both marriage and Catholicism are experiencing at the turn of the twenty-first century, the Catholic understanding of marriage is again undergoing development.

A single chapter in a book on divorce is not the place to treat the whole history of marriage and divorce in the Catholic Church.[4] What can be done in a single chapter, however, is to relate in a summary fashion how the modern Catholic theology of marriage developed through the Middle Ages, reached a point of solidification at the Council of Trent, and found its legal expression in the Code of Canon Law.

A NOTE ON ASSUMPTIONS

It has become virtually a truism in our postmodern culture that every belief rests on assumptions, and indeed that every perception of fact rests on assumptions.

Assumptions are ideas that we take to be true and do not question when we are trying to understand things; assumptions provide the knowledge base for seeking new knowledge, the background information for acquiring further information, the familiar understanding that we take for granted when we explore the unfamiliar. When we walk into a library, we bring with us certain assumptions about what a library is and how it works; on the basis of those assumptions, we are able to find the book we want, we can research the topic we are interested in, and so on. When we have a problem, we go to experts (mechanics, physicians, therapists, etc.) because they have taken the time to acquire specialized knowledge that functions as a set of assumptions when they try to understand and solve our problem.

In human society, all goes relatively well when people share the same assumptions: they have the same values, the same ethical standards, the same beliefs about reality. When people argue, it is often because some of their assumptions differ. Christians who argue about homosexuality share the assumption that sexual behavior is important, but they often have very different assumptions about the role of sex in human life as well as about the significance of the Bible and what it says about homosexual behavior. Some countries use tax money to support private schools, even religious schools, while others forbid it, based on different assumptions about the role of government, the purpose of education, and so on. Even the "fact" that Columbus discovered America is based on the tacit assumption of a Eurocentric perspective on history; Native Americans who operate with a different set of assumptions perceive that same event as the beginning of an invasion by Europeans.

Whenever we think about human institutions such as marriage and divorce, we cannot avoid making certain assumptions about the nature of marriage, the effects of divorce, and so on. Moreover, if we ask whether all societies and cultures have the same assumptions about marriage and divorce, familiarity with cultural anthropology compels us to say that they do not. Many Christians do assume, nonetheless, that when the Bible speaks of marriage, when medieval theologians treat marriage, when Protestant reformers write about marriage, and so on, they are all talking about the same thing. That is, we often assume that marriage in biblical times, in the Middle Ages, during the Renaissance, and in modern times was the same as it is in our culture today. To say the same thing a bit more accurately, we often believe that people in the past shared the same assumptions about marriage—and, consequently, divorce—that people might share today. Very often, however, this is a mistaken assumption.

A great deal of the argument of this chapter will be to the effect that the traditional Catholic theology of marriage (i.e., the understanding of marriage that developed in the Middle Ages and solidified after the Council of Trent) is based on assumptions that many Catholics today would reject, or at least question.

CHRISTIAN MARRIAGE AND DIVORCE IN THE MIDDLE AGES

The title of this section suggests that it is possible to generalize about what Christians did and church leaders said with regard to marriage during the Middle Ages. During this long span of almost a thousand years, there were variations in practice from region to region (sometimes from family to family) and from century to century (sometimes from decade to decade). Likewise, Christian thinkers were not uniform in what they wrote about marriage from one period to the next, and indeed in any given period there were writers who disagreed with one another. Although it is necessary to speak in general terms, therefore, what was generally true was not always true, and there were exceptions to almost every rule. Readers interested in a more detailed picture of medieval practice and thought may refer to the larger scholarly works that were used as sources for this section.[5]

Europe in the Middle Ages was a conglomeration of small kingdoms and principalities loosely united by a common faith and to some extent a common culture. The common faith was Christianity, spread by missionaries among the Germanic tribes that had invaded and caused the downfall of the Roman Empire in the fifth century. The common culture was therefore Germanic or Teutonic, with variations from Celtic Ireland to Lombard Italy. The older Roman culture still survived, however, especially in southern Europe, which had once been a part of the Roman Empire. People of the two cultures communicated through the medium of the Latin language, the only written language of the time, and the language of the Roman church and its clergy. While the Germanic culture was geographically dominant, covering a greater extent of Europe, the Roman culture had the advantage of possessing the language of international communication and religious discourse. The theologians of the Middle Ages thought and wrote in Latin, even though most of them came from Germanic backgrounds.

Both cultures had their own marriage customs; that is to say, they had their own assumptions about the nature and purpose of marriage, about how marriage was entered into, about how it might be ended, and so on. The medieval Catholic understanding of marriage developed out of a dialogue between these two cultures in the context of Christian faith. Needless to say, the Christian religion brought additional assumptions into the conversation.

Marriage among the "Barbarians"

Among the Germanic tribes, marriage was a family matter.[6] Marriages were arranged by parents for their children: boys for reasons such as ensuring the perpetuation of the family line and securing its property into the future, girls for reasons such as making alliances with neighbors and extending the network of family relationships that was so important in a feudal society. Offspring were essential in this approach to marriage; from the parents' point of view, if there were no offspring (especially male heirs to inherit property), the marriage was a failure. Boys were therefore chosen for their virility, girls for their fertility. The process of marrying began with betrothal or the initial agreement between the parents, it proceeded through an exchange of vows between the boy and girl when they were deemed old enough to live together and produce offspring, and it culminated with the first act of sexual intercourse.[7] Custom sometimes dictated that if the boy and girl had sex before the formal exchange of vows, their marriage was consummated even though there was no wedding ceremony.

Also common was an arrangement between a man who was no longer under his father's jurisdiction and the father of a girl he wanted to make his wife. The steps were the same, the main difference being that the wedding took place when the girl was old enough to bear children—usually not younger than twelve.

Under this system of marriage, divorce was rather infrequent because, like marriage, it depended in large measure on the will of the parents. Children who were betrothed by their parents were considered to be married in effect, even though it might be years before they would begin living together. It might happen, though, that their parents would have a falling out and the marriage would be canceled; in other words, the espoused couple would be divorced. It could also happen that one of the children would decide not to go along with the arrangement, persuading the parents to call it off. After the consummation of a marriage, divorce was more difficult, but it could be accomplished—usually by a man dissatisfied with his wife, rather than the other way around. The most acceptable reasons for the dismissal of a wife were infertility and infidelity.

The Roman Tradition of Marriage

Marriage in the former Roman Empire operated out of a different set of assumptions.[8] While many marriages were indeed arranged by parents, as they were in the northern culture (and for many of the same reasons), laws had been passed which allowed men and women who were no longer under the guardianship of their parents to contract their own marriages. A marriage was deemed to come into existence when two people said to each other, in effect, "I give myself to you in marriage and I accept you as my spouse." No waiting time was needed, no formal ceremony was needed, and no witnesses were needed. Indeed, Roman law assumed that a woman and man were married (i.e., that an exchange of marriage vows had taken place) if they had lived together for at least a year.[9]

In a system in which parental consent was not needed for marriage, it was also not needed for divorce. According to Roman law, either spouse could end a marriage simply by withdrawing his or her consent. There were, of course, social pressures and family expectations to contend with, so divorce in fact was not all that common.[10] But it was legally possible, it was in the hands of the spouses themselves, and it did occur.

That it occurred among Christians can be inferred not only from Roman civil records but also from the writings of churchmen who disapproved of divorce on theological grounds. In addition, bishops penalized what they called the sin of divorce (especially unjust divorce, that is, a divorce that was not justified by adultery on the part of the spouse[11]), which they would not have had to do if Christians had not been committing it.[12]

Christian Beliefs and Values Affecting Marriage

Christianity, then, brought into the medieval discussion of marriage a third set of assumptions. One assumption was that the Bible contained information and directives that were highly relevant to the discussion because they were revealed by God for the good of humankind. Another was that Scripture passages were to be interpreted literally; they might also be interpreted figuratively or analogously (for example, the erotic love poetry in the Song of Songs was taken as symbolic of the spiritual love between Christ and the church), but the basis of any further interpretation was always the literal meaning of the text. Thus Christians assumed that the Genesis story of the creation and fall of the first human parents was literally true, as were all the other stories in the Old and New Testaments, including stories that related what Jesus had said about marriage and divorce.

Another operative assumption about divine directives in the Bible was that they were to be read legalistically, as though they were commandments. Not every directive in the Bible was taken this way; for example, no one took literally the directive to cut off one's hand or to pluck out one's eye if they led one into sin (Matt. 5:29–30), and few took the directive to turn the other cheek (5:39) as a legalistic demand. But it was generally assumed, for whatever reasons, that all the texts relating to sexual morality were to be taken this way.

Christian thinkers and writers in the Middle Ages also assumed that marriage was a sacrament, and this for three reasons. First, the Latin text of Ephesians 5:32 read, "*Sacramentum hoc magnum est.*" St. Jerome, who had made the translation in the fourth century, had used *sacramentum* to translate the Greek word *mystērion*. It was a perfectly good translation at the time, when both words could refer either to sacred signs or to sacred mysteries. St. Augustine, however, who used Jerome's Latin translation because he himself could not read Greek very well, took Ephesians 5:32 to mean, "This is a great sacrament." And since the Pauline text occurs in a discussion of marriage, Augustine interpreted it to mean that there is a sacramentality to marriage in the same way that there is a sacramentality to baptism.[13]

The second reason why medieval theologians assumed that marriage was a sacrament was the authority of St. Augustine. Augustine was arguably the greatest of the church fathers who wrote in Latin, and he was certainly the most prolific. His writings (not only about marriage but also about every other topic of interest to Christians) were therefore more available and more influential in the Latin-speaking Middle Ages than were those of the Greek-speaking fathers, not all of which had been translated into Latin. Augustine's opinion that marriage is sacramental was therefore very influential.[14]

The third reason was the common usage by the twelfth century of a church wedding ceremony. Earlier, in the Roman Empire and in barbarian Europe, marriage had been a civil matter and wedding ceremonies were presided over by heads of households. From the sixth to the eleventh centuries, however, the breakdown of Roman law and the christianization of the Germanic tribes led first to ecclesiastical demands that weddings be witnessed by the clergy and eventually to the development of a marriage ritual presided over by a priest. It was not difficult for canonists and theologians to view this ritual as sacramental, analogous to baptism and ordination.[15]

Church leaders had their own reasons for regarding marriage as a sacrament. After the fall of the empire to the barbarians and the disappearance of Roman law courts, bishops were often called upon to act as judges in civil disputes, including marriage cases. Some of these cases involved families that disagreed about betrothal arrangements; others involved the legitimacy of children and their right to inherit property; others involved women who had been dismissed by their husbands, and so on. The situation was complicated by the simultaneous existence of two different traditions—the Germanic and the Roman—with quite different assumptions about marriage, and by the fact that social rules could vary widely from one region to another and from one tribe to another.

The church's effort to regulate marriage and family life among Christians was motivated by the philosophical assumption that the moral law is uniform for all of humankind; extreme variations in marriage customs and practices throughout Europe, therefore, could not be moral. The effort was also motivated by the paternalistic assumption that the church's thinkers and lawgivers had the responsibility to discover the true nature of marriage and to legislate the correct moral behavior for all Christians. If marriage were a sacrament, the church's ability to regulate marriage and family life would be enhanced.

Blending the Three Traditions into One

When scholastic theology was developing during the rise of the medieval universities and theological schools, there was much debate as to whether marriage should be considered a sacrament and, if so, what in the wedding ceremony or the marital relationship should be considered sacramental.[16] By the late twelfth century the first question was assumed to be settled in the affirmative: since there existed a church ritual for marriage, since Augustine's interpretation of the Epistle to the Ephesians was taken for granted, and since a growing body of ecclesiastical law dealt with marriage, there was common agreement among church leaders, lawyers, and academics that marriage is a sacrament.[17] The only questions that remained dealt with the nature of the sacrament, its effects, and so on.

The canonist Francis Gratian contributed much to the discussion and its eventual outcome. His influential *Concordia discordantium canonum*, first published around 1140, attempted to collect and harmonize church laws and regulations then in effect in many parts of Christian Europe. Aware of both the Roman and the Germanic traditions regarding marriage, Gratian suggested that a marriage came into existence when the couple (not their parents) promised themselves to one another, and that the marriage was consummated through the first act of intercourse. Pope Alexander III (1159–1181), himself a canonist, adopted Gratian's compromise and reshaped many of the church's marriage laws in accordance with it.[18]

By the mid-twelfth century, the academic approach to theology practiced at medieval universities had reached a level of maturity that its basic assumptions were well established: the scholastic method of posing theological questions, the use of Aristotelian philosophical categories for intellectual analysis, the authority of Augustine, and so on. With regard to marriage, the foundations for a solid theology were in place: biblical and patristic texts on marriage and divorce, a rite of Christian marriage, and canon laws regulating marriage and its consequences. The scholastic theologians of the period (notably Thomas Aquinas and John Duns Scotus) built their theologies of marriage on these foundations.

The scholastics never completely agreed with one another; as is the case with academics today, their reputations were earned in part by taking issue with other scholars and arguing for what they considered to be a better solution to theological problems. What they did agree on were the assumptions mentioned above, the questions that needed to be answered, and the general parameters within which acceptable (i.e., nonheretical) answers needed to fall. With regard to marriage, for example, it was agreed that marriage has an essential nature that can be understood by human intelligence, that marriage was instituted by God and should be regulated by the church, that marriage is a sacrament, and that marriage is in some sense indissoluble. These assumptions also carried forward, despite social and cultural changes, into the Catholic theology of the twentieth century.

Some of the questions that were asked about the nature and purpose of marriage are very illuminating. Is sexual intercourse, for example, part of the nature of marriage? If so, then Mary the mother of Jesus (to whom the medievals attributed perpetual virginity) was not really married to Joseph —which contradicts the testimony of Scripture. Marriage therefore needed to be defined as a union of wills rather than as a physical union between persons. At the same time, however, marriage had to be open to the possibility of having children, and so married persons had to be capable of sexual intercourse, which presumably Mary and Joseph were. Is the purpose of marriage the procreation of children? The answer in the Middle Ages was obviously yes. At the same time, however, children could not be considered essential to marriage or childless couples would not be really married. Is friendship an essential part of marriage? Aquinas, among others, argued that it is not, since friendship is not unique to marriage, and what keeps a marriage together is not friendship but a contract.[19]

Augustine had argued that one effect of the sacrament was its permanence. While pagans in the Roman Empire could divorce at will, Augustine wrote, Christians were bonded together for life because their sacramental marriage was a sacred sign of the relationship between Christ and the church. The full text of Ephesians 5:32 (translated from the Latin) reads, "This is a great sacrament; I say this, however, about Christ and the church."[20] If Christian marriage is a sacred sign of the Christ–church relationship, reasoned Augustine, then since the Christ–church relationship is indestructible, the husband–wife relationship must also be indestructible.[21]

Augustine's theory of indissolubility fit in very nicely with medieval churchmen's desire to regulate marriage more closely and reduce the social harm and family alienation caused by marital breakdown. It also squared with a literal interpretation of such Scripture texts as, "Whoever puts away his wife and marries another, commits adultery against her; and if the wife puts away her husband and marries another, she commits adultery" (Mark 10:11–12).[22] Church leaders before Augustine had used the biblical texts to argue that Christians *should not* divorce and remarry; armed now with Augustine's theology of marriage, they argued that Christians *could not* divorce and remarry.[23]

Cracks in the Theory of Indissolubility

Despite the theological conclusion that a Christian marriage could not be dissolved, separation and remarriage were able to continue, if only on a limited scale, thanks to a variety of medieval assumptions.

One assumption was the "power of the keys," the belief that the pope as the successor of St. Peter had to power to make decisions on earth that would be honored by God in heaven, based on Matthew 16:19, where Jesus says to Peter, "I will give you the keys of the kingdom of heaven. Whatever you bind on earth shall be bound also in heaven, and whatever you loose on earth shall be loosed also in heaven." On this basis, Alexander III and later popes decided they had the power to dissolve marriages before they were consummated but not afterward. They also declared that an unconsummated marriage was automatically dissolved if one of the spouses entered the monastic life.[24] In this regard, Catholic teaching and practice respected the Germanic marriage tradition, which made divorce relatively easy before consummation but not after it.

At the same time, the church honored the Roman tradition that a marriage was created through the mutual consent of the spouses, regardless of the wishes of their parents, and even regardless of church laws requiring a ceremony and witnesses. Church courts consistently ruled that clandestine marriages were valid even if they had been contracted illicitly, because some of the rules for legal marriage (e.g., the posting of banns, the presence of witnesses) had not been observed.[25] The popes and canonists left it up to theologians to explain how an indissoluble union could be dissolved before consummation and why sexual intercourse produced an indissolubility that was impervious to the power of the keys.

The second way that separation and remarriage were able to continue in the Middle Ages was through marriage annulments. Technically, an annulment is a legal judgment rendered by a court that a particular contract is invalid and nonbinding. The reasons for the invalidity may vary, but in general they point to the absence of some ingredient needed for a binding contract. If a valid marriage required both parties to be of a certain age, to be currently unmarried, to enter into the agreement of their own free will, and to be capable of sexual intercourse, then a marriage could be declared null and void if it could be shown that either one of the parties had not been old enough to marry, was already married to someone else, had been coerced into the marriage, or was impotent. Once a marriage was annulled, the partners could remarry—provided of course that they now met the legal requirements mentioned above.

Christians in the Middle Ages, however, assumed that there were other factors that could annul a marriage. The most common of these concerned relatedness through family or other ties. Siblings of course were prohibited from marrying, as were first and second cousins, but in some parts of Europe relationships as distant as a seventh degree of affinity could prevent —or void—a marriage. Among the nobility, for whom the selection of spouses was limited to persons of rank, marrying a distant relative was sometimes unavoidable. Then, if the marriage fell apart, one of the parties (usually the husband) could seek an annulment based on the forbidden degree of kinship and make the case that the marriage had failed because a law of nature (or of God) had been violated.[26]

By the end of the Middle Ages, then, Catholic law and theology with regard to marriage were well developed, even if their observance was sometimes imperfect, and even if in some respects they were conceptually flawed. The notion that a bond is indissoluble but that at the same time it can be dissolved by papal authority for certain reasons was not really self-consistent, although postulates such as the power of the keys did much to conceal the defect. It was not until the Reformation that critics of the church used the imperfections and inconsistencies of the medieval theory and practice of marriage to question some (though not all) of the assumptions on which they were based.

THE REFORMATION AND THE COUNCIL OF TRENT

Once the sixteenth-century Reformers began to question the church's sacramental and judicial systems, it was not long before they pointed to what they felt were gross errors in the Catholic teaching and practice of marriage. Of the early leaders of the Reformation, Martin Luther was a Scripture scholar and John Calvin was a lawyer turned theologian; both read Greek and both were familiar with early church writings.

Luther was the first to point out that the Vulgate *sacramentum hoc magnum est* is a poor translation of the Greek *to mystērion touto mega estin*, and that the author of Ephesians is saying that the relationship between Christ and the church is a great mystery, not that marriage is a great sacrament. According to Luther, marriage was instituted by God at the time of Adam and Eve, as described in the book of Genesis; it was not instituted by Christ during his earthly ministry, and no text in the four Gospels can be used to prove that it was. For Luther, then, marriage is an important human institution which God blesses and the church celebrates, not an ecclesiastical ritual that canon law should regulate.[27]

Calvin accepted the medieval Catholic understanding of a sacrament as a spiritually effective ritual that had been instituted by Christ and, like Luther, he could find no New Testament support for a Christian wedding ceremony. His familiarity with patristic and early Roman legal texts, moreover, led him to conclude that no such ceremony existed in the early church either—a position still supported by historical scholarship. The sacrament of marriage therefore had to be, it seemed to Calvin, an invention of the medieval church. He agreed that marriage as a human institution needed to be regulated, and he found rules for husbands and wives revealed in the Scriptures, but he believed that in the modern world the legal regulation of marriage should be left to the state, so that the church could concern itself with the pastoral dimensions of marriage.

To the world's Catholic bishops gathered at the Council of Trent (1545–1563), the claims being made by the Protestant Reformers were both inaccurate and heretical. To their way of thinking, it was not necessary to prove the existence of a Christian wedding ceremony from the Bible, for the sacrament from a theological perspective was not a ritual but a spiritual reality created by a ritual. Moreover, the essential ritual was understood to be the exchange of wedding vows between the spouses, and so the absence of a church ceremony in early Christian writings proved nothing.[28] What was needed, therefore, was a clear restatement of Catholic doctrine.

In terms of positive doctrine, the council was very succinct:

> Inspired by the divine Spirit, the first parent of the human race proclaimed the perpetual and indissoluble bond of matrimony when he said, "This is now bone of my bones, and flesh of my flesh. For this reason a man will leave his father and mother and cleave to his wife, and they will be two in one flesh" (Gen. 2:23–24; see Eph. 5:31).
>
> Christ our Lord taught even more clearly that only two persons are joined and united by this marriage bond. Referring to the last sentence above as words spoken by God, he said, "Therefore now they are no longer two, but one flesh" (Matt. 19:6). Immediately after this, he confirmed the solidity of that same bond which had been declared by Adam so long before with the words, "What therefore God has joined together, let no man put asunder" (Matt. 19:6; Mark 10:9).
>
> Indeed, Christ himself, who instituted and brought to perfection the venerable sacraments, merited for us by his passion the grace that perfects the natural love [in marriage], strengthens the indissoluble unity, and sanctifies the spouses. The Apostle Paul implied this when he said, "Husbands, love your wives, just as Christ loved the church and delivered himself up for her (Eph. 5:25), adding shortly afterwards, "This is a great sacrament; I say this in reference to Christ and the church" (Eph. 5:32).[29]

This brief statement does not prove the sacramentality of marriage but assumes it; in logical terms, it begs the question. The proof texts cited from Scripture speak of marital unity, fidelity, and even permanence, but not indissoluble permanence. And citing the Latin translation of Ephesians to prove the existence of the sacrament since biblical times is of dubious value in light of the original Greek.

The council was more elaborate in its negation of doctrines it considered heretical, listing them in twelve canons that threatened excommunication to anyone who held them. Among those it condemned were anyone who taught that (1) marriage is not a sacrament instituted by Christ; (2) Christians may be polygamous; (3) the degrees of consanguinity which impede marriage are limited to those listed in the book of Leviticus; (4) the church cannot determine impediments to marriage; (5) heresy, incompatibility, and desertion are grounds for divorce; (6) an unconsummated marriage is not dissolved by the profession of religious vows by one of the spouses; (7) the church is mistaken in teaching that not even adultery provides grounds for divorce; (8) the church is mistaken in teaching that spouses may live separately for serious reasons; (9) priests and persons in religious orders are able to marry, despite their vows to the contrary; (10) marriage is better than virginity and celibacy; (11) the church cannot regulate the performance of weddings; and (12) church courts do not have jurisdiction over marriage cases.[30]

Each of the positions listed above had been taken by one or more of the Protestant Reformers and, in its original wording, each was carefully crafted to condemn heretical teaching while not condemning legitimate theological discussion. Others, such as canons 7 and 8, were worded in such a way that they excommunicated those who attacked the Catholic Church for what it taught, but they said nothing about those who taught differently— the Orthodox churches, for example.[31]

Again here, however, the canons rest on a raft of assumptions that the Reformers would not accept, and that Catholics today might not accept either. In their original wording, if not always in the above summary, it is clear that the formulators of the canons assumed that Scripture texts should be taken literally, that the church can authoritatively interpret ambiguous texts, that church teaching is irreformable, that church practice is correct, that the church should be in complete control of marriage laws, and that questioning the church's position on certain matters is not to be tolerated.

One of the problems with the church's regulation of marriage in the Middle Ages had been the persistence of clandestine marriage. Since the church had accepted the Roman assumption that marriage could be contracted privately between two individuals, young people who wanted to thwart their parents' plans could secretly give themselves in marriage to each other and then publicly announce they were married. Such marriages were illicit because they violated church regulations, but they were regarded as valid because they were based on the mutual consent of the couple. Other social ills were also connected with clandestine marriage (a man could abandon a woman and her children, for example, claiming that he had never vowed marriage to her), but in the Germanic society of northern Europe, the main complaint was that the church allowed children to marry without their parent's consent.[32]

After lengthy debate, the bishops at the Council of Trent decided to address these ills by putting an end to clandestine marriage once and for all. In chapter 1 of a separate decree on the reform of marriage practices, they announced that henceforth more than mutual consent would be required for validity: to be valid, any marriage contracted in the future would have to be performed in front of a priest and two other witnesses. To ensure that every marriage be publicly knowable before and after the fact, they decreed that every wedding had to be announced three times before it took place, and that every wedding had to be recorded in the parish in which it occurred. These latter regulations were not requirements for validity, but priests who ignored them were subject to ecclesiastical sanctions.[33]

In summary, the Catholic Church neither changed nor developed its doctrine of marriage at the Council of Trent. It reaffirmed the sacramentality of marriage and its institution by Christ. It reiterated the doctrine that marriage is indissoluble while retaining the understanding that in certain cases an unconsummated marriage can be dissolved. It defended its right to regulate marriage and adjudicate marriage cases. Since the twelfth century the church had declared that celibate priests could not validly marry; they could only "attempt" marriage. Now in the sixteenth century the church declared that lay people could validly marry only in the presence of a priest and two witnesses; they too could only "attempt" marriage unless this condition were met. Again here we see the assumption of the power of the keys at work: the notion that the church has the ability to declare what is true or valid in God's eyes and what is not.

What developed, therefore, was not doctrine but practice, and the ecclesiastical regulation of marriage. Theology (understood as the explanation of doctrine) likewise did not advance. The council did not attempt to explain how an indissoluble sacrament could be dissolved in certain cases, nor why a bond created by the spouses themselves could be prevented from coming into existence by church laws. More basically, the church continued to operate on the assumption that it and it alone had the right and the power to define the reality of marriage and regulate the practice of marriage for all Christians.

Indeed, by the sixteenth century, the Catholic Church was beginning to assume that it had the right and the ability to define the reality of marriage not only for Christians but for all humans as well. Theologians in the Middle Ages had theorized not only about Christian marriage but also about marriage before the coming of Christ, basing their reasoning on what was said about marriage in the Jewish Scriptures (especially Gen. 2:21–24) and on the words that Jesus had spoken to Jewish audiences (especially Matt. 19:3–9 and its parallels in other Gospels). Their conclusion was that marriage is an undivided union, an indivisible relationship of its very nature, and that God had permitted the Israelites to divorce (even as he had permitted the Old Testament patriarchs and kings to have more than one wife) as a special exception to the law of nature.[34] By the Renaissance, Catholic theologians were assuming that they correctly understood not only Christian marriage but all human marriage, and Catholic churchmen were assuming that they had the responsibility to defend the law of nature against the beliefs and practices of Jews, Muslims, and other non-Christians.

The church was also operating under the assumption that marriage in the Renaissance was essentially the same institution that it had been in the Middle Ages. To a large extent, this assumption was correct, since parental consent was still needed in order to marry; moreover, romantic love was not an important factor in the decision to marry, whereas the desire to have children (whether to work the family farm or to inherit the family wealth) was. But to some extent, the pendulum of history was swinging back to where it had been in the early church, when marriage was a secular institution governed by family traditions and civil laws. During the modern centuries, marriage would become increasingly secularized in practice, despite the Catholic contention that marriage is a religious institution governed by ecclesiastical laws.

CATHOLIC THEOLOGY AND CANON LAW IN MODERN TIMES

By the close of the Council of Trent, the Catholic position on marriage as regards divorce was clear. Validly married Christians are united in an indissoluble sacramental union. In certain circumstances, however, papal authority may dissolve unconsummated sacramental marriages, though not consummated ones.

This rather simple picture was complicated by two major factors. First, the Catholic Church still viewed itself as the rightful legislator for all baptized persons (including heretics and schismatics), but Protestants did not regard themselves as subject to Catholic canon law. Second, the church believed itself to be the rightful interpreter of natural law—the moral law as it applies to all human beings, not just Christians. Non-Christian marriage practices did not always conform to this interpretation of natural law, however, especially in the areas of polygamy and divorce. As long as Protestants and non-Christians remained outside the Catholic Church, there were no problems. Nor were there problems with converts who had never been married. But complications sometimes arose when married people wanted to join the church.

Protestant Complications

Trent had decreed that henceforth one of the requirements for a valid marriage would be that the wedding take place in the presence of a priest and two additional witnesses. The council understood that this legislation would be easier to implement in countries and regions that remained Catholic than in those that had become largely Protestant, and for this reason the decree stated that the law would go into effect only in those places where it was promulgated.[35]

By the Catholic logic of the time, Trent's decree was binding on all Christians, even heretical ones. If the council declared that the new law went into effect all over the world on a certain date, let us say, then Protestants who ignored the law after that date would not be validly married. Likewise, Catholics in Protestant areas without access to a priest could not be validly married. In other words, both Protestants and Catholics who did not follow the law would not really be married; they would be living in adultery. By allowing for the law's partial and gradual implementation, the council hoped to escape this consequence.

Indeed, the council did avoid this consequence in the short run, but eventually the rivalry between Catholics and Protestants subsided, and most European countries practiced religious tolerance to a greater or lesser degree. When the decree was finally promulgated throughout Europe, Catholics had no difficulty in finding a priest to witness their marriage, but Protestants who married before a minister were technically violating the law. The same was true of persons who had been baptized earlier in their life but who no longer practiced their religion, whether Catholic or Protestant, and who got married in a civil ceremony. From a Catholic legal and theological perspective, therefore, all marriages between baptized persons that did not follow the required form were invalid. This remained the church's policy until early in the twentieth century, when it at last recognized the validity of non-Catholic marriages.[36]

Even in the sixteenth century, though, some theologians recognized the problem that was posed by Protestant marriages: put crudely, the Catholic Church was saying that Protestants were not really married and their children were bastards. Before the Council of Trent, Melchior Cano and others had proposed that a valid marriage and the sacrament of marriage were two different things: Christians could validly marry simply by exchanging wedding vows (as in a clandestine marriage or a marriage before a Protestant minister), but they received the sacrament of marriage only if their union was blessed by a priest. The priest, in Cano's view, was the minister of the sacrament, just as he was for other sacraments.[37] Adopting this view would solve the problem, it seemed, for it suggested that Protestants were validly married but only Roman Catholics, who were wed before a priest and two witnesses, received the sacrament of marriage.

Rome, however, resisted this view for a couple of reasons. First, civil governments from the seventeenth century onward passed their own laws regulating marriage and divorce, and in non-Catholic countries these civil laws sometimes contradicted the church's laws. Admitting that marriage in the absence of a priest was not a sacrament would give governments control over many marriages between baptized persons—which was condemned by the twelfth canon of the Council of Trent. Second, the church had taught for a long time that a consummated marriage is indissoluble. If marriage were separable from the sacrament, however, marriage (unless performed in a church ceremony) would be a purely secular matter and people could obtain a civil divorce even if in the church's eyes they were still married—which the church could not in good conscience tolerate. If it did, it would be allowing the creation of laws that gave people legal permission to sin.

Catholic theologians also questioned whether every marriage was necessarily sacramental. Some pointed out that, according to Catholic theology, one requirement for the validity of a sacrament was the intention of the minister and the recipient. A priest who was merely demonstrating the mass for seminary students, for example, would not actually consecrate the Eucharist, and a woman who did not want to be baptized would not receive the sacrament even if the ritual were performed on her. In the case of marriage, moreover, the prevailing theological opinion (different from Cano's) was that the couple were both the ministers and recipients of the sacrament. If they intended to marry one another but not to administer or receive the sacrament, it seemed that they would be validly but not sacramentally married.[38]

Rome did not definitively address these issues, however, until the nineteenth century. In 1852, Pope Pius IX stated for the first time that "there can be no marriage between Catholics, which is not at the same time a sacrament."[39] The same pope in 1864 issued a *Syllabus of Errors*, listing beliefs that were contrary to Catholic doctrine, including eight on marriage. Among these were Cano's opinion that the priest's blessing bestows the sacrament, the idea that Catholics can intentionally prevent themselves from receiving the sacrament, and indeed any notion that the sacrament can in any way be separated from the marriage bond. Pius IX also asserted the natural indissolubility of all marriages, even civil marriages and marriages between non-Christians, by condemning the claim that civil authorities have a right to dissolve marriages. His *Syllabus* deliberately left open the possibility, however, that marriages could be dissolved by papal authority.[40]

Pope Leo XIII reiterated the doctrine of natural indissolubility in 1878 when he wrote that marriage was "instituted by God as indissoluble from the beginning of the world."[41] Two years later, he reaffirmed the inseparability of the sacrament and the marriage bond or contract: "Certain it is that in Christian marriage the contract is inseparable from the Sacrament, and that, for this reason, the contract cannot be true and legitimate without being a Sacrament as well."[42] Nevertheless, argued Leo, even natural and nonsacramental marriages should be regulated only by the church and not by the state, for marriage is God's holy institution and not simply a human invention.[43]

Again here we can discern a number of assumptions at work, some of which have not been previously noted. One is that tradition or longstanding church practice is a sound basis for theology. Thus, the tradition of dissolving certain types of marriages and not others was regarded as a legitimate practice for which a theological explanation could be found (e.g., the reason why a consummated marriage is more indissoluble than an unconsummated one), rather than as a questionable practice that might be mistaken. Indeed, it was to bring Catholic theology in line with an ancient practice—the tradition of recognizing the exchange of vows as creating a valid marriage bond—that the popes had to insist that the bond and the sacrament were one and the same thing. Another assumption was that, whereas merely human practice might be mistaken, traditional church practice is guided by the Holy Spirit and is therefore correct. In other words, God is with the church in its ecclesiastical practice and does not permit it to go astray, so what has been done in the past must be God's will or, at the very least, not against God's will. This is one reason why, as was said above, practice precedes theory, and the practice is not questioned.

Two other general assumptions of the modern period were the infallibility of the church and the unchangeableness of doctrine. It was understood that God's guidance extended especially to the teaching function of the church, and so nothing that was authoritatively taught by the church could be erroneous.[44] Moreover, because truth does not change, true doctrine could not change. Since in fact previous popes had declared that consent is all that is needed to contract a valid marriage,[45] therefore, later popes believed they could neither contradict nor change this teaching. For the sake of consistency, they had to declare that for Christians the sacrament of marriage comes into existence at the same time that the marriage bond or contract comes into existence.

Non-Christian Complications

The European discovery of the Far East and the New World was not the first time that Christianity had encountered married people who were not baptized. In the very first decades of Christianity, Paul the Apostle had counseled converts to remain married if at all possible, but he had also allowed that it might sometimes be necessary to divorce a pagan partner in order to follow Christ (1 Cor. 7:12–16; 2 Cor. 6:14–18). This apostolic advice proved very helpful in the early Middle Ages, when Christian missionaries brought the faith to the Germanic tribes of Europe. The so-called Pauline privilege permitted converts with disapproving and uncooperative spouses to divorce and seek Christian partners.[46]

As long as the Catholic Church's control over marriage was incomplete, and as long as church law was not organized (prior to Gratian's *Concordia discordantium canonum*), it did not matter that the application of the Pauline privilege was uneven; local bishops decided each case without much regard to what other bishops were doing. By the beginning of the sixteenth century, however, Rome had assumed exclusive jurisdiction over marital matters, and canon law was increasingly viewed as a legal system in which all the parts should be consistent with one another.

The fifteenth century brought new complications to church law regarding marriage from the conversion of married pagans in the Americas, Africa, and Asia. Missionaries working in those areas had to deal with converts who had uncooperative spouses, with converts in plural marriages (polygamy), and with converts who had been divorced prior to asking for baptism. Bishops in the mission lands were not authorized to apply the Pauline privilege in such cases. Instead, the cases had to be sent to Rome for a decision, and over the years Rome developed a consistent if sometimes intricate set of policies regarding the dissolution of marriage.

In 1537, Pope Paul III issued a policy document for Catholic missionaries in foreign lands. The pope reasoned that a pagan man who had many wives was actually married only to his first wife, for God had said in Genesis that only two persons can become one flesh in marriage. The other so-called wives were therefore nothing more than concubines or "kept women" in the eyes of the church, even though in their native society they may have been considered legitimate spouses. A man in a plural marriage who wanted to convert to Catholicism, therefore, had to dismiss all but his first wife before joining the church. The pagan marriage to the first wife was essentially indissoluble (according to Gen. 2:21–24 and Matt. 19:3–9), which is why the man was not free to dismiss her and choose one of his other wives as his Christian spouse. At the moment of their baptism, the pagan marriage to the first spouse would automatically become a sacramental marriage because it would now be a marriage between two Christians.

To this simple application of the Catholic tradition, however, the pope added a complication. If a man could not remember which woman was his first wife, he could appeal to Rome for a dispensation, and the pope would dissolve the pagan marriage to that unnamed wife. Thereupon, the man would be free to marry any of his wives in a Christian wedding ceremony and enter a sacramental marriage.[47] Strictly speaking, this was not an exercise of the Pauline privilege since it was not the case of a Christian married to an uncooperative spouse. Rather, the pope was extending his use of the power of the keys to cover a new situation caused by the encounter of Christian missionaries with polygamous societies. One of the pope's assumptions, of course, was that he could use the power of the keys to dissolve marriages that according to Catholic theology were indissoluble by nature, namely, first marriages between unbaptized persons.[48]

In 1571, Pope Pius V invoked the power of the keys even more clearly when he extended it to cases in which the first wife was in fact known but refused baptism. Such cases did not exactly fall within the scope of the Pauline privilege if the woman was declining to become a Christian but was not making life difficult for the spouse who wanted to join the church. Citing his "certain knowledge of the fullness of apostolic power," the pope declared that men "who have been baptized or who shall be baptized may retain, as their legitimate wife, the one who has been or will be baptized with them, after dismissing the others."[49] The ability to petition for the dissolution of a nonsacramental marriage in order to contract a sacramental one became subsequently known in canon law as "the privilege of the faith," but it was also called "the Petrine privilege" by those who wished to emphasize that the power to dissolve nonsacramental marriages came not from what Paul had written to the Corinthians but from what Jesus had said to Peter (in Catholic eyes, the first pope) in Matthew 16:18–19.

A little more than a decade later, Pope Gregory XIII in 1585 addressed the problem of married people who were captured in Africa, enslaved and sent to the New World, and then wanted to marry in the Catholic Church. (Such scenarios played out primarily in Latin America and in Louisiana.) Here was another case where the natural first marriage (essentially indissoluble) did not fit the pattern required for the Pauline privilege, namely, a disbelieving and uncooperative spouse. In this instance, the spouse was either still a pagan in Africa or a slave somewhere else in the Americas, but in either event he or she could not be found. To address this circumstance, Pope Gregory gave local bishops permission to grant converts a dispensation from their first marriage if they wanted to marry in the church.[50]

Two things made this development importantly different from what had been previously decided. First, local bishops were given authority—an extension of the pope's authority—to dissolve natural marriages; previously, they had to appeal to Rome for a decision. Second, Gregory decreed that the second marriage would be valid even if the first spouse had been baptized during the time between the slave's initial abduction and subsequent baptism. In theology and canon law up to Gregory's time, a marriage between baptized persons was considered sacramental and absolutely indissoluble if it was *ratum et consummatum*, that is, ratified by the spoken vows of the spouses and consummated by sexual intercourse. It did not matter which of these two components came first: in most Catholic marriages, the vows pronounced in front of a priest and two witnesses came first, but in the case of married converts, sexual intercourse occurred prior to their Catholic wedding. Gregory's decree, however, seemed to imply that local bishops might dissolve sacramental marriages in those instances where, unbeknown to the bishop, the absent spouse had gotten baptized, thereby turning what had been a pagan marriage into a Christian one (for now both spouses were baptized, even though they were separated) as soon as the spouse joining the church was baptized.

Canonists and theologians therefore had to adjust the Catholic theology of marriage to say that intercourse consummated a Christian marriage only when it was performed *after* the wedding vows were pronounced. Once again, however, no explanation was given as to how or why intercourse after the wedding turned a marriage from one that could be dissolved by the pope (i.e., a marriage between baptized persons that was not yet consummated) into a marriage that not even the pope could dissolve. At the same time, though, Catholic theology had no difficulty in explaining why what had been true before 1585 was not true after 1585: the pope, exercising the power of the keys, had simply changed the requirements for a valid Christian marriage.

Again here we can discern assumptions similar to those mentioned in the previous section: that church practice is a sound basis for theology; that church doctrine and practice—especially papal teachings and decisions—are guided by the Holy Spirit and therefore correct; that the pope can exercise the power of the keys to change church practice; and that true doctrine does not change, although it can be amended and nuanced, if need be.

The 1917 Code of Canon Law

Until the beginning of the twentieth century, the Catholic Church was governed by canons and decrees issued by councils and popes that were periodically published in collections (such as Gratian's, the first such collection) which made them more accessible. Under Pope Benedict XV in 1917, however, the church set aside this patchwork of laws and issued the Code of Canon Law, a unified body of legal definitions and regulations governing all aspects of Catholic life, including marriage. In the 1917 Code, the theological and canonical developments regarding marriage that had occurred from the twelfth century to the nineteenth were encoded in canons 1012–1143. Those pertaining to marriage and its dissolution may be summarized as follows:[51]

- Marriage is a binding contract for the purpose of having children and allaying concupiscence (i.e., relieving sexual tension) (canons 1012, 1013).
- Marriage is naturally indissoluble by divine law, and marriage between baptized persons is more firmly indissoluble because it has been made a sacrament by Christ (canons 1012, 1013, 1110).
- Marriages therefore cannot be dissolved by any merely human power, but in certain cases they can be dissolved by God's power acting

through the church, namely, marriages between unbaptized persons and unconsummated marriages between baptized persons (canons 1118–20).

- There are certain legal requirements for marriage (e.g., banns, records, time and place) which, if not observed, make a marriage illicit. Permission to waive one or more of these requirements can in some cases be granted, making the marriage licit (canons 1017–34, 1108–9).
- There exist certain impediments to marriage (e.g., impotence, consanguinity, prior marriage) which prevent a marriage from being valid. A dispensation to marry despite the existence of an impediment can in some cases be granted, making the marriage valid (canons 1035–80).
- There are also some essential requirements for a valid marriage (e.g., knowledge, consent, absence of coercion), from which no dispensation can be given (canons 1081–93).
- Baptized persons must be wed in front of a priest and two witnesses. This requirement must be met for validity. Non-Catholic Christians, however, are exempt from this requirement (canons 1094–1107).
- Apparently valid sacramental marriages are subject to judicial review for serious reason, and they may be declared null and void if it is proven that an impediment was present or a requirement for validity was absent at the time of the wedding (canons 1118–27).
- The church recognizes civil laws regarding marriage insofar as they do not contradict divine law or canon law (canon 1016).[52]

With this codification of church law, Catholicism brought to a close developments in the practice and understanding of marriage that had been taking place for about eight hundred years. Before the twelfth century, marriage was largely a family or civil matter; now in the twentieth century, it was primarily an ecclesiastical concern. Before, the sacramentality of marriage was an Augustinian concept and, in the eyes of some, theologically problematic; now, it was a Catholic dogma. Before, divorce was possible although relatively rare, and it was generally regarded by the church as sinful; after, divorce in most cases was impossible, for marriage was considered indissoluble. Before, divorce occurred mostly in the secular sphere, decided by the spouses themselves or granted by some civil authority; after, divorce (called a dissolution in church language) was entirely an ecclesiastical matter (the church did not recognize the authority of civil governments to grant divorces), and it was granted only under very limited circumstances. Before, annulments were virtually unheard of; after, annulments were the only way that Catholics in apparently valid marriages could separate and remarry, and, like church-granted dissolutions, they were relatively rare.

CONCLUSION

The code had been in development since 1904, and it was promulgated on May 27, 1917. It appeared to the Catholic hierarchy that they had at last pulled together all the loose ends of canon law into a coherent system that mirrored the orderliness of the civilized world. But that coherence and orderliness had already begun to unravel. In 1914, a war had broken out that eventually devastated much of Europe and destroyed the illusion of European civilization; it was first called the Great War, and later, World War I. Afterwards, people's understanding and practice of marriage began to change, slowly at first, then with increasing rapidity as media technology (radio, film, records, television), economic displacement (the Great Depression), military disaster (World War II and Cold War conflagrations), and personal mobility (assisted by car, rail, bus, and plane travel) successively influenced how men and women thought about themselves, their relationships, their sexuality, and their commitments. At the Second Vatican Council in the 1960s, the Catholic Church recognized that the world had changed and, among other things, talked about marriage in ways that mirrored the contemporary experience of marriage. This change in Catholic thinking was in turn incorporated into the 1983 Code of Canon Law, which attempted to retain the narrow limitations on divorce while broadening the definition of marriage to a "covenant, by which a man and a woman establish between themselves a partnership of the whole of life,"[53] echoing Vatican II's description of marriage as an "intimate partnership of married life and love."[54]

The church's attempt to keep a tight control on divorce, however, has not been successful. In today's pluralistic and secular society, Catholics can bypass the church's restrictions and obtain a civil divorce, and the 1983 Code, while not explicitly acknowledging the state's power to grant divorces, implicitly recognizes that a civil divorce has both legal and social legitimacy. As noted at the beginning of this chapter, Catholics now divorce with the same regularity as their non-Catholic neighbors, and the overwhelming majority of divorced Catholics disregard the requirement to seek an annulment before remarrying. How long the current contradiction between theory and practice can be maintained is a question that has yet to be answered.

Notes

1. See Steven Priester, "Marriage, Divorce and Remarriage in the United States," *New Catholic World* 229 (1986): 17; also Terrence Sweeny, *A Church Divided: The Vatican vs. American Catholics* (Buffalo: Prometheus Books, 1992), 132–33.

2. Edward Schillebeeckx, O.P., *Marriage: Human Reality and Saving Mystery* (New York: Sheed & Ward, 1965). The original Dutch edition was published two years earlier.

3. Theodore Mackin, S.J., *Marriage in the Catholic Church: What Is Marriage?* (New York: Paulist Press, 1982); idem, *Marriage in the Catholic Church: Divorce and Remarriage* (New York: Paulist Press, 1984); idem, *Marriage in the Catholic Church: The Marital Sacrament* (New York: Paulist Press, 1989).

4. For a one-chapter summary of the history, see Joseph Martos, *Doors to the Sacred: A Historical Introduction to Sacraments in the Catholic Church* (Liguori, Mo.: Triumph Books, 1991), ch. 11.

5. Among others, see James Brundage, *Law, Sex and Christian Society in Medieval Europe* (Chicago: University of Chicago Press, 1987); and Philip Lyndon Reynolds, *Marriage in the Western Church: The Christianization of Marriage During the Patristic and Early Medieval Periods* (Leiden: E. J. Brill, 1994).

6. See Reynolds, *Marriage in the Western Church*, 66–100.

7. See John Witte, *From Sacrament to Contract: Marriage, Religion, and Law in the Western Tradition* (Louisville, Ky.: Westminster John Knox Press, 1997), 32.

8. See Reynolds, *Marriage in the Western Church*, 3–65.

9. Some authors argue that the basis of Roman marriage was not so much an exchange of vows, explicit or implicit, as "marital affection," that is, the will to be in a marriage relationship and the feelings that go along with that. See Brundage, *Law, Sex*, 41–42, 94.

10. The situation was sometimes quite different among upper-class Romans, who, because of their wealth and independence, could afford to divorce and remarry without much difficulty.

11. Some bishops during the time of the Roman Empire interpreted Matt. 5:32 and 19:9 ("Anyone who puts away his wife, except on account of fornication, and marries another, commits adultery") to mean that men could divorce wives who had committed adultery. The same bishops often did not allow wives to divorce unfaithful husbands because the text does not explicitly say anything about men's infidelity.

12. On divorce in the Roman Empire during Christian times, see John T. Noonan, "Novel 22," in William W. Bassett, *The Bond of Marriage: An Ecumenical and Interdisciplinary Study* (Notre Dame, Ind.: University of Notre Dame Press, 1968), 41–90. Also Brundage, *Law, Sex,* 94–98.

13. Augustine never claimed that marriage is a sacrament in the same way that baptism is a sacrament, but his attribution of sacramentality to marriage was an important precedent for later theologians who argued that marriage is indeed a Christian sacrament. For Augustine's theology of marriage, see Reynolds, *Marriage in the Western Church,* 241–311, especially 280–308. On the sacramental quality of marriage, see Mackin, *What Is Marriage?* 139.

14. "What Augustine certainly provided were the ingredients of a theology of the marital sacrament that invited ensuing centuries' theologians to work them into a coherent teaching" (Mackin, *Marital Sacrament,* 227; see also Schillebeeckx, *Marriage,* 281–86).

15. See Schillebeeckx, *Marriage,* 244–79, 303–12.

16. Ibid., 312–32; also Brundage, *Law, Sex,* 260–78.

17. See Mackin, *Marital Sacrament,* 274–90.

18. See Brundage, *Law, Sex,* 331–37.

19. See Mackin, *What Is Marriage?* 181–83, also 112–14 on Aristotle, and 139–41 on Augustine regarding friendship in marriage.

20. The Scripture quotations in this article have been translated by the author from the Latin Vulgate, which is the text that was used by Catholic scholars from the time of Augustine to the 1917 codification of canon law.

21. See Mackin, *Marital Sacrament,* 217–28. If Augustine considered a sacramental marriage indestructible, then logically he should have drawn the conclusion that since the spiritual bond between the spouses is eternal (reflecting the eternal bond between Christ and the church), they remain husband and wife even after one of them goes on to the afterlife, and that therefore they are never free to marry again in this life. Augustine does not draw this conclusion, however, insisting only that they remain married until one of them dies. This reflects a cultural assumption that people are free to marry after the death of their spouse, which Augustine does not question even though the practice contradicts the logic of his theology.

22. See also Luke 16:18; Matt. 5:31–32 and 19:9. The exceptions in the Matthean texts were treated as allowing a man to "put away" his wife (i.e., separation from bed and board) if she was immoral, but not to divorce her and marry someone else.

23. "According to the church Fathers the dissolution of marriage was not *permissible;* but according to the schoolmen its dissolution was not *possible*" (Schillebeeckx, *Marriage,* 284).

24. See Schillebeeckx, *Marriage,* 287–302, especially 295–96; also Mackin, *Divorce and Remarriage,* 302–17.

25. See Mackin, *What Is Marriage?* 146–54, 168–70.

26. Lawyers sometimes "proved" their cases by appealing to somewhat dubious records of family relationships reaching back two or three generations. Oral history and Old Testament texts were also invoked as testimony regarding forbidden degrees of kinship. See Georges Duby, *The Knight, the Lady and the Priest: The Making of Modern Marriage in Medieval France* (New York: Pantheon Books, 1983).

27. See Martos, *Doors to the Sacred,* 373–74. For a more thorough account of Luther's and Calvin's positions on marriage, see Witte, *From Sacrament to Contract,* 47–53, 78–92.

28. The Council of Florence about a century previously had drawn up a bull of union with the Armenian church, summarizing the Catholic doctrine on the sacraments. About this one it said, "The seventh is the sacrament of matrimony, which is a sign of the union of Christ and the Church according to what was said by the Apostle, 'This is a great sacrament; I say this in reference to Christ and the Church' (Eph. 5:32). The efficient cause of matrimony is mutual consent ordinarily expressed through words referring to the present"—not a consent to marry in the future (translated from Denziger-Schönmetzer, *Enchiridion Symbolorum* [Freiburg: Herder, 1962], 1327).

29. Denziger-Schönmetzer, 1797–99.

30. Ibid., 1801–12.

31. See Mackin, *Divorce and Remarriage,* 390–94.

32. On the problem of clandestine marriage and Trent's solution to it, see Schillebeeckx, *Marriage*, 363–67; also Mackin, *What Is Marriage?* 194–97.

33. For the entire decree, see *The Canons and Decrees of the Council of Trent*, trans. H. J. Schroeder, O.P. (New York: Herder, 1941), 183–89.

34. For the evolution of the notion that marriage is of its nature permanent, indivisible, and even indissoluble, see Mackin, *Divorce and Remarriage*, 326–61.

35. See *Canons and Decrees of the Council of Trent*, 185.

36. "Benedict XIV in 1741 . . . declared that in the Netherlands the decree *Tametsi* was binding only when two Catholics marry each other. Pius X in 1906 extended the same ruling for Germany, in 1909 for Hungary. Then, in 1907 with his decree *Ne temere* he imposed the canonical form on all marriages where one of the parties was Catholic, except in Germany and Hungary." The 1917 Code of Canon Law went further, declaring all baptized persons bound to observe the canonical form of marriage, but at the same time granting an exemption to non-Catholic Christians (Ladislas Örsy, S.J., *Marriage in Canon Law* [Wilmington, Del.: Michael Glazier, 1986], 159).

This simplification of the law, retained in the 1983 Code of Canon Law, nevertheless gives rise to legal (and theological) complications. Since the requirement to marry before a priest applies to all persons baptized in the Catholic Church, (1) nonpracticing Catholics who do not marry before a priest are regarded as not validly and sacramentally married, and (2) Catholics who marry Protestants before a minister or justice of the peace are regarded as not validly and sacramentally married, but (3) all Protestants, by virtue of their baptism, whether they are practicing their religion or not, are regarded as validly and sacramentally married. In a sense, it is easier for Protestants to receive the sacrament of marriage (even if they deny the existence of the sacrament) than it is for Catholics!

When it comes to divorce and remarriage, therefore, divorced Catholics from situations (1) and (2) can obtain an annulment quite easily; they only need to show that their first marriage was invalid because they married outside the church. Divorced Protestants from situation (3), however, find things much more difficult. If they want to marry a Catholic in a Catholic wedding ceremony, they must first go through a lengthy legal investigation of their first marriage in the hope of having their marriage annulled.

For similar reasons, complications also arise when divorced and remarried Protestants want to join the Catholic Church: before they can be Catholics in good standing, they must have their first marriage annulled.

37. See Mackin, *Marital Sacrament*, 409–10.

38. For more detail, see George Hayward Joyce, S.J., *Christian Marriage: An Historical and Doctrinal Study* (New York: Sheed & Ward, 1933), 203–4.

39. Cited in ibid., 204.

40. See Mackin, *Divorce and Remarriage*, 422–23; idem, *Marital Sacrament*, 517ff.

41. Encyclical *Quod apostolici*, trans. Michael J. Byrnes in *Papal Teachings: Matrimony* (Boston: St. Paul Editions, 1963), 125.

42. Encyclical *Arcanum Divinae Sapientiae*, in *Papal Teachings*, 149.

43. "As, then, marriage is holy by its power, in its own nature, and of itself, it

ought not be regulated and administered by the will of civil rulers, but by the divine authority of the Church, which alone in sacred matters professes the office of teaching" (*Papal Teachings*, 146).

44. For a clear statement on the infallibility of the church, see the first draft of the constitution on the church prepared for the First Vatican Council, in *The Church Teaches: Documents of the Church in English Translation* (St. Louis: Herder, 1955), 92–93. Although this statement was deleted from the final draft of the constitution, the infallibility of the church was nonetheless regarded as the basis of papal infallibility: "The Roman Pontiff, when he speaks *ex cathedra,* officially functioning as the shepherd and teacher of all Christians, and when he defines by virtue of his supreme apostolic authority a doctrine of faith or morals to be held by the universal church, is strengthened, through the divine assistance promised to him in St. Peter, with the infallibility which the divine Redeemer willed his Church to possess in defining doctrine regarding faith or morals" (Denziger-Schönmetzer, 3074).

45. This tradition goes as far back as Pope Nicholas I in the year 866. See Mackin, *Marital Sacrament*, 277–78.

46. See Schillebeeckx, *Marriage*, 155–60. Note that during the first centuries of Christianity, when the legalities of marriage and divorce were civil matters, Christians who invoked the Pauline permission to dismiss an unbelieving spouse obtained a civil—not an ecclesiastical—divorce, although some may have asked for advice and received permission to do so from their bishop.

47. Apostolic constitution, *Altitudo,* in Denziger-Schönmetzer, 1497.

48. According to Mackin, *Divorce and Remarriage,* 396, "The availability of this dispensation is also reported to have been the cause of suspicious failures of memory on the part of men who not unexpectedly preferred a younger wife."

49. Constitution, *Romani Pontificis,* in Denziger-Schönmetzer, 1983.

50. Constitution, *Populis ac nationibus,* in Denziger-Schönmetzer, 1988. See the analysis of the three papal documents discussed in this section in Mackin, *Divorce and Remarriage,* 393–401.

51. See T. Lincoln Bouscaren, S.J., Adam C. Ellis, S.J., and Francis N. Korth, S.J., *Canon Law: A Text and Commentary,* 4th ed. (Milwaukee: Bruce, 1963), 461–650.

52. Bouscaren et al. point out that this provision of the code implies that, although civil marriages between non-Christians are valid, all civil divorces are, in the eyes of the church, null and void: "To dissolve the bond of a valid marriage, even between unbaptized persons, is entirely beyond the power of the state, since it is contrary to the divine law" (*Canon Law,* 471).

53. Canon 1055, in *Code of Canon Law, Latin-English Edition* (Washington, DC: Canon Law Society of America, 1983), 387.

54. *The Church Today (Gaudium et spes)* §48, in Walter M. Abbott, S.J., ed., *The Documents of Vatican II* (New York: Herder & Herder, 1966), 250.

7

Not Made in Heaven: Marriage and Divorce in the Anglican Tradition

WILLIAM H. SWATOS, JR.

T HE PURPOSE OF THIS CHAPTER is to provide a historical survey of the Anglican position on divorce from the time of the separation of the Church of
England from that of Rome in the mid-sixteenth century to the present practice in the Episcopal Church in the United States. To do that in a presentation of this length will require some considerable leaps in terms of both time
and space. These leaps, however, can also be justified as accurately reflecting what actually happened in Anglican practice. That is, while the issue of
divorce and remarriage was one of significance both at the time of the
Reformation and is so today, it would be wrong to assume that there is a
clear historical development from the 1550s to the beginning of the third
millennium. There are historical connections more than continuities.

THE TUDOR BACKGROUND

Struggles over fine points notwithstanding, it can hardly be denied that the
Church of England—*re-formed* Anglicanism—as we know, it came into
existence over the issue of divorce. To say this is, on one hand of course, to
minimize important political and economic questions throughout the late
medieval and early modern periods. Nevertheless, the weight of liturgical
and ecclesiastical legislation during the Henrican period makes it quite clear
that Henry VIII had little sympathy for Protestant Christianity. What he
wanted was a male heir, and he believed that his path to that end was being

frustrated by his marriage to Catherine of Aragon. That modern under-standings of conception and genetics would almost certainly find him wrong on this point is sociologically unimportant. "A situation is what it is defined to be" by the participant actors within it, and certainly when one of the actors is the king, what he says carries great weight in the system of social action.

When it is said that Henry wanted a "divorce" from Catherine, however, we must also be quite clear that what that term meant then would be called an "annulment" today. Henry did not invent the divorce issue. He peti-tioned the pope for a divorce/annulment because divorce/annulment was possible in the sixteenth-century Western church. But a reason had to be invented that could sustain the pope's approbation—hence the convoluted argument put forward by Henry and Cranmer about Henry marrying his brother's wife. If, in fact, Henry had not been trying to have the marriage declared invalid from its point of origin (hence annulled), this style of rea-soning would not have been required; hence the modern Anglican position on divorce is only loosely connected to the Henrican precedent. Henry's convoluted reasoning did not work with the pope, who was of course also feeling enormous political pressure from Spain. Nevertheless, the argument was itself theologically weak. It was, for example, equally rejected by the Lutheran theologian Melanchthon, who noted that there was more biblical evidence to support polygyny than there was for Henry's proposal!

What can be said about divorce in the Tudor period following the Refor-mation is only bits and pieces. One of the most important of these was the homily "Against Adulterie" by Thomas Becon (ca. 1547), where he blames adultery "for the many divorces" that are prevalent in the mid-sixteenth century. How many was many? We do not know, but it was enough to allow the homily credible official publication by the Church of England into the Stuart period. The role of the Homilies as a part of the Church of England's theological corpus and, perhaps more important, liturgical life is not to be minimized by their desuetude today. For generations these printed sermons were read year in and year out to congregations throughout the realm. This in some ways makes the mention of "the many divorces" the more interest-ing, since it also became part of the lore of the land, and in some small way may have even legitimated divorce as a possible option for unhappy mar-riages. It also suggests that the Matthean exception ("except for adultery") may have been an acceptable basis for divorce at some point during the sec-ond half of the sixteenth century in the Church of England, though the sub-sequent Canons of 1603 did not allow remarriage on this ground.[1] We know there was clerical divorce and remarriage in the Tudor period, includ-ing the episcopal bench (Throckmorton of Limerick).[2] All divorces, how-ever, up until 1857 were in any case by a private act of Parliament.[3]

Over against this, however, must be laid the mistress/paramour culture—more clearly documented in the case of mistresses, but certainly there were also paramours—that persisted at least until the time of Victoria and Albert. Much of Becon's and other English Reformers' concerns about marriage were actually centered on this culture, which the Reformers associated with Catholic laxity regarding the biblical model of marriage. As I read the evidence, at least, what was so shocking to the general populace of Henry's day, for example, was not that he was comporting with Anne Boleyn, but that he was going to put aside his lawful wife—a princess—to marry Anne. Similarly, Princess Mary's legitimacy was never in doubt at the popular level, while Elizabeth early on constantly had to prove herself a "true" princess. If we look forward to the seventeenth century, furthermore, we know that the Restoration monarch Charles II (1660–1685) made no secret of his mistresses, that they were popularly known, and seemed to represent the conflicting course of England between Protestantism (Nell Gwynn) and the Catholicism (the Duchess of Portsmouth) in whose arms Charles found his final rest—thanks, indeed, to none other than his mistress's perspicacity.

"Looseness" was clearly a "social problem" in Tudor England. Elizabeth's reservations about married clergy reflect no doubt her own personality, but her concern as well that the clergy might marry "loose" women, who might tarnish not only their husband's ministries, but also the authority image of the Reformation. That the priests themselves might err in more than their choice of women is only implicit in these texts, yet it is clear that the conditions for their straying from their chaste call were never far off. If (male or female) looseness were rare, or unknown, in Elizabethan times, why all the fuss? It seems more fair to conclude that throughout the society there ran at least enough infidelity to make the problem worth addressing. This would include both consensual adult relations, paid and unpaid, as well as sexual relations with younger people that would now fall under the rubric of child molestation.

It is the homilies, too, that make us aware of the prevalence of wife beating in this same society. How much? We don't know, but enough, again, to make the homily on marriage creditable for at least a century. Marital union was often imperiled. Less certain is the level of remarriage when those unions were broken, but that it occurred at least sometimes is certain.

Was marriage understood as a sacrament by the Reformation? In what would become typical Anglican fashion, it equivocated. My reading is that marriage was regarded at most as a "natural sacrament," at least as a divinely sanctioned legal contract. The concept of contract, as David Zaret has shown, was signally important to Reformation Puritan thought, and therefore should not be taken lightly (that is, as "merely" a contract), since Christians were understood to have entered into a "heavenly contract" in their lives with God.[4] On the other hand, such a view led away from the mystical endowments of Catholicism. In the Reformation prayer books up to the Restoration, the marriage ceremony was always (rubrically) to be accompanied by a celebration of holy communion in which the bride and groom were to participate. Although the evidence on this is skimpy, it seems as though this rubric was often laid aside. What we can say, certainly, is that it was dropped at the Restoration. Some will say "as a concession to the Puritans," but others will reply that it was an easy concession because it was already gone in actual practice. I am inclined to accept the latter view because of the tenacity with which the Restoration church fought for the wedding ring—a deeply offensive custom to the Puritans.

Although Anglicanism is known for its theological inconsistencies, it nevertheless seems odd that if the ring and the communion were equally used prior to the Great Rebellion (1642–1648), the bishops would fight for the ring and let the communion go. Yet here the Anglican genius for doubletalk was certainly manifest: the Puritans at the Savoy Conference (1661) accused the Anglicans of holding that marriage was "a sacrament," because the Anglicans demanded the ring. No, said the Anglicans, the ring does not mean that marriage is a sacrament. Note the peculiarity here—the Anglicans neither affirmed nor denied that marriage was a sacrament; rather, they asserted the authority of the church to ordain "godly customs and ceremonies." However, they also had popular sentiment on their side; the wedding ring was part of popular as well as official religion, as the communion apparently was not. Thus, although anything is possible in religious history, it strains credulity on my part to think that if the communion had been constantly and faithfully observed at weddings prior to the Rebellion, the bishops would have been so quick to let it go at the Restoration, while taking their stand on the ring. No, the communion was *already gone*, so the bishops were quite willing to concede it. They lost nothing they had not already lost.

The Thirty-Nine Articles (1563), the closest thing there is to an Anglican "Confession of Faith," made a clear distinction (Art. XXV) between the "two Sacraments ordained of Christ" and the "five commonly called Sacraments," matrimony being one, which qualify as "states of life allowed in the Scriptures," which "are not to be counted for Sacraments of the Gospel." Marriage in the Tudor world was a preeminently *political* act—that is, an act of *civil administration,* which the church both facilitated and blessed.[5] Church and state simply were one at this time, and parish ministers acted as civil servants in a divinely sanctioned order. To grasp this signification leads to a relatively negative conclusion, namely, that neither the founding documents nor personages of Reformation Anglicanism have much to say to us today about the issues of divorce and remarriage in the lives of our people.

That is, we have jettisoned the foundational assumption of Anglican theology, perhaps without even recognizing it as a theological assumption—that is, the understanding of marriage in the Church of England's original textual corpus clearly and unmistakably derives from the prior theological "certainty" of the divinely sanctioned nation-state. Hence the foundational Anglican posture on marriage was one directed not primarily to a theology of relationship but to a theology of governance.

Both Puritan and Anglican divines during this period shared this view of the state. Where they disagreed was in the question of the personal morality of state functionaries ("the royal supremacy" versus "godly magistrates"). The Anglican view held that the state was a transcendent concept that in Christ was itself *right*. Whether or not such a view is correct, it is certainly not true in North America as we approach the third millennium. Under the conditions of secular pluralism that affect our states, issues of marriage, divorce, and remarriage become *adiaphora* ("things indifferent"), since that is the only theological principle of the English Reformation left intact. That is, the Anglican position held that things not specifically prohibited by Scripture could be enjoined by the state or the church, whereas the Puritans held that only those things enjoined by Scripture could be enforced by the state or the church. Adiaphorism, however, need not degenerate into nothingness in our own day; rather, it leaves the Episcopal Church *free* to employ the dynamics of Scripture, tradition, and reason that are at the heart of the Anglican "*via media*" to the best effect it can amidst the continued shortness and uncertainty of human life.

THE PLURALISTIC SYNTHESIS

Because the Anglican Communion is a relatively loose union of "national" churches, it is impossible today to speak of "the" Anglican position on divorce and remarriage within its faith community. For example, in England, it is still very difficult for a divorced person to be admitted to candidacy for ordination to the ministry, while there are some who quip that it's a prerequisite in the United States! In Africa debate centers far more on polygynous converts—keeping multiple wives—rather than on divorce and remarriage as we know it. In this section, I will review developments specifically in the United States, though much of what I say can be extended fairly to Canada.[6]

Church of England partisans in the United States were by and large unprepared for the pluralism that was thrust upon them by disestablishment at the time of the War of Independence. The Episcopal Church became a struggling minority. Whereas in England matters of divorce and remarriage, though always conducted in reference to the church, were essentially enforced by the state, the American situation early on allowed for civil marriage, and eventually civil divorce. The Episcopal Church had no immediate strategy for handling this. For almost the first quarter of a century of its existence the Episcopal Church had neither canon law nor policy covering divorce and remarriage. The matter first came before the General Convention when the Diocese of Maryland inquired of the advisability of adopting the English canon (from the Canons of 1603) on marriage. The matter was referred from the House of Deputies (a total of twenty-seven men) to the House of Bishops (two men), who sidestepped the issue as a whole, while the convention ultimately issued a joint resolution that Episcopalian clergy "shall not unite in matrimony any person who is divorced, unless it be on account of the other party having been guilty of adultery."[7] Discussion of the question of divorce and remarriage continued through the first half of the nineteenth century, but no formal action was taken until 1868, when a canon on the subject was finally enacted, the substance of which was identical to that of the resolution of 1808. The 1868 canon, then, represents "the first law of the American on the remarriage of a divorced person."[8]

Only in 1877, however, was the effect of the canon given teeth in regard to the laity, when a revised canon was adopted making it clear that persons married "otherwise than as God's Word doth allow" were to be barred from the sacraments except for "a penitent person in imminent danger of death," unless the diocesan bishop rendered a favorable godly judgment on their behalf. Previous to this time, the only prohibition specifically created by the convention was with regard to the conduct of the marriage service itself: persons who divorced for reasons other than the Matthean exception (or persons "guilty" under the Matthean exception) could and did marry outside the Episcopal Church and then present themselves for normal sacramental ministrations. Clergy did have at this point recourse to the "open and notorious evil liver" rubric in the communion service, but apparently this was not used in a significant number of cases, since the problem of communicants remarried outside of the church was adduced repeatedly in the debates of the 1877 convention. The 1877 canon also was the first to recognize the distinction between annulments and divorces; that is, it permitted the remarriage of persons whose marriages had been dissolved for causes existing *before* the marriage was solemnized. Not clear at all was who was to determine this temporal sequence, though the canon made explicit reference to the bishop as settling "questions" in such cases.

The matter of divorce and remarriage continued to be on the agenda of virtually every General Convention thereafter. Included in these debates, furthermore, was the question of whether even the Matthean exception should be allowed; that is to say, that while there were those who favored liberalizing the Episcopal Church's rules, there were also those who wished to make them more strict. In 1922 a slight modification was made regarding the conduct of the laity to state specifically that it was not "lawful" for any Episcopalian "to enter upon a marriage when either of the contracting parties" is a divorced person whose spouse is still living—except on the grounds of the Matthean exception or a defect prior to marriage. The Convention of 1931 set out for the first time a list of specific impediments that a person holding a civil dissolution might use to apply to the bishop or ecclesiastical court for remarriage on bases other than adultery or conditions prior to the marriage; these included such considerations as insanity, mental deficiency, undisclosed impotence, and venereal disease. Although by today's standards these would constitute a highly limited list, this was the opening wedge for all subsequent canonical changes. A crucial point of clarification was added in 1946, when it was stated that these impediments need *not* have existed prior to the contracting of the marriage; however, this language did not require a favorable judgment in any case. Hence, those bishops who rejected the possibility of dissolution for causes arising after marriage were free to withhold their permission—and did. This dual procedure (some bishops allowing, some not allowing, remarriages when nullity was not established *ab initio*) was specifically acknowledged and accepted by the Convention of 1949 as consistent with Anglican practice (i.e., adiaphorism).

Contemporary Episcopalian practice was innovated in 1973, when the listing of specific impediments was dropped and the concept of "termination" of a prior marriage was added as an apparent alternative to nullity as the basis for the possibility of remarriage. Such a judgment must come from the bishop prior to the performance of any subsequent marriage by Episcopalian clergy or else by the bishop in cases where divorced Episcopalians have married outside the church and wish to be admitted to the sacraments. Termination is often expressed as the "spiritual death" of the prior marriage. More radical suggestions have been proposed to deal with the matter of divorce, including some liturgical expression of divorce,[9] but these have not been acted upon, nor does action upon them appear likely. Current issues before the church focus much more on the blessing of same-sex unions.

In evaluating contemporary Episcopalian practice, we can note several dynamics that have consistently run through the discussions. On the one hand, there is a theological recognition that there is strong New Testament support for marital permanence and the prohibition of marriage following divorce, and that this view has been consistently upheld by the Western church; on the other hand, there is the view that both the Protestant churches, which historically hold a high view of Scripture, and the Eastern Orthodox tradition allow remarriage after divorce in at least some cases— making it clear that there are Christian groups of both strong biblical piety and strong traditional reverence that do not share the view of marital indissolubility that is particularly prominent in the Roman church. At a practical level, additionally, Episcopalians are quite aware that American pluralism is such that people who cannot be married in one church will simply seek out another. Indeed, recent research has shown that denominational loyalty among Episcopalians is quite low.[10]

The solution that the Episcopal Church has chosen is consistent with the Anglican *via media* position: namely, to permit remarriage on a case-by-case basis, but always requiring reference to the diocesan bishop. This procedure in effect takes a Protestant view toward divorce and remarriage but imposes a Catholic discipline, by taking the matter outside the context of the local congregation. Because the Episcopal Church is a federation of dioceses, there is no central authority beyond the diocesan bishop, while simultaneously the bishop has wide discretionary authority within his diocese to determine the procedures by which a favorable godly judgment may be obtained. Nevertheless, I do not know of any other non-Roman Catholic tradition wherein the authority of a figure beyond the local congregation is imposed in the decision-making process toward remarriage, and the process of referral, even at the simplest level, makes clear to the parties to the new marriage the "exceptional" character of their intentions over against the Christian norm.

Notes

1. The Canons of 1603, though published with James I's sanction, were not ratified by Parliament. "Thus, although they were generally followed, they were not literally binding on the laity and may not have been binding on the clergy either" (Colin R. Chapman, *Sin, Sex and Probate*, 2nd ed. [Dursley, U.K.: Lochin, 1997], 6). Thus, the American church might rightly hold that these canons were not definitive standards for its own decision making, for example, in what did or did not constitute adequate grounds for divorce.

2. I deal with this and related questions in greater detail (including full references) in my essay "Ave Virginia, Regina Terræ," in *Equal at the Creation*, ed. Joseph Martos and Pierre Hégy (Toronto: University of Toronto Press, 1998), 96–113.

3. See Colin R. Chapman, *Marriage Laws, Rites, Records & Customs* (Dursley, U.K.: Lochin, 1996), 91–94; Chapman also notes that, although illegal, the sale of a wife "at the local market place" was popularly accepted at least among "the labouring classes" from at least the 1700s until the early years of the twentieth century. Although it sounds quite bizarre at the turn of the third millennium, this form of divorce was apparently partially negotiated in advance between the husband and

the suitor, whose intentions were known, and was done in the market place to achieve suitable publicity for the new "marriage," which was a "requirement from earliest times."

4. See David Zaret, *The Heavenly Contract* (Chicago: University of Chicago Press, 1985). I do not think it is necessary to accept Zaret's tendency toward economic determinism to appreciate his contention about the importance of the concept of contract in Puritan theology.

5. In this respect, by the way, I think the Papal bull *Apostolicae curae* on Anglican orders is also absolutely correct in saying that there was no *intention* in the Church of England to create a "Catholic" (i.e., Romish) priesthood in the "commonly called" sacrament of "Orders." Anglicans created what they openly called "the Protestant succession." Of course, I also think that *Apostolicae curae* is wrong in holding that such a succession is not a "true" succession, but that is another story.

6. The historical details in this section are generally derived from the standard commentary on canon law in the Episcopal Church, Edwin Augustine White and Jackson A. Dykman, *Annotated Constitution and Canons for the Government of the Protestant Episcopal Church in the United States of America otherwise known as The Episcopal Church* (New York: Seabury Press, 1981).

7. Resolutions of General Convention are not canons, but are advisory only. An 1877 General Convention committee reporting on the question of divorce and remarriage stated this to be the case specifically with regard to this resolution of 1808: "the House of Bishops treat it as an opinion only, and there is no trace in our Church of its having been treated as a law." (This observation in this report, in fact, constitutes one of the major precedents for understanding the legal status of General Convention resolutions.)

8. The introduction of the Matthean exception into canon law was an American innovation, without precedent in either Western canon law generally or the English canons of 1603; however, the (Presbyterian) Church of Scotland, over which the same monarch was head from 1603 forward, allowed divorce on the basis of adultery from 1563 on.

9. See John S. Spong, *Living in Sin?* (Nashville: Abingdon, 1988).

10. See Wade Clark Roof and William McKinney, *American Mainline Religion* (New Brunswick, N.J.: Rutgers University Press, 1987).

APPENDIX
A STUDY IN APPLICATION

Because every diocesan bishop in the Episcopal Church (they number 113 at this writing) has wide latitude to interpret and apply the marriage canons, there can be considerable variation, especially at extremes. On the other hand, there are also central tendencies. The following section contains the current approach of the Diocese of Central Florida (Orlando) and may be taken as an example of how divorce and remarriage cases are handled—or at least intended to be handled—at the local level in the Episcopal Church in the United States at the turn of the third millennium.

DIOCESE OF CENTRAL FLORIDA
BACKGROUND STATEMENT RE: CHRISTIAN MARRIAGE

At the beginning of creation God made them male and female. For this reason a man will leave his father and mother and be united to his wife and the two will become one flesh. So they are no longer two but one. Therefore, what God has joined together, let no one separate.

Mark 10:6–9

Christian marriage is the lifelong union between a man and a woman in which they make vows before God and the Church and receive the grace of God to help them fulfill those vows. The Church considers marriage to be sacramental in character, expressing something of the nature of Christ's love and commitment to his Church. The purpose of marriage is for "their mutual joy; for the help and comfort given one another in prosperity and adversity; and when it is God's will for the procreation of children and their nurture in the knowledge and love of the Lord." (BCP p. 423) Jesus said that when two people marry they leave their fathers and mothers and become one flesh. To live as one flesh means to regard each other's security, happiness and personal growth as important as one's own. In the view of the Church, this is accomplished through agreement of both parties to establish the gospel of Jesus Christ as authority over themselves and their lives together. In practice the study of scripture, daily prayer, regular worship and the support of consistent Christian fellowship enables the couple to be successful in determination of the will of Christ in all decisions affecting them individually or corporately. The sacrifice of dying to one's self and living in Christ is the heart of every Christian marriage.

Since scripture plainly states that "God hates divorce" (Malachi 2:16), the provision for remarriage must not be seen as condoning or approving of divorce, but rather a pastoral response to the fact that divorce does occur. The Episcopal Church seeks to help people make a new life when their marriages are clearly and irreversibly broken. When both partners seek to follow the redemptive path of Christ they discover that such a commitment not only works, but brings great joy to themselves and others.

Christian marriages are begun with the sacramental grace of holy matrimony and are strengthened through the grace extended to God's people in baptism, the Eucharist, and reconciliation of a penitent. Through baptism we are made members of God's family, we are given the Holy Spirit, we are promised forgiveness and forgiven, and we are enabled to embark on a pilgrimage of faith in which we die to self and are raised as new people in Jesus Christ, our Lord. We can be sure that God will nurture us on our journey through participation in the sacraments and interacting with other members of the body of Christ, and corporately we become lights to the world in our generation. As expressed in the Book of Common Prayer, every member of the body of Christ has responsibility to encourage and assist those who are married in the Church to grow in their capacity to love, forgive and affirm one another.

Revised 5/98

It is the policy of the Diocese of Central Florida that:

1. At least one member of the marriage must be baptized.
2. Regular attendance at worship is required.
3. In a situation of remarriage, at least one year shall have passed from the date of the divorce decree.
4. Pre-marital instruction shall include the items mentioned on the petition form.
5. The judgment of the Bishop shall be requested at least 30 days prior to the date of the marriage.
6. The approved petition form shall be used by the clergy in obtaining a judgment.
7. When either person seeking the Bishop's permission to marry following divorce (or annulment) has had more than one previous marriage, it is the policy of this diocese that in addition to the pre-marital pastoral counseling given by the clergy, there shall be evaluation by a professional psychological counselor. We recognize there are no guarantees as to the "success" of a proposed marriage, but our concern is to ensure—so far as is possible—that a pattern of marital failure not be repeated. We seek the assurance of a professional counselor that the current relationship is a healthy one, and there are no obvious psychological impediments resulting from the previous marriage(s).

CONCERNING CLERGY DIVORCE AND REMARRIAGE

A member of the clergy whose marriage is in jeopardy shall inform the Bishop. The Bishop shall be made aware of the problems and the measures taken to resolve them. Plans for remarriage will not be given consideration until at least one year has elapsed after the final divorce decree, except in those cases in which an extremely lengthy separation has preceded the final legal decree.

The diocesan guidelines for remarriage after divorce are in all cases to be followed. The Bishop, Priest, and intended spouse will mutually agree on a marriage counselor to conduct premarital preparation and submit an application to the Bishop for judgment. Inasmuch as the clergy guide and counsel persons seeking remarriage, their own preparation under such circumstances should be a model for the process which the church intends. In his counseling with the priest intending marriage, the Bishop will usually advise against remaining in the parish served prior to the divorce.

Under no circumstances will a marriage be recognized unless it has complied with canonical procedures.

We recognize the clergy to be leaders of the congregations and as such they must be models of reconciliation. If the clergy are involved in scandalous or immoral behavior their resignation will be required.

DIOCESE OF CENTRAL FLORIDA 1017 E. Robinson Street, Orlando, Florida 32801
Petition to the Bishop Regarding Judgment of Termination
of a Marriage, Annulment, and/or Consent to Solemnize a
Marriage after Divorce or Annulment

Petition submitted by:
The Rev'd _____ Date _____
Address _____
Church _____

To the Bishop:

( )   I petition for a judgment of termination in the marriage of:
( )   I petition for annulment of the marriage of:
( )   I petition for consent to solemnize the marriage of:

Name _____ Age _____
Address: _____
Please furnish dates for the beginning and termination of any prior marriages:
1st Marriage: Wedding _____ Divorced _____ Annulled _____ Widowed _____
2nd Marriage: Wedding _____ Divorced _____ Annulled _____ Widowed _____
3rd Marriage: Wedding _____ Divorced _____ Annulled _____ Widowed _____
Other? _____
Ages of children from prior marriage(s) _____

Name _____ Age _____
Address: _____
Please furnish dates for the beginning and termination of any prior marriages:
1st Marriage: Wedding _____ Divorced _____ Annulled _____ Widowed _____
2nd Marriage: Wedding _____ Divorced _____ Annulled _____ Widowed _____
3rd Marriage: Wedding _____ Divorced _____ Annulled _____ Widowed _____
Other? _____
Ages of children from prior marriage(s) _____

Note: If both addresses are the same—i.e. if this couple is already cohabiting—the member
of the clergy preparing this form is to describe in writing to the Bishop the nature of
the pastoral counseling being given to the couple regarding this decision on their part.

Each petitioner shall furnish the following information concerning prior marriages.

What do you believe to be the true cause of the breakdown of your prior marriage in terms
of your own involvement as well as that of your spouse? Your statement should include the
following:
    a.- Describe your attempt at marital counseling before and after the divorce.
    b.- Describe your spiritual life during the process of your separation and divorce.
    c.- Describe what repentance, forgiveness and healing you have experienced.
    d.- What is your intention toward involvement in the life of the church after your marriage?

The clergy person submitting this petition shall answer the following question:

Yes   No   I have personally examined the final decree(s) of divorce or civil annulment
listed above, and I certify that on the basis of my examination the prior
marriage(s) (is) (are) dissolved.

If you are petitioning for Judgment of Termination or Annulment without requesting consent
to marry, you may stop here.

Revised 5/98

TO BE COMPLETED BY CLERGY IN ALL APPLICATIONS FOR CONSENT TO
REMARRY. CIRCLE YES OR NO TO EVERY QUESTION. WHERE NO IS CIRCLED
PLEASE ATTACH FULL EXPLANATION

Yes   No   1.   I have met personally with both parties and they are engaged in a pro-
                       gram of premarital counseling satisfactory to me, or they have met in
                       person with a priest of this church satisfactory to me and I have con-
                       sulted that priest and am assured that they are engaged in a program of
                       premarital counseling.

Yes   No   2.   Each person has signed the Declaration of Intent.

Yes   No   3.   At least one person is baptized.

Yes   No   4.   I have inquired of the parties whether they have consulted any other
                       priest of this church regarding the proposed marriage and have per-
                       sonally contacted that priest. If a priest has declined to officiate, a state-
                       ment concerning the circumstances of that priest's decision is attached.

Yes   No   5.   I have inquired of the priest of the former parish (if applicable) to ascer-
                       tain pertinent pastoral information. (A letter is attached.)

Yes   No   6.   I have thoroughly discussed with both parties their personal readiness
                       for marriage. (Or such discussion has occurred in a counseling program
                       satisfactory to me.)

Yes   No   7.   I believe each person has realistically faced and evaluated the cause(s)
                       of the death of the previous marriage.

Yes   No   8.   I am satisfied that each party has an adequate continuing concern for
                       the previous spouse(s) and children and is acting responsibly to fulfill
                       moral and legal obligations.

Yes   No   9.   I believe the marriage of this couple is likely to be a demonstrable sign
                       of the spiritual union between Christ and His Church.

Yes   No   10.   I am satisfied that the couple (or at least of one person with the support
                       of the other) intends to live out their marriage with the support of the
                       Christian community as participants in some congregation of the
                       Church.

Yes   No   11.   At least one calendar year has elapsed since the date(s) of the final
                       decree(s).

Yes   No   12.   I have discussed with the couple, to the degree that I believe appropri-
                       ate, the spiritual aspects of:
                       FAMILY RELATIONSHIPS: Equal partnership in marriage, in-law
                       relationships, blended families, parenting concepts.
                       COMMUNICATION: Sharing feelings, how do you deal with anger,
                       is there mutual affirmation?
                       SPIRITUAL: Family rule of life, daily prayer, scripture reading, rela-
                       tionship to God.
                       FINANCIAL: Legal and insurance matters, will, planning budgets,
                       who pays bills, stewardship.
                       SEXUAL: Discuss the sacramentality of marriage, fidelity, honesty,
                       openness to communication and discussion of sexuality.

Yes   No   13.   I am willing to solemnize the marriage if consent is granted.

Yes   No   14.   I am requesting judgment at least 30 days prior to the date of the marriage. Proposed date of marriage _____ .

THE FOLLOWING QUESTION IS FOR SITUATIONS WHERE EITHER OR BOTH PERSONS HAS/HAVE BEEN DIVORCED OR HAD THEIR MARRIAGES ANNULLED MORE THAN ONCE.

Yes   No   15.   I have received from a professional counselor a statement concerning this couple and that statement is attached along with an explanatory letter from me.

WHERE QUESTIONS 1-14 ARE ANSWERED YES AND QUESTION 15 IS NOT APPLICABLE, NO ADDITIONAL MATERIAL IS REQUIRED TO ACCOMPANY THE PETITION.

I request consent of the Bishop for me to solemnize this marriage.

_____

Clergy submitting Petition   Parish   Date

8

Divorce among
Protestant Clergy

ADAIR T. LUMMIS

PROTESTANT CLERGY ARE NOW DIVORCING at about the same rate as lay persons in American society, and many are remarrying, especially divorced clergy men.[1] The Catholic divorce rate (in terms of legal dissolution of marriage) is not much lower than that of Protestants, Jews, and "nonaffiliates."[2] During the last forty years the divorce rate has risen worldwide, even in countries with a heavy Catholic population.[3] With the increase in the divorce rate, there has also been growing acceptance of both divorce and remarriage.

What kind of model of personal and religious morality can clergy and lay church leaders who divorce still provide parishioners, friends, and family members? Just how serious is the incidence of clergy divorce and remarriage? What is the response of top church executives to the issue of clergy divorce? Is there anything the Catholic Church can learn from clergy divorce and denominational responses? These are some of the questions that will be explored in this chapter.

In the Catholic Church, there are no married priests (or very few), but the number of lay women and men employed by the church as parish leaders, school teachers, college professors, hospital nurses and administrators, and so on, by far exceeds the total number of priests, diocesan and religious. Hence the chances are very high that now or in the near future there will be prominent lay leaders in parishes, schools, or hospitals who will divorce. What effect will divorce have on their career?

ARE DIVORCE AND REMARRIAGE NOW
COMMON AMONG CLERGY?

Denominations typically do not keep records of clergy who are presently divorced, and none to our knowledge keeps records of clergy who have married after divorce. However, divorce and remarriage statistics were collected in 1993–94 as part of a large survey study of approximately 4,600 clergy in fifteen denominations, ranging from the very liberal Unitarian Universalists and moderately liberal mainline Protestant denominations to the more conservative Southern Baptists and very conservative Holiness or Spirit-centered denominations. Most of the numerical data presented in this chapter are drawn from this 1993–94 fifteen-denominational survey.[4]

Before presenting some findings about the divorce rate, one important caveat needs to be stated: divorce is not the norm among Protestant clergy. In fact, in the modal group of clergy, 75 percent of the clergy men and 50 percent of the clergy women are in their first (and probably only) marriage, with at least half the remainder never married, or remarried after the first spouse died. Divorce among clergy has become an issue for Protestant denominations because until about thirty years ago, it was fairly rare for a divorced person to be a pastor in any congregation. Married Protestant clergymen, the preferred pastor type, were expected to provide models of the ideal Christian marriage.

In the past, divorce virtually ended the careers of clergy in almost all denominations. The increasing divorce rate in secular society and concomitant greater acceptance of divorce as an unfortunate, not immoral, ending of a marriage, has resulted in more divorced and remarried persons contributing their time, money, and energies to the life of the church in many denominations. While congregations still seek married clergy on the whole, they are not quite as reluctant at the end of the twentieth century as they were in the middle of this century to hire a pastor who has been divorced. This greater acceptance of clergy divorce by those who hire and pay pastors means that there are now many more clergy who have gone through a divorce serving congregations than even twenty-five years ago. Still, the greater number of once-divorced clergy, even though a small proportion of all clergy, is sufficiently novel to raise the specter, in the eyes of some denominational church executives, of their clergy becoming models not of marital harmony but of marital dissolution.

Despite these fears, there is no evidence that clergy are divorcing at a greater rate than lay persons. In the 1993–94 fifteen-denominational study referred to earlier, about 18 percent of all the clergy men and 24 percent of

the clergy women considered actively engaged in ministry by their denominations had been divorced at least once, which closely parallels the national
divorce rate of 22 percent of the men and 23 percent of the women in the
United States.[5] Divorced clergy men are more likely to remarry than clergy
women, like divorced men generally,[6] with the result that more clergy
women surveyed in 1993–94 were currently divorced than clergy men, 13
percent versus 3 percent. Since in religious institutions, especially given
strictures in some denominations against remarriage after divorce, the
ever-divorced rate is a better measure of the prevalence and meaning of
divorce than the currently-divorced rate. The divorce rate in the remainder
of this paper refers to the proportion of all active clergy who have ever been
divorced.

Clergy women are more likely to have gone through a divorce than men.
Three out of ten clergy women's marriages ended in divorce, compared with
two out of ten of the men's marriages. Although more married clergy
women than men have been divorced, women tend to seek ordination after
a divorce, while the reverse is true for men. Among ever-divorced clergy, 68
percent of the men as opposed to 35 percent of the women went through
their only or most recent divorce after ordination. In other words, clergy
men are more likely than clergy women to go through the kind of divorce
that most upsets their denomination, that is, divorce while they are serving
as parish ministers.

CAUSES OF CLERGY DIVORCE

Do married pastors face greater pressures on their marriages because of
church work in contemporary times than previously? One of the greatest
changes among married clergy in the mainline Protestant denominations is
the increase in the proportion of pastors' wives who work outside the home
and the church. The traditional clergy wife who devoted most of her time
serving as an unpaid staff member at her husband's church is becoming
rarer each year. In a recent national study of Episcopal clergy, fully 58 percent of the wives of parish ministers are secularly employed, at least part
time.[7] Across denominations, clergy wives who work outside the home indicate that making family income meet family expenses is the primary reason
for their seeking employment, but a strong second reason given by clergy
wives is that employment gives them a career of their own.[8] Wives with jobs
may have some greater difficulties balancing family, work, and church life
than clergy wives who are not in the labor force. However, for working
clergy wives, the added income and the escape from some of the demands

put on them by parishioners are a source of personal satisfaction and perhaps marital harmony. At any rate, there is no evidence that clergy marriages where the wife is employed are any more or less happy than those where the wife is not earning a salary.

Ministry is a very time-consuming and demanding occupation. Pastors are on call twenty-four hours a day—but "after hours" for emergencies only (lay persons may forget this when calling about less than crucial matters, or they may forget that clergy too need time away from the concerns of the congregation). Single clergy, because they do not have a family, may be subjected to greater demands than married clergy in some congregations. However, single clergy do not have spouses who may feel neglected because of church pressures. Half of the ever-divorced clergy men said that at least to some extent their divorce was caused by the time taken by or the nature of their ministerial work (a few were not sure, and the remaining 47 percent said their divorce was totally unrelated to their ministerial work). A similar distribution might obtain if we had data on reasons given for divorce by men in other time-demanding occupations, such as surgeons, corporation executives, and top politicians.

Scandal around the divorce of highly placed persons in the secular world, especially if they are guilty of flagrantly objectionable actions or litigable offenses, may derail their careers for many months or forever. However, in the absence of egregious behavior by professional and civic leaders, the fact that they are undergoing divorce while in such prestigious positions is more likely to incur indifference or sympathy than social opprobrium from their publics. Similarly, in the more secularized, liberal Protestant denominations, there seems to be a growing acceptance of divorce by ordained church executives and lay leaders; the latter are less likely to see divorced clergy as guilty of moral turpitude rendering them unfit to be spiritual leaders.

This orientation is exemplified in the following remarks in an interview of a regional church executive who sees the divorce rate as unfortunate, but also sees the acceptance rather than condemnation of divorce, even among clergy, as a more humane response. He compares his stance to that of some Roman Catholic colleagues in the area:

> I am with the Roman Catholics in that I say scripture is the final authority. . . .
> But the church has made many stupid pronouncements. . . . the whole issue surrounding marriage and divorce is an example. The church because it was not willing to be more gracious and accepting isolated an awful lot of folk who for good reasons came to a place of divorce in their lives. And though I would not wave a flag for divorce, I recognize that divorce is going to take place. We are not going to break communion with a wife or a husband [when they divorce].
>
> We have a majority of clergy in this church who are in their second marriage, a few in their third. . . . There is a high incidence in this jurisdiction of

clergy who are remarried after divorce, and have been remarried since they were ordained. . . . Yet, in talking to those clergy who are in their second marriage, they say they learned all the mistakes about themselves in the first one and do seem serious about correcting those mistakes in the second marriage. In the largest congregation here, the senior minister went through a divorce last year, and that congregation really came behind him and behind her. They never knew the causes of that divorce, but I think their feeling was: "You are going the way many of us had to go and it is painful." So they did not add to that. But if you have a situation where there is scandal—if a minister is divorcing his wife and it is obvious that he has been carrying on with another woman in the congregation, then not only does he have to go, but you have a lot of work to do in healing that congregation. However, I have found in this part of the world that congregations are much more forgiving now of clergy divorce.

DIFFERENCES AMONG DENOMINATIONS
IN ACCEPTANCE OF DIVORCE

The church executive quoted above is part of a denomination that, less than thirty years ago, insisted not only that clergy who divorced (for whatever reason) resign their church positions but also leave the regional jurisdiction. Currently, there are great differences among denominations in the degree to which these bodies permit divorced persons to be ordained or divorcing clergy to stay in a ministerial career. Generally the theologically conservative Protestant denominations are less accepting of divorce among clergy than the liberal Protestant denominations. In the fifteen-denomination survey, less than 10 percent of the clergy of either gender had divorced in the theologically conservative denominations of the Assemblies of God, Church of God, Free Methodists, Nazarenes, and Wesleyans. At the opposite extreme, approximately 45 percent of the clergy in the very theologically liberal Unitarian Universalists have been divorced. No other denomination comes close to this rate. The second highest clergy ever-divorced rate is found among Episcopalians, with approximately 27 percent of the priests divorced. Several other liberal Protestant denominations (the Disciples of Christ, the Presbyterians, the United Methodists, and the United Church of Christ) cluster around a divorce rate of approximately 20–23 percent. The more conservative Brethren, Lutherans, and Baptists have a clergy divorce rate close to 12–15 percent.

These divorce rates are based on samples drawn from lists of clergy considered active by their denominations; part of the low divorce rates found in the more conservative denominations may be due to the fact that divorced clergy have been forced out of active ministry. It is possible that denominational differences in clergy divorce rates are less indicative of happy or unhappy marriages, or even possibly of clergy's own values about the sanctity of marriage vows, than the career consequences of divorce in these different denominations. Clergy, both men and women, are twice as likely to report that their divorce has hurt their career if they were divorced after they were ordained than before. A clergy divorce which takes place while serving a congregation involves not just the divorcing couple in the pain of marital breakup; many members of the congregation share in the grief or turmoil, as do other clergy colleagues in the jurisdiction. This is true for both clergy women and clergy men. However, since among ever-divorced clergy, men are nearly twice as likely as women to have been divorced after ordination, the career effects of divorce are reported for clergy men only.

THE EFFECT OF DIVORCE ON A CHURCH CAREER

From clergymen's own reports, it is apparent that divorced clergy in the liberal denominations are considerably less likely than those in the conservative denominations to report that their divorce definitely hurt their ability to get church positions. While only 11 percent of the Unitarian Universalist and Presbyterian clergymen said their divorce had deleterious career consequences, fully 46 percent of the American Baptist and 100 percent of the few divorced Southern Baptist clergy men (still active in ministry) said their divorce had hurt their getting church jobs. However, among ever-divorced Episcopal clergymen, the denomination with the second highest clergy divorce rate, 37 percent of the priests also said that their divorce had hurt them in their careers.

This last finding may be accounted for in part by the differences among U.S. dioceses in how strongly the bishop feels about clergy divorce and the culture affecting the congregations' views about divorce. Formal authority in the Episcopal Church rests in the dioceses rather than in the national church. Bishops have the legal power to restrict clergy from working as priests in the diocese, and they have much influence in what particular church position a clergyman gets. The consequences for clergy who divorce while serving as parish ministers, for example, are likely to differ according to the bishop's own views and the general climate of opinion concerning divorce among congregations and clergy in the diocese. Bishops are not only pastors to pastors, they are clergy judges and chief deployment officers. Whatever a bishop's own feelings about clergy divorce, he may be reluctant to recommend a priest for a plum parish if the priest has gone through a divorce, or perhaps worse, has a shaky marriage that might soon end in divorce. A congregation afflicted by the divorce of its rector may not be as willing in the future to financially support the ministries of the diocese. Among the Episcopal clergymen surveyed between 1987 and 1995 in over twenty-five dioceses, differences among dioceses were apparent in the proportion of clergy in each diocese who agreed with the statement: "Generally clergy in this diocese are reluctant to tell the bishop if they are having marital or family problems," though a minority in every diocese strongly disagreed.[9] The fear on the part of clergy is that confessing marital problems or divorce to their judicatory executive will have negative career consequences for clergymen in many denominations. If so, two results can be expected to ensue: the actual clergy divorce rate is likely to be underreported; and those whose marriage might be saved through counseling are unlikely to get help.

The more authority executives such as bishops have to control clergymen in their jurisdictions, the more likely divorce is to curtail clergy career mobility. Church executives in the United Methodist, Lutheran, Episcopal, and the Presbyterian denominations have far more formal control over which clergy go to which congregations than their counterparts in the Southern Baptist and Unitarian Universalist denominations. Hence, if judicatory executives personally object to divorce, divorced clergymen in the former denominations potentially have more difficulty in getting parish positions than in the latter denominations. However, there are great differences between Southern Baptist and Unitarian congregations in the likelihood of their hiring a divorced pastor. In the Southern Baptist denominations pastoral search committees are unlikely to knowingly call an ever-divorced man as senior pastor, while in the Unitarian Universalist congregations the ordained man's divorce is not likely to have any effect on the hiring decisions of the search committees. Regional norms also impact the hiring of ever-divorced clergy. Episcopal, Lutheran, Presbyterian, and United Methodist congregations in the deep South and in certain parts of the Midwest are typically less likely to accept a divorced pastor than those on East Coast or West Coast. States are not isolated islands, however; they are themselves affected by divorce norms in other parts of the country.

PRESS REPORTS

Newspaper reporters have been quick to pick up on the changing norms about clergy divorce.[10] Their stories are a barometer of changing attitudes toward clergy divorce, as well a potential means of gaining greater social acceptance of clergy divorce. Reporters also report differences among Episcopal bishops in their response to divorce. One reporter quotes an Episcopal bishop as having said:

> Episcopal clergy must obtain the bishop's permission to divorce. Requirements include a written review of the relationship, evidence of counseling, and assurance that the interests of the spouse and children are protected. I also take into account the impact of the divorce on the pastor's congregation and the morale of other clergy. Remarriage in most cases is permitted, but we do not give permission lightly.[11]

Talking with a bishop of a different diocese, another reporter found that the bishop authorizes payment for clergy marital counseling but, if divorce occurs, the priest must offer his resignation from his/her position. It is then up to the bishop, in consultation with the congregation, to accept or reject the offer.[12] Remarriage of the priest following divorce, in this and most other Episcopal dioceses, is at the discretion of the individual priest. Note that these incidences are only applicable to priests who divorce while in parish ministry; there is now little stigma in most Episcopal dioceses and parishes in hiring a priest who was once divorced. Furthermore, subsequent remarriage of divorced clergy is typically seen positively rather than negatively by parish pastoral search committees, since congregations typically prefer married clergy.

National leaders of the Unitarian Universalists, the denomination with the highest divorce rate (nearly double that of the Episcopal clergy), told reporters that they are a caring and open denomination that does not stigmatize either clergy or laity for undergoing the pain of marital breakup.[13] Clergy divorce for the Unitarian Universalists has therefore few negative consequences. On the other hand, the promulgations against clergy divorce and especially remarriage in the Assemblies of God do diminish their credibility in light of the very publicized sexual misadventures of some of their most prominent clergymen.[14] Thus, having preached for several decades that "any man who gets a divorce is unfit to be a pastor," Rev. Charles Stanley, a former president of the Southern Baptist Convention and co-founder of the Moral Majority, sent "spiritual shock waves through the evangelical community" (as one reporter put it) when he refused to leave his pulpit when his wife sued for divorce.[15] Publicity about the prevalence of clergy divorce through public media, typically accompanied by statements from church leaders calling for forgiveness and inclusion rather than shunning of divorced clergy and laity, is likely to contribute to the softening of attitudes toward divorce.

CATHOLIC ATTITUDES TOWARD DIVORCE

Survey data on divorce are presented in the 1996 book *American Catholic Laity in a Changing Church* by W. V. D'Antonio, J. D. Davidson, D. R. Hoge, and R. A.Wallace. They state:

> With divorce and remarriage becoming ever more common in the late 1960's and 1970's, Catholics moved away from the orthodox church teaching. . . . In the 1992 survey, 72 percent of the Catholics said divorced and remarried Catholics should be allowed to receive communion. . . . In the 1993 survey, 87 percent of young Catholics said that remarriage after divorce could be a morally acceptable act. Even among the most committed Catholics in 1993 (those who say they go to Mass every week, that the church is one of the most important forces in their lives, and that they would never leave the church) 44 percent said that one could be a good Catholic without obeying the church's teaching on divorce and remarriage.[16]

These authors, citing other studies, indicate that some Catholic priests over-looked rules about refusing communion to divorced and remarried parish-ioners; otherwise they would have difficulty attracting and keeping committed Catholics in their parishes.

DENOMINATIONAL ATTITUDES TOWARD DIVORCE

Divorce is objectionable to denominations in part because it is seen as undermining the traditional nuclear family. If divorce is viewed as the pri-mary cause rather than the result of the dissolution of the nuclear family, then clergy counseling will focus on keeping marriages intact, even at the cost of the physical or psychological well-being of one or both spouses and their children. Divorce ends marriage, to be sure, but does it destroy the nuclear family?

The dramatic doubling of the U.S. divorce rate between the mid-1960s and the mid-1970s, Cynthia F. Epstein explains,[17] is due to women's grow-ing financial independence and moral support from the women's groups to end abusive marriages. In this perspective, is it better for the churches to take a firm stand against divorce, thereby perhaps diminishing its preva-lence slightly, whatever cost this entails? Or should churches assist in insti-tutionalizing divorce, making it less destructive to families when it does occur, even though this may increase the likelihood of divorce?

According to William J. Goode, the "stable high-divorce rate systems" among both literate and nonliterate societies outside the Western world are actually protective of the family.[18] Even though the divorce rate in Indonesia, Japan, Taiwan, and some of the Arab countries is high, the family is relative stable, because, Goode explains, "by following tradition and custom, they did take care of the problems created by divorce, with rules of custody, child-care, support and remarriage for the mother, and so on."[19] Goode goes on to explain that while marriage is institutionalized in the contemporary Western world, being "surrounded by laws, rituals, local or ethnic customs, expectations and approval of friends, family and co-workers," this is not true of divorce. Rather than stigmatize divorce, Goode suggests, divorce too should be institutionalized with rituals, rules, and social pressures undergirding its use for the dissolution of marriage. This would result in greater family stability in our high-divorce system than presently obtains.[20] The more strongly a religious body inveighs against divorce, the more stigmatized by divorce adherents of the particular faith are likely to feel. Individuals can feel socially stigmatized by divorce either because they feel guilty for ending the marriages they had promised to continue until death, or, as Helen Rose Ebaugh put it, because they assume others think that "divorce connotes failure, irresponsibility and a threat to the basic social system."[21]

DIVORCE AS A THREAT
TO THE INSTITUTIONAL CHURCH

Divorce is a threat to the religious institutions because it terminates a marriage contract celebrated under the auspices of the church. The consequences of divorce for religious institutions depend in large part on whether marriage is viewed as a indissoluble contract "till death do you part" or as an open-ended relationship based on mutual commitment "as love shall last." In the former case, marriage involves a man, a woman, and the church, whereas in the latter case, the church (if it is involved at all) only blesses the legal contract which two people have entered into. The more a church sees itself involved in the marriage contract between two members, the more difficulty these members are likely to have in getting their divorce accepted by the church. Divorce and remarriage are unacceptable to the Catholic Church, but are viewed with approval by Unitarian Universalist denominations and are accepted by most other Protestant denominations. Given that the Catholic Church takes a strong stand against divorce, it would seem that divorce among Catholics would have more negative consequences for the Catholic Church as an institution than it would have for many of the liberal Protestant denominations.

Negative consequences for the church as an institution, however, do not seem to greatly deter individual church members from seeking to end their marriages. The Catholic Church deals with unhappy marriages in part through annulment, perhaps thereby diminishing the negative consequences to the institution. Even so, Catholics in the United States are undertaking divorce without church consent at about the same rate as those of other religions. In terms of institutional viability alone, it might seem better for the Catholic Church to be more tolerant of divorce among Catholics. Furthermore, if preserving a healthy nuclear family is also a value to the church, it would appear that accepting as full members divorced Catholics who are now remarried would be a positive and prudent step.

The findings of this study suggest that church leaders in all Christian faiths would strengthen the well-being of their members, families, and congregations by showing more pastoral attention to their divorced and remarried members.

Notes

1. Barbara Brown Zikmund, Adair T. Lummis, Patricia M.Y. Chang, *Clergy Women: An Uphill Calling* (Louisville, Ky.: Westminster John Knox Press, 1998), 40–43.

2. Wade Clark Roof and William J. McKinney, *American Mainline Religion: Its Changing Shape and Future* (New Brunswick, N.J.: Rutgers University Press, 1987), 156–57.

3. William J. Goode, *World Changes in Divorce Patterns* (New Haven: Yale University Press, 1993).

4. This study, conducted at Hartford Seminary, was supported by a grant from the Lilly Endowment. Some of the data are reported in Zikmund et. al., *Clergy Women*, 40–43.

5. Ever-divorced rates for all adults are from the 1985 Census Bureau statistics, provided courtesy of the Associated Press.

6. Goode, *World Changes,* 142.

7. R. C. Walmsley and A. T. Lummis. *Healthy Clergy, Wounded Healers: Their Families and Their Ministries* (New York: Church Publishing, 1997), 95–103.

8. C. Lee and J. Balswick, *Life in a Glass House: The Minister's Family in Its Unique Social Context* (Grand Rapids: Zondervan, 1989), 192–94 et passim; Liz Greenbacker and Sherry Taylor, *Private Lives of Ministers' Wives* (Far Hills, N.J.: New Horizons Press, 1991), 120–35. Walmsley and Lummis, *Healthy Clergy,* 95–103.

9. This was a question in a survey answered by clergy and spouses in twenty-five dioceses as part of an action research project in which I was principal researcher, carried out under the auspices of the Episcopal Family Network.

10. The Hartford Seminary study is the most current and probably the only record of clergy divorce across denominations. David Briggs of the Associated Press

and Gerry Reiner of the *Hartford Courant* were the first reporters to write stories on clergy divorce using the Hartford Seminary results. Their stories were picked up by other news media, and several reporters called me for more information. At least two enterprising reporters used our data as a basis for interviewing denominational executives in their areas about what they felt about clergy divorce (Julia McCord, "Stigma against divorced clergy eases," *Omaha World Herald,* January 21, 1995; and J. Michael Parker, "When Pastors Divorce," *San Antonio Express News,* January 20, 1996).

11. McCord, "Stigma."

12. Parker, "When Pastors Divorce."

13. Many reporters who used the Associated Press release about the clergy divorce rates found in the Hartford Seminary study attempted to call executives at the Unitarian Universalist national headquarters in Boston for a response. This is the response of one Unitarian Universalist executive given to both McCord ("Stigma") and to Parker ("When Pastors Divorce").

14. Margaret W. Poloma, *The Assemblies of God at the Crossroads: Charisma and Institutional Dilemmas* (Knoxville: University of Tennessee Press, 1988).

15. Parker, "When Pastors Divorce."

16. W. V. D'Antonio, J. D. Davidson, D. R. Hoge, and R. A. Wallace, *Laity American and Catholic: Transforming the Church* (Kansas City: Sheed & Ward, 1996), 52–53.

17. Cynthia F. Epstein, *Deceptive Distinctions* (New York: Russell Sage Foundation, 1988), 203–5.

18. Goode, *World Changes,* 15–17, 328–30 et passim.

19. Ibid., 16.

20. Ibid., 330.

21. Helen Rose Ebaugh, *Becoming an Ex: The Process of Role Exit* (Chicago: University of Chicago Press, 1988), 159.

9

Church Teaching
on Sexuality and Marriage

E D W A R D   S C H I L L E B E E C K X

ELEMENTS OF THE CURRENT PROBLEM

NOWHERE IS THE DISCREPANCY between the official teaching of the Catholic Church and the actual convictions of many believers so great as in the domain of sexuality and marriage. Yet nowhere do faith and life touch each other so closely as in this domain. For Christians, marriage is part of God's creation, a secular reality that is not sacred but profane. At the same time, however, marriage for Christians is something that is not just profane; it is also somehow sacred, a religious reality.

Because of this connection in marriage between the profane and the sacred, between the secular and the religious, changes in one of these dimensions inevitably has an effect on the other. More precisely, changes in society, culture, and human self-understanding with regard to marriage and relationships between the sexes pose a severe challenge to the church's traditional views on marriage and sexuality, since the latter happen to have arisen in an earlier culture. It would be good, therefore, to look at sexuality and marriage as human phenomena before going on to examine their specifically Christian meaning. As it turns out, the secular realities of sexuality and marriage become part of the process of salvation, as Christian theology

Editor's note: Although this article is not directly related to divorce, its conclusions about church teaching on sexuality and marriage can easily be applied to church teaching on divorce.

understands it, in rather specific ways. Nonetheless, it is not easy to determine what is specifically Christian in marriage.

The Judeo-Christian faith tradition, that is, the ongoing Jewish and Christian interpretation of human experience, is intentionally universal and applicable to all people. In that sense it is transcultural, or not bound to any specific culture. At the same time, however, this tradition is a living reality only insofar as it is embedded in concrete cultural contexts, and thus it has all the limitations of a specific actual history. In the same way, there is a continuous dialectic between the universality of the Christian gospel, which challenges and transcends every culture, and the concrete cultural forms that historically embody that gospel. It seems on Christological grounds that the gospel can be the universal revelation of God's salvation only in particular cultural expressions. Indeed, the special genius of the Judeo-Christian tradition is its insistence that what is universal and absolute can be expressed only in what is historically particular and radically contingent in persons, cultures, and societies.

This characteristic of the Christian gospel has far-reaching consequences with reference to sexuality and marriage. For if the gospel is always culturally situated, then we must ask about the cultural form of the Judeo-Christian tradition. Since the gospel, or the good news proclaimed by Jesus, has come down to us in a Western cultural form, we should not confuse gospel norms and values with those of the Western culture in which they are embodied. Determining what is specifically Christian with respect to sexuality and marriage thus appears to be a problem that arises from the encounter of two cultures. On the one hand, there is the Christian gospel in its traditional Western form, and on the other hand, there is the contemporary cultural situation in the West, not to mention the situations in the non-Western cultures of Asia, Africa, and elsewhere.

Essentially, the problem arises from the unavoidable interaction between a gospel that is always lived out in culturally embedded churches and a cultural situation that is always changing. Christian faith appropriately displays the gospel's critical and liberating power in human realities such as marriage when churches and their leaders have a clear understanding of the relationship between marriage as a secular reality and marriage as a means of salvation.

In contrast to animal sexuality, human sexuality has a certain amount of indeterminacy and plasticity that is shaped by what we call culture. This is clear from contemporary human sciences such as sociology and anthropology, and it is also clear from history. In the Western intellectual tradition, for example, philosophers through the ages have developed theories about many aspects of society such as government and economy, marriage and sexuality. Even a great Christian thinker such as Thomas Aquinas in the

Middle Ages suggested that human nature was not as unchangeable as most people assumed,[1] and he observed that marriage could be found in culturally diverse forms.[2]

As a secular reality (or in faith language, a reality of creation), human sexuality and marriage, then, exist only in concrete historical and cultural realizations. When the Christian message confronts various aspects of human existence, therefore, the universal gospel is able to be a critical and liberating force both within every culture and across the historical changes that take place within any particular culture. While the church can criticize cultures from the perspective of its universal message, however, the same cultures can also criticize the cultural forms in which Christ's good news is being brought to them. Through such mutual criticism, cultures can be said to encounter each other. As a result of such cultural interaction, Catholic teachings on marriage and even Catholic marriage laws have evolved over the course of time.[3] Admittedly, for example, the church only partially and with difficulty succeeded in preserving gospel ideals with regard to marriage at times when the surrounding culture was strongly dualistic. At the same time, however, the church in those centuries constantly defended marriage against those who were hostile to sexuality and who disparaged anything having to do with the body.

Today, Christianity with its traditional Western views concerning sexuality and marriage is being confronted by profound changes in society and people's understanding of themselves. During the modern period, the West evolved from a rural agricultural society into an urban industrial and technological civilization in which the private sphere of life was kept rather separate from the public sphere.[4] In earlier centuries, marriage existed primarily in the public sphere, an arrangement to produce workers for the farm and descendants for the patriarchs of a large extended family. Today it is anything but that, being mainly a personal commitment of two individuals in the framework of a small nuclear family, and the domain of marriage and family is separated from that of work or profession, so that the wife often works outside the home. Thus the focus of marriage today is on the interpersonal love relationship, particularly with its possibilities for spiritual and physical fruitfulness.

This new situation leads to developments in two very different directions. On the one hand, the privatization of marriage makes it possible for the marital relationship to be more personal; on the other hand, it also allows for greater depersonalization in some ways.

First, privatization leads to greater personalization because, as Max Horkheimer and Jürgen Habermas (among others) have suggested, marriage and family life can be experienced as "a reservoir of power to resist the modern loss of meaning in the world."[5] Marital and familial relationships provide a place of security and a corrective to the increasing rationalization, bureaucratization, and anonymity of the public sphere in which people live.[6]

On the other hand, at the same time that marriage is reduced to the private sphere, sexual relationships, also pushed into the private sphere, become freed from their former economic and even biological consequences and so find themselves in danger of becoming disengaged from the public sphere altogether. Contemporary marriage is more vulnerable than its cultural predecessors because it does not have the social support of publicly held norms to protect it against the pressures and influences exerted by the surrounding society. In addition, tensions generated by work, which is in the public sphere, can come to explosive expression at home, or at least they can unconsciously embitter interpersonal relationships within the family. Today, therefore, middle-class values such as prestige, profit, and consumption penetrate more easily into marriage and family life, so that there are scarcely any significant differences between Christian homes and those of other people. So we can see that privatization does not automatically lead to a greater personal connection and solidarity within marriage and the family, but can actually lead to more impersonal and banal relationships as well.

Finally, the second half of the twentieth century has witnessed what is often called a sexual revolution, which deeply if not always obviously has affected the moral norms of everyone in the Western world, including Christians. One of the results of this revolution is the tendency to separate sexual activity not only from the institutional form of marriage and other forms of social control, but also from "nature" and its given limitations.

In the West this new phase in the cultural formation of sexuality and interpersonal relationships gives rise to a broad range of questions about official Catholic teaching and, for that matter, about the traditional teaching of other Christian churches on sexuality and marriage. The wide variety of these questions is an indication that the important issue is not any of the topics, taken in isolation, that are usually the subject of discussion, such as birth control, premarital sex, co-habitation, and so on. These particular matters are all manifestations of a more fundamental cultural shift in the West's understanding of human sexuality and, ultimately, of human existence.

From the perspective of revelation, the church has the responsibility to interact with cultures in a way that is both sympathetic and critical. It needs first of all to listen carefully for the possibilities of greater human development emerging in a new culture, but second, to discern there things that could signify a cultural regression or even a debasing of authentic humanity.

As a result, the church can only form particular norms on the basis of an encompassing vision of Christian marriage put in confrontation with a clear insight into what is really going on now. If the church does not do this but instead chooses to attack current practices from the cultural perspective of the Middle Ages, let us say, its pronouncements will be either felt as repressive or dismissed as irrelevant. But, in accepting this challenge, the church's task is not simply to adapt traditional teachings to modern times. Rather, the task is to help adapt, so to speak, contemporary individuals and society to the perduring gospel. As Christians leave behind premodern, Western forms of marriage based on an agrarian culture, what is at stake here is maintaining Christian identity through cultural transition.

OFFICIAL TEACHING IN THE CHURCH

In General

Theologically speaking, the foundation of Christian life and church teaching is the Lordship of Jesus Christ, which is active in the community through the Holy Spirit.

Hence, official authority in the church is not itself the norm but rather the "entrusted pledge" of the gospel as the apostles have interpreted it, "the teaching of God our Savior" (Titus 2:10). This evangelical content is also found in the life of Christian communities themselves; it is, as Paul said, a message written not only in books but also in the hearts of believers, and expressed in their lives (2 Cor. 3:2–3). In this sense, the Catholic Church's official teachings are dependent on the faith life of Christian communities, authentically lived under the guidance of the biblical witnesses to the person and teaching of Jesus, confessed as the Christ.

When the church speaks officially, proclaiming something for all its members to accept, even its most absolute statements are relative in various ways. That is, if these pronouncements are to be authentic and normative, they must relate to important criteria of their truth and relevance. First, church teachings must be related to the life and ministry of Jesus as recorded in the scriptures, especially his announcement of the reign of God. (This basic message must inform any church teaching if that teaching does not want to exceed its own competence.) Second, they must be related to the larger context of the Judeo-Christian scriptures and the salvation history they narrate. Third, they must have a connection to the church's past history, particularly to the concrete situations in which official church teachings proclaimed the church's faith. (Every church teaching has its own historical location and cannot be understood apart from it.) Fourth, they must be related to the contemporary situation in which people find themselves.

When we look into the New Testament itself, we find not only proclamations of faith (for example, Jesus is Lord) but also exhortations to lead a life of faith, as well as instructions about how to do this in various situations. Such biblical admonitions suggest to Christians how they should live the gospel, how they ought to translate the good news into action. It is here especially that we discover the dialogue, mentioned earlier, between the gospel and culture, in this case the culture of first-century Mediterranean civilization, resulting in a critical synthesis of the universal gospel and a particular culture that we can call a theology (e.g., Pauline theology).

Interestingly, there are places in the New Testament where the scriptural authors indicate that not every statement in biblical theology is equally authoritative. In other words, there is a gradation of authority in biblical teachings that is acknowledged in the Bible itself. So, for example, Paul says at times, "Not the Lord, but I say to you . . ." (1 Cor. 7:12; cf. 1 Cor. 7:10). In other places he presents arguments to justify his directives for specific Christian conduct, but he appreciates that his readers might not be convinced by these arguments. In still others, he freely admits that he is basing his argument on custom (see 1 Cor. 11:16). Clearly in places like these, the church's leadership is not claiming absolute authority for its teaching, and it is therefore not absolutely binding on the community.

Therefore personal viewpoints (as in Paul's case) obviously play a role at times in official teaching—which can be a temptation for all officeholders who (rightly) carry out a synthesis in their own lives between the gospel and their entire personal experience and thinking. The critical question is only how far they can prescribe their personal synthesis as the model for others. I myself am always hesitant about doing this, unless I expressly add: "At least that's the way I see it as a Christian." In a papal encyclical, for example, the pope may expresses his personal theology (or that of his advisors), and what presents itself as the official teaching of the church may therefore not be as free of personal opinion as it appears to be. Official teaching is necessarily more restricted than personal theology.

Another consideration is that ethical instructions require some type of cultural mediation between the universal gospel and the present concrete situation. Therefore this instruction is dependent on the cultural form of, for example, marriage in a particular period, while in another cultural period ethical instruction will have to have another tone derived from the same gospel, if it still wants to strike home in a real, living situation. In matters like these the church addresses a definite situation here and now and does not speak for all ages. In this kind of teaching, the continuing and fundamental inspiration of the gospel can indeed come to expression; sometimes the church can give guidelines that specify what is Christian ethical behavior in this concrete situation (which may no longer be ours). But even the church's rules and regulations do not escape from history.

It is not only the Catholic Church that has to wrestle with issues such as these. In 1955, the Dutch Reformed Church issued a pastoral letter in which it distinguished between three different levels of church teaching. In its official teaching, the letter says, the church can "confess" (i.e., profess in faith), it can also declare "a conviction of the church," and finally it can present "an opinion of the church." These distinctions are equivalent to what the Catholic Church calls *notae theologicae* or theological qualifications. Even the Second Vatican Council's Dogmatic Constitution on the Church, *Lumen Gentium*, has an official note which says that the theological qualification and thus the authoritative value of this document must be understood according to the rules of interpretation that were in use in the church before then. If nothing else, this means that unless the council clearly defines something as a matter of Catholic faith, statements in the document need not be taken to be such. Implicitly, then, the council recognizes diverse levels of teaching in its own documents, and the same would have to be said for official teachings that come from individual church leaders rather than from a gathering of the world's bishops.

Here we are reflecting not on confessional statements—what Catholics call dogmas or doctrines of faith—but on the consequences of such doctrines for the behavior of Christians, and thus on official teachings about the ethical direction of their actions. Although the gospel is primarily a religious message, gospel faith naturally has ethical consequences, as the New Testament itself suggests when it says, "Seek first the reign of God and its righteousness" (Matt. 6:33). Ethics is an area where the church does not pronounce dogmas except when doctrine and practice are closely intertwined (for example, the Catholic doctrine that marriage is a sacrament).

Since the ethical character of an action depends in large measure on the social and cultural situation in which the activity takes place, the official teaching of the church about such an action is likewise dependent on the church's ability to discern right and wrong in very specific cultural and even political situations. This ability to discern right and wrong is not unique to the church, and hence is a somewhat foreign element which nevertheless mediates between the gospel and church teachings about the behavior of believers. For this reason it seems to me that official teachings about most types of human behavior must be either a conviction of the church or an opinion of the church, even though such behavior may have some connection with a doctrine of faith.

Generally, an official teaching that is a conviction of the church can make a serious claim on the conscience of each of its members. An official teaching that is an opinion of the church, on the other hand, calls for serious consideration as a position that should not be ignored when the matter is discussed, but church members need to decide for themselves whether they can identify with the church's opinion.[7] That the church in certain cases can give only an opinion implies that believers actually hold very diverse views on a matter, and in such cases the official teaching is simply symptomatic of the diversity. An official teaching that is a conviction of the church points to stronger evidence and greater certainty on the part of the church's leadership, but even here there can be a sharp polarization among believers.

A complication arises when an official teaching that was a conviction of the church in an earlier period becomes an obviously dated position in changed cultural circumstances. For example, the 1930 encyclical *Casti Connubii*, which taught that the primary end of marriage is the procreation and education of children, was based on a very different view of humanity and was directed to believers with a different experience of marriage than what most Catholics have today. Thus it would be an anachronism and an error to claim that this historical document is still binding in all its particulars on the Catholic conscience. Given Vatican II's acknowledgment of intimacy as vital to contemporary marriage, we can say in retrospect that what seemed to be a religious conviction early in the twentieth century was in fact only a common opinion based on cultural conditions.

This suggests that official teachings that come out of the church's convictions need to be based on adequate information, communication among members of the church, and dialogue between the hierarchy and the laity. If this does not happen, official teachings have a tendency on their own to repeat what has been said in the past, often in a different social and cultural setting. The great religions of the world, not just Christianity, in fact have this same tendency: they all came into existence during a period of agrarian culture, and they all experience some difficulty maintaining themselves in postagrarian cultures.

Sometimes it may not be easy for church leaders to determine whether what they are teaching is a conviction or an opinion. As we know from the study of ethics, people who have to make moral judgments about complicated matters can seldom be certain that they are absolutely right, and yet they do have to make those judgments. This suggests that church leaders must sometimes be willing to offer tentative or hypothetical judgments, and at times they should even have to courage not to say anything at all.

In the Roman Catholic Church, the doctrine of papal infallibility has played a rather limited role in church history, but today it tends to surround official teachings with an aura of quasi-infallibility, and church officials tend not to speak in ways that sound provisional or uncertain. The unwillingness to appear less than completely correct has also led church leaders to be more concerned with remaining in line with the teachings of past popes than with facing the facts that challenge the church from new social and cultural locations. But even in the area of official church teaching about social problems the greatest power of this teaching lies in its critical and liberating language, which, based on an inexpressible and positive affirmation of faith, has always marked the highest points of the church's wisdom.

On Sexuality, Marriage, and Family

A great deal of talk about what is human has been less objective than it has purported to be. Not long ago, one could find communist literature that equated what is truly communist with what is truly human. And even today one can find Christians who believe that what is human is Christian, and what is Christian is human. These are examples of bias and even ideological thinking, although there is also a tendency today to go in the opposite direction and focus exclusively on cultural differences and ignore people's common humanity. But ideological misuse should not lead us to abandon the real question about the relationship between humanity and the deepest convictions of religion; it is rather a warning against premature identifications and syntheses on our part.

Whatever else it may be, Christianity has to do with human beings, and being Christian is one particular way of being human. No religion or culture, however, has a patent on being human. There are as many ways to be human as there are cultures—or even individuals, each of whom is unique. Indeed, the concept of humanity is an abstraction; concretely, only individual and cultural forms of humanity actually exist, although they do this on the basis of genetic information that is common to all human beings and each person's possibility for freedom within the ecological and social-cultural structures which human beings have themselves constructed over time. The dominance of one specific culture is therefore wrong, although this conclusion need not lead to cultural indifference, as if each view of humanity and the world were of equal value. But when it comes to expressing what is really human, each person really does have a say.

Through their contact with different cultures, then, people today are beginning to realize that their experiences of marriage, family, and sexuality are largely determined by social and cultural conventions, even if these conventions are based on factors that all humans have in common. This realization in turn has implications for the Catholic Church's official teachings in these areas.

Now, Christian discourse is in many respects a second-order language; that is, it is language that is used to talk about experienced realities that are first talked about in nonreligious discourse. What Christians first see as a purely human reality, they then also talk about either with regard to its meaning or value from a religious perspective.

Christian discourse is therefore a way of speaking about what is transcendent and absolute (for example, God) in relation to what is particular and transitory (for example, human behavior). Indeed, in the Christian view of things, the transcendent is in the particular and the absolute is in created, transitory realities. In other words, from a Christian perspective, human activity is a locus of God's presence and action in the world, and this is why the reign of God must be brought about through particular actions of individual human beings. Although God's presence and power on earth cannot be reduced to human activity, it is still true that the absolute and total character of our faith commitment can only be expressed in very specific actions, done in a very specific context.

Christian discourse about any human activity with a theological dimension is always talk about human well-being. What is called salvific or saving activity is that which creates or enhances human integrity and healthy relationships, and what is called sinful is that which diminishes integrity and destroys relationships. This does not mean that theological realities are being reduced to human realities, nor that what is properly human is being called Christian for ideological reasons. Rather, it means that theological realities are always found in particular historical instances, when what is understood by faith involves human relationships and behavior.

And if this is the case, then the Christian dimensions of marriage, as well as the theological aspects of sexuality, are able to be found in human forms of marriage and human sexual behavior.

MARRIAGE AS CULTURAL REALITY AND SACRAMENT

For Christians, all human realities, whether individual, social, or cultural, have theological significance. Concrete events and actual processes are never neutral, for they always have either a positive or a negative relationship to the God of salvation and liberation. For this reason, in the Catholic view of reality, worldly things can be sacraments; that is, they can be special mediators of grace and salvation. The Catholic understanding of marriage as a sacrament is a particular case of this more general outlook.

According to Catholic theology, the secular human reality of marriage, when it is a relationship between two Christians, is a sacrament. (Although Protestant churches do not use the word "sacrament" when talking about marriage, they have basically the same understanding of this human reality that the Catholic Church has.) In other Christian sacraments, there is always some natural or worldly element (water, for example, or bread and wine) that is part of the ritual. The same is true with regard to marriage, but in a unique way. In the Catholic understanding, it is not the wedding ritual that is the sacrament, but the marriage itself, or the marital relationship. This means that in the case of marriage, the cultural reality (in its vast plurality of forms) and the salvific or grace-giving reality coincide with one another.

In his teaching about marriage, especially in the Gospel of Mark (10:2–9), Jesus regards marriage as a human reality formed by cultural norms (Jesus sees marriage, in Luther's words, as "a worldly matter"), and at the same time he regards it as a saving reality. According to Mark, Jesus does not describe the marriage bond using legal language, but as a promise of the power of grace and salvation for those who are married "in the Lord."

According to Paul, Christians live out their marriages "in the Lord" (1 Cor. 7:39; see Col. 3:18). Marriage is taken up into the new Christian way of being, the life in the Lord, which has been initiated by baptism. The sacramentality of marriage is therefore not an extrinsic label that gets imposed on marriage from outside, as it were. Looked at in the light of the gospel message and the Christian way of living, the sacramental bond between husband and wife reveals a religious potential that is already present in a secular, human marriage. Calling the marriage relationship a sacrament is a creative redefinition, so to speak, of what is already present, although in an undefined and unrecognized way, in every human marriage. Arguably, this is why marriage in every culture is solemnized with religious symbols. These cultures sense that in the solemn, definitive, and irrevocable commitments of marriage, sexuality, and family life, people somehow make contact with something transcendent, ultimate, and absolute—what Christians call God.

From a Christian perspective, if two people want to dedicate themselves to each other and want to accept each other definitively and unconditionally, this is possible only because both people are already definitively and unconditionally accepted and affirmed by God. (This is what is affirmed and celebrated in baptism.) Thus, for believers, the fidelity of marriage is a participation in God's own fidelity. This is not a matter of legalities, however, but a matter of grace as proclaimed by Christ's gospel. It therefore says nothing in itself about how marital breakdown should be dealt with legally, that is, in civil or church law.

Now, the Catholic interpretation of marriage and its sacramentality presupposes that marriage is a secular reality, one that has been culturally desacralized. Historically, this desacralization took place in ancient Israel, where the Jewish understanding that everything was created by God stripped away the more ancient perception that sexual activities were sacred realities, divinely ordained and performed in religious rituals such as fertility rites and intercourse with temple prostitutes. Because of this desacralization in the Judeo-Christian tradition, sexuality on the one hand was able to be understood and experienced as something good, a gift of creation from God, and on the other hand could not be regarded as something of ultimate value.

Through the sacramentalization of marriage, then, this human reality that is valuable in itself acquires a further value as a means of salvation within an economy of salvation that embraces many other possibilities for the redemption and liberation of human life. When they marry, Christians engage in a process that they do not control but in which they participate, namely, their individual and mutual salvation. The sacramentally married, therefore, live from a hope and expectation whose foundation is not the two partners themselves. The sole foundation for this hope is God's fidelity in Christ to human beings; the faithful Christian lives of married people then share in this. The foundation of Christian fidelity in marriage is therefore not a juridical form (the marriage vow they make during the wedding ceremony) but the Christian way of living that they have entered through baptism and to which they are faithful as Christians.

The Catholic Church's official teaching about marriage as a sacrament must above all be a teaching about Christian faith. The best kind of marriage preparation that the church can provide, therefore, is to help believers learn how to lead a Christian life of committed love in the context of marriage.

THE HUMAN AND CHRISTIAN ETHOS OF MARRIAGE

In the epistles of the New Testament, there are two strands of teaching about behavioral norms related to sexuality and marriage. On the one hand, some passages (e.g., 1 Cor. 7:39) speak about marriage "in the Lord," implying that there is a certain way of living in a marriage relationship that is simply a consequence of living in a Christian lifestyle. On the other hand, other passages show that the New Testament churches (critically) accepted the social morality dominant at the time and that the church's leadership urged these standards for marriage and family life on Christians. So we have on one side the conduct of Jesus as norm and direction for all Christian action, the standard of Christian discipleship, and, on the other, a critical assimilation of the ethics of Greco-Roman and, even more so, Jewish culture. This ethical pluralism in the New Testament is nevertheless held together and brought to a fundamental unity through *agapē*: the twofold commandment of the love of God and of one's neighbor, preferably the poor and isolated, the outcasts of society. This is not without consequences for the Christian ethos of marriage.

Ethics as a study of moral behavior covers inner dispositions as well as concrete actions. Because of this, there are in any system of ethics or morality two different types of norms. First, there are formal norms, which are general and dynamic guidelines that in one way or another tell people how to behave in order to promote individual and social well-being, regardless of changing circumstances. Second, there are substantive norms, which embody formal norms within the culturally conditioned views that people have of themselves and the world, and within people's efforts to manage the diverse and always ambiguous situations of their lives.

As was just mentioned, formal norms hold true for all ethical behavior in all societies and cultures. In tribal societies, for example, members are always expected to behave justly toward others. In most instances, however, the persons who are the objects of ethical behavior are the members of one's own tribe, and so substantive norms of justice do not necessarily apply to dealings with strangers, who are regarded as nonpersons and therefore not worthy of ethical consideration. This indeed is generally true of all societies and cultures as well. Thus, for a long time white Europeans regarded people of other races as inferior human beings, and they even regarded indigenous peoples in Africa and the Americas as nonhuman. The substance given here to the absolute formal norm was therefore socially and culturally determined, but even within these limitations the fundamental human ethical sense was active. Those formal norms, which express in the abstract our basic drive to achieve a full human life, therefore continuously generate new ethical ideas. For example, gradually people came to realize that being human is more encompassing than tribe, race, or skin color.

In contrast, substantive norms are culturally situated and historically conditioned. Although absolute formal norms only express their value concretely in substantive norms, which then share in their absolute quality, these substantive norms hold only conditionally, at least when seen in a broader perspective. This is because our understanding of ourselves and our own concrete action is always ambivalent and we can never survey beforehand the totality of the effects and side effects of a particular action. This is also true because each of our attempts to formulate what is really human and just remains largely abstract since these realities can only appear in concrete situations. For these reasons we often can give different answers to the ethical questions raised by a particular situation.

Another distinction that needs to be made in a discussion such as this one is a distinction between moral values and what are usually referred to as premoral values. Moral values are found in ethical norms, whether formal (such as truthfulness) or substantive (the rules for appropriate truth telling in a particular culture). Premoral values are all the good things in human experience (life, health, pleasure, security, possessions, etc.) about which moral judgments and decisions can be made, and premoral disvalues are all the bad things (death, sickness, pain, insecurity, poverty, etc.) that likewise can become the content of moral judgments and decisions. Premoral values and disvalues are neither virtues nor vices (it is not ethical to be healthy or immoral to be sick), but they are important because we make moral judgments and decisions about them (what we think about wealth, or how we treat the sick).

If the purpose of any moral code or ethical system is to maintain and increase people's humanity, or in other words, to preserve and enhance the quality of human life, then it becomes a moral obligation to protect and multiply premoral values as well as to decrease and eliminate premoral disvalues. This obligation extends, moreover, not only to oneself and one's immediate group (family, co-workers, etc.) but also to larger institutions and to society itself. Nevertheless, since the effective possibilities for increasing the good things in life and decreasing the bad ones are dependent on individual, social, and technological resources, substantive ethical norms for doing these sorts of things are necessarily going to vary. So, for example, what must we do now about world hunger, in view of the possibilities of our modern technology and economy? Given this modern technology and economy, the contacts between cultures become therefore a challenge for each particular culture; they require each specific culture to transcend itself precisely *in* and *as* its own culture, which means without having to betray its own ethical unity. If this appears impossible in the short or long term, it raises the question whether this specific culture does not have a flaw somewhere in its fundamental structure.

When two cultures come in contact with one another, they face many challenges, not the least of which are ethical challenges. In the determining of ethical priorities this encounter of cultures and the reciprocal criticism that it brings can also bring people to the disclosure of more refined ethical insight and action. The determination of a culture's priorities is itself an ethical decision. For example: Is life in itself more or less valuable than freedom in itself? In addition, we must think about how far the concrete evaluation of priorities, for example, in affluent societies, is socially and economically conditioned. The so-called philosophical, rational scale of values drawn up in a book like Abraham Maslow's *Humanistic Phychology* clearly betrays the aspirations of modern American middle-class people and in no way is a universal scale of values.

Examples such as these show that it is possible for there to be differences in ethical norms between cultures. Moreover, these differences can occur simultaneously, when two societies exist in the world at the same time, or they can occur historically, when the culture of a society changes from one period of time to another. Clearly, this general observation about cultures and ethical norms has implications for cultural norms related to sexuality and marriage. It is quite possible that norms that are ethically important in one culture may not be very relevant in another culture, whether the two cultures exist side by side in the world today or are two stages in the social and economic evolution of a single society. The realization of the connection between cultural practices and ethical norms has important implications for the church's teachings on faith and morals.[8]

NATURE, CULTURE, AND HUMAN INTELLIGENCE

In discussions of sexuality and marriage, culture is often contrasted with nature. This contrast is not as simple as it appears to be, however, since nature can be thought of in three ways.

First, one can talk about nature in a rather concrete and environmental sense when what is meant is the world of forests and fields, rivers and streams, mountains and valleys. In this sense of the word, one says that most people today live in cities rather than in nature. Second, one can talk about nature in a somewhat more general sense when one refers to the wind and tides, rain and snow, light and gravity as natural phenomena. Third, one can talk about nature in a very abstract sense, and it is in this sense that nature can be contrasted with culture. Nature in this sense includes everything that is not made by human beings, which works through definite and unalterable laws that can be discovered and used to human advantage. Nature in this third sense is objective: it can be investigated but it cannot be changed.

Notice, however, that the boundary between nature and culture, or between the natural and the humanly produced, is not natural but artificial. That is, the line between the two is itself a product of culture, and the location of the line reflects the limits of human control over the environment and things within it. The contrast between nature and culture is always dependent on culture and society. For example, what is clearly a human creation can take on the qualities of a natural phenomenon, as happens when those of us in Holland think about the Dutch train system operating as inexorably as the tides: they are "naturally" on time.

As a result of modern scholarship, nature has been demythologized, but culture is still regarded as mysterious. In reality, though, cultures operate according to rules and laws just as natural phenomena do. For example, in cultures where paternity and inheritance are of paramount importance, there is great social control over sexuality. Contemporary Western society, by contrast, places great stress on individual power and achievement, and so it sees less need to maintain rigid controls over sexual activity. As a result, our society has become more tolerant toward behavior that used to be regarded as deviant.[9]

Appealing to human nature as a way of measuring morality is an appeal not to nature in itself, therefore, but to nature as interpreted by human intelligence working in some sort of cultural location. Moral norms are not found objectively in nature, but they are the human mind's interpretation of nature in some intellectual framework or another.

> What nature itself contributes to guaranteeing the universal nature of morals, which the intellect determines, results from the structure and type of this intellect itself. The intellect is in nature, and therefore is located in a gigantic and complex referential framework of regularities which co-determine each step that the intellect makes, either by making these steps possible and advancing them, or by limiting them.[10]

The ultimate source of morality is therefore never nature, which simply opens possibilities and sets limits, but human intelligence itself.

Christian faith, moreover, is not simply ethics, nor can it be reduced to ethics. This is not to deny that there is a close relationship between faith and morality, for there is an intrinsic connection between Christian beliefs and the kind of ethical life that Christians are supposed to lead.

Ethical discourse, however, is a different language from religious discourse. Moral labels such as "good" and "bad" are more fundamental and even logically prior to religious labels such as "in accordance with the will of God" and "contrary to the will of God," when it comes to evaluating human behavior. In other words, moral behavior is primarily and basically judged with regard to its value or disvalue in human terms. Secondarily, Christians may observe the same behavior and make the theological judgment that it is or is not in accordance with God's will. From this we can see that pronouncements about God's will are historically mediated, and unavoidably so.

For this reason, ethics is somewhat independent of faith, and, as a result, believers and unbelievers can dialogue together about the ethical merits of certain types of behavior without reference to religion. Nevertheless, from a Christian perspective, God's absolute freedom is the ground of human freedom, which is truly free even if less than absolute. Similarly, God's unconditional value is the ground of the unconditional quality of formal norms that are found in ethics, even though human actions are themselves never unconditioned. In this light, Thomas Aquinas and other scholastic theologians perceived natural law as proceeding from God's will (which he called eternal law) and providing a basis for ethical judgments. In this same light, the Catholic Church perceives that its official teaching about morality extends to matters of natural law in ethics.

CONCLUSIONS ABOUT OFFICIAL CHURCH TEACHING

Based on what has already been said, it seems that a few observations are in order.

First, the primary and proper domain of the Catholic Church's official teaching on sexuality and marriage is marriage understood as a reality of faith, that is, the marital relationship as a sacrament of faith, hope, and love.

Second, the official teaching of the church about marriage, like all religious discourse, is a second-order language, as explained above. That is, church teachings speak about human realities that exist only in historical societies and particular cultures. Whenever the church speaks about marriage and sexuality in a universal manner without reference to any society or culture, therefore, it is speaking in a vacuum. Moreover, since the church has an obligation to proclaim a gospel that is not tied to any one culture (even though it is always expressed in some cultural form or other), church leaders need to keep in mind that official pronouncements directed to all Christians around the world cannot be naively based on a European understanding of marriage and sexuality. If they were, they would conflict with the Catholic understanding that the human, culturally conditioned reality of marriage is a sacrament. From the outset, then, church leaders need to respect (critically) the different forms of marriage in different cultures: otherwise, official teachings are likely to be seen as examples of Western bias and even Roman ideology.

Third, the pope and the Roman congregations that head the Catholic Church can certainly issue official teachings for the whole church if they listen very carefully to Catholics and especially bishops around the world, for the bishops have primary responsibility for local churches, they live in and know them from the inside out, and they are responsible for inculturating the Christian message and church practices in their own social settings.

Fourth, however, as much as teaching from the top seems necessary and sometimes even urgent, it should never be so abstract that it prescinds from every human culture, for teachings of that sort would not really benefit the people in any local church. If the concrete cultural reality of marriage is the sacrament of marriage, then church leaders necessarily have to take into account a certain amount of ethical and cultural pluralism around the world. Otherwise, they are bound to treat culturally relative features of marriage (whether it be marriage in the ancient Middle East, marriage in medieval Europe, or marriage in the modern West) as though they were transcultural absolutes that can never change.

Fifth, church leaders should not pick and choose the information that they get from the human sciences. Too often it appears that they appeal to scientific research only when it supports conclusions that they already hold, and they ignore or even discount any research that calls traditional views into question. Interestingly, it is only in the latter case that the tentative and hypothetical nature of scientific knowledge is pointed out, whereas this is not mentioned when there is research that supports official teachings.

Sixth, however, the gospel of Christ gives the church something very important to say about the Western (but spreading) belief that all the problems of human life can be solved by purely technological means. The church should let its voice be heard and should insist that what is technologically possible is not necessarily ethical, nor is it always possible to find technological solutions for existential human problems. Since the truth that is reached by modern science is neither the only truth nor the norm of all other truth, the church must always, without belittling the validity of science, articulate and defend truth that is not just scientific hypothesis and theory.

Seventh, church pronouncements about marriage and sexuality need to let go of their tendency to overspiritualize when they talk about the joy of married life and the beauty of the conjugal relationship. On the other hand, church pronouncements also need to stop being overly materialistic in the sense that they often focus on the physical when they talk about sexual morality, for example, and on the biological when they talk about birth control. This sort of dualism is not culturally justifiable, for it does not reflect the way marriage and sexuality are experienced in Western society.

Eighth, when the church teaches that marriage "actualizes the covenant love between God and his people" or "between Christ and his church," it needs to keep in mind the source of this teaching. This image has ancient pagan roots and stems from a culture in which sexuality was understood as a function of the gods, or as a human participation in divine activity. Israel, however, demythologized this image and understood sexuality simply as a human activity. When biblical authors used this image as a metaphor for the relation between the divine and the human, moreover, the original image was turned around, and the human marriage relationship became regarded as a symbolic expression of an inexpressible divine–human relationship. The scriptural metaphor thus gives God a human appearance that is uniquely imaged in each unique culture. If the metaphor is reversed, however, and the church makes the claim that a certain image of the divine–human relationship (based on a culturally conditioned vision of marriage) presents an absolute norm for marriage, the claim is probably hiding an ideological agenda. For in fact, God can be imaged differently in different cultures, and the divine–human relationship can be understood differently when a culture changes over time. It is important to realize this when considering what the church should be teaching about marriage in this century.

Ninth, even if the official teaching presents ideals based on a vision of the reign of God, that is, where the human cause is God's cause (and for human beings God's cause must be the human cause), it must be remembered that these ideals always have juridical consequences in a church community, even though the gospel cannot be restricted to juridical thinking.

Personal Reflections on the Future

It seems to me that in the future, church leaders ought to listen more closely to what is coming out of the diversity of cultures around the world. Indeed, the Judeo-Christian belief in creation—that everything comes from and is sustained in existence by God—implies that human cultures and society also have a theological significance. For even before the churches bring the gospel to people, God's absolute saving reality is already actively present in each people and in every person.

In talking about sexuality and marriage, therefore, those who speak in the name of the Catholic Church need to realize that diverse cultures implicitly contain diverse theologies—local theologies, if you will, that may or may not be very different from one another. On the one hand, those cultures (like all cultures, including our own) stand to be critiqued by the gospel of Christ, which is transcultural and for all peoples of all times. On the other hand, those same cultures are in a position to help us critically examine our own culture and thus help us to recognize our own cultural additions to the gospel. Through this mutual criticism, we can come to a greater assurance that what we believe is the good news for all peoples is truly transcultural.

Applied to what the church says about marriage, this means that in the future church leaders should pay more attention to the traditional Catholic belief that Christian marriage which is lived "in the Lord" is a sacrament. For if the marriage relationship is concretely lived in diverse cultural forms, it is these cultural forms of marriage that provide the living contexts for whatever can be said theologically about the sacrament of marriage.

This vision of how theology should proceed implies that those who speak in the name of the church should constantly bear in mind the distinctions that were introduced earlier about the weight and force of official teachings. In other words, church leaders need to be asking themselves whether what they are saying is a matter of church doctrine, a conviction of the church, or an opinion of the church. If it is a matter of doctrine, then is their teaching a true confession of faith, a transcultural expression of the gospel of Christ? If it is a matter of conviction, is it a conviction of the whole church, of the European church, or of some other local church? Or is it a matter of opinion, when one is aware of speaking hypothetically, gropingly, provisionally? Are church leaders honestly convinced that they should teach honorably and conscientiously within all these limitations?

If church leaders become convinced that they can and should talk about marriage with such nuances in mind, I am convinced that church teaching will gain credibility and authority in the minds of believers. On the other hand, if they disregard distinctions such as these and speak as though every pronouncement were a matter of universal doctrine, what the church says will lose credibility and neither believers nor people in general will benefit from this teaching.

Church members expect their leaders to address important issues such as marriage and the family, but they also expect them to support their statements with arguments that are understandable and meaningful. Earlier in history, the church could appeal to its own authority and claim a divine right, as it were, to make pronouncements that had to be accepted by all Catholics, but those days are over. Today it is no longer possible to cover over weak arguments with a strong appeal to the Holy Spirit's guidance of the church and its leaders. I certainly believe in divine assistance, but I also believe that such assistance works best, if not only, when leaders have listened carefully to the voice of the Spirit in the voices of the faithful. If leaders stop listening because of an unreflective fidelity to a past form of culture, they cannot claim to be heeding the Spirit when they issue church teachings. What will be crucial, if the church is to speak credibly in the future, is fidelity to the truth of the gospel and openness to the people of many cultures.

Translated by Daniel Thompson

Notes

1. Thomas Aquinas, *Summa Theologiae*, Supplementum, q. 41, a. 1, ad 3 (with references there to Thomas's earlier writings).

2. Ibid., q. 42, a. 2; q. 65, a. 2.

3. H. Dombois, *Kirche und Eherecht: Studien und Abhandlungen 1953–1972* (Stuttgart, 1974); J. Freisen, *Geschichte des kanonischen Eherechts bis zum Verfall der Glossenliteratur* (3rd ed.; Paderborn-Aalen, 1963); E. Schillebeeckx, *Het huwelijk: Aardse werkelijkheid en heilsmysterie* (Bilthoven, 1963; Eng. trans. *Marriage: Human Reality and Saving Mystery* [New York, 1965]); G. H. Joyce, *Die christliche Ehe: Eine geschichtliche und Dogmatische studie* (Leipzig, 1934); P. Adnès, *Le mariage* (Tournai, 1961).

4. H. Begemann, *Strukturwandel der Familie: Eine sozial theologische Untersuchung über die Wandlung von der patriarchalischen zur partnerschaftlischen Familie* (Hamburg, 1960); J Höffner, *Ehe und Familie: Wesen und Wandel in der industriellen Gesellschaft* (Münster, 1959); H. Schelsky, *Soziologie der Sexualität: Über die Beziehungen zwischen Geschlecht, Moral und Gesellschaft* (Hamburg, 1955); P. Bourdieu, *La reproduction: Eléments pour une théorie du système d'enseignement* (Paris, 1970); idem., *La distinction: critique sociale du jugement* (Paris, 1979).

5. M. Horkheimer, "Autorität und Familie," in M. Horkheimer, *Kritische Theorie: Eine Dokumentation* (Frankfurt am Main, n.d.), 1:277–360.

6. See P. L. Berger, B. Berger, and H. Kellner, *The Homeless Mind: Modernization and Consciousness* (New York, 1974).

7. Why is it not possible for churches and communities of faith to have only opinions about complicated problems that have no clear solution?

8. The phrase "faith and morals" comes from Augustine, who puts the sacramental practice of the church under the heading of "morals." See P. Fransen, "'Geloof en zenden': notitie over een veelgebruikte formule," *Tijdschrift voor Theologie* 9 (1969): 316–26.

9. Bourdieu, *La reproduction*.

10. W. Korff, "Het criterium voor het universele karakter van de zedenwet," *Concilium* 17, no. 10 (1981): 92–99, especially 96.

10

Divorce and Remarriage
as Second Chances

PIERRE HEGY AND JOSEPH MARTOS

SINCE THE BEGINNING OF CHRISTIANITY, the remarriage of divorced persons has been a disputed question because an absolute ban on divorce often seems unfair to one of the parties. We know from Origen and Jerome that in early Christianity remarriages took place, as in the case of the famous Fabiola. We also know from history that the rich and powerful could remarry after obtaining an annulment, although wealth and power were no guarantee of success in annulment proceedings. In more recent times, the remarriage of Catholics has become much easier in the United States than in the past, yet resentment has increased both among those who went through the annulment procedures and among those who refused. Let us consider the possibility that, in prohibiting remarriage and creating an annulment process to find a way to circumvent the prohibition, the Catholic Church was engaged in deception. With this in mind, we first review the previous chapters from the perspective of deception. Next, we briefly summarize the findings of attachment research on inner healing. Finally, we turn to remarriage as a second chance.

Discussion of Previous Chapters

1. "Catholic Divorce, Annulments, and Deception" defined deception as unintentionally misleading others, often with the best intentions. One can also intentionally mislead others with the worst intentions, but such cases will not be considered here. To let oneself be deceived always involves some

personal responsibility. Thus, from the profession of faith, "I believe in the holy catholic church," one may come to believe that the church is existentially and universally holy. If one is not aware of the difference between theological discourse and everyday language, one is likely to be deceived because religious language tends to be prescriptive and metaphysical (the church is holy as Christ's bride), rather than factual and descriptive (local churches being all holy). In any deception there is self-deception and individual responsibility. Deception may easily result from too much faith, unenlightened faith, or simply excessive credulity.

2. "Testimonies." "It was not fair to expect Mom to hold up her end of the contract/commitment when the other end was no longer there. Was she supposed to cast herself upon the funeral pyre? Why? Was this a ruling that gave witness to any of the attributes of our loving Father?" Is there deception here? Maybe this person expected too much. She expected that the church address the issue of the innocent marriage partner unfairly divorced. We know from history that Roman Catholicism—as opposed to Orthodoxy—has refused to do so for centuries. She also expected to find solace and comfort from the local priest when her mother was severely depressed. But can one expect priests to be shepherds when they have a thousand sheep? If one only expects priests to be sheepdogs barking when sheep stray away, then maybe one will not be deceived. But should we lower our faith in the church? Should we conclude with the writer: "I have come to believe that to marry legally or in the church is less important than to commit to each other's well-being and that of their children"? Does marrying in the church make any difference at all?

In the second testimony we read: "The Monsignor who was conducting the proceedings repeatedly tried to get me to say that I thought from the very beginning that the marriage wasn't going to last forever or that I wasn't committed from the very beginning. I never agreed to that because it wasn't true. . . . Had I written how much the marriage had actually benefited me by moving me along on my own growth trajectory and how, by ending this marriage, I finally found out who I was, there would have been no annulment." Everybody gets deceived here. The theology of annulments becomes deceitful when a declaration of invalidity is based on false or misleading testimonies. The judges deceive themselves when they induce others to tell lies. And the petitioner is also deceiving herself in order to get an annulment. Was the annulment worth the price? "I would never do this again" is her redeeming conclusion, and her indirect advice to others to do the same.

Can one receive communion without an annulment and without deception? Yes, according to the priest who tells his penitent: "[You] have a choice. [You] can take communion," and no priest can deny such a right. His position is as clear as canon law itself on three points. Remarried Catholics can be considered *public* sinners only in the parish in which they are known; in any other parish they become—like most people—anonymous. Second, although remarried Catholics are not supposed to receive communion, no priest can stop them. Finally, canon law is not binding in conscience but under the penalty of the law, and laws are only as binding as the sanctions attached to them. A law without sanctions (e.g., a speed limit that is never enforced) is no more than a suggestion. The only sanction against remarried Catholics is that their unions are not recognized by the church. This is the only sanction, and it has nothing to do with receiving communion. Hence, knowledge of the law may shield one from the deception that results from misinterpreting it.

If everyone were perfectly rational and logical, perhaps there would be much less deception. The judicial vicar quoted in the *Long Island Catholic* seems to have reached the ultimate conclusion of the Catholic praxis of marriage and annulments: all marriages should be considered nonsacramental (or "simulation[s] of marriage") until proven otherwise. This position is logical: the ideal of marriage as covenant is so high that most people, because of immaturity, cannot achieve it (as a proof: most petitions for annulment are granted). Also logical is the conclusion of the writer of her letter: "The price to pay is much too high for what may later be declared only a 'simulation of a sacrament.' I would strongly urge them [her grandchildren] to have a civil ceremony only, because at least it would give them the assurance that the union is really legal and with certainty." Both the vicar and the writer recognize the deceptiveness of church laws and practices, to which officials and lay people turn a blind eye, ordinarily.

"It took twenty-eight years of being turned away, before I finally was granted an annulment. Remarriage was not the issue with me. All I wanted was the right to live a single life without feeling guilty." The breakup of a marriage is often experienced as a guilty failure. Waiting twenty-eight years for an annulment may be worth it, in order not to feel "in bondage with someone who freely chose to divorce me and remarry." Yet the annulment may also add insult to injury. In this case "It gave the other party the chance to get his third marriage validated in the church," and at the same time it conveyed the feeling that "I am unfit for marriage, or as he used to tell me, that I am worthless." An annulment based on supposedly proven psychological immaturity only adds oil to the fire. Hence having too much trust in the church may prove self-deceiving. In parishes of several thousand people, priests are administrators most of the time, and shepherds only sometimes. There is room for much deception.

3. In "Disputed Biblical Interpretations about Marriage and Divorce" we learn that the scriptural basis of the Catholic position on divorce is not as monolithic as one would expect. The theological knowledge of most Catholics is based on their catechism remembrances and the Sunday homilies. Obviously children are taught at the level of children, but the church still considers most adult Catholics to be children. Still prevalent in the church is the attitude common two centuries ago about women: too much instruction is dangerous; it may lead them to become "fresh" and "smart." Thus in the semi-official *Catechism of the Catholic Church*, readers are shielded from any knowledge of opposite views. In spite of the wealth of references and footnotes, controversial issues (sexual morality, divorce, ordination of women, original sin, etc.) are systematically presented as monolithic and unchallengeable doctrines, at the level of maturity (or naïveté) of the child. Such an attitude may seem normal in many parts of the world where social inequality still prevails, but presenting unsettled matters as settled is nevertheless deceptive.

At the beginning of Christianity there was pluralism, that is, tension and conflict between opposite views. Failure to recognize this historical reality exposes one to much deception. Some of Paul's letters were not written by Paul; the letters of Peter and John were probably not written by Peter and John. The author of the Acts shows no knowledge of the letters of Paul. John the evangelist shows no knowledge of the Synoptics. There are even discrepancies between the three Synoptic Gospels. Tensions and controversies resulting from these discrepancies only started when Christianity began to institutionalize Jesus' teaching into an organized religion. Any institutionalization involves ideological and political power struggles that result in the suppression of diversity.

4. In "Christian Marriage and the Reality of Complete Marital Breakdown," Edward Schillebeeckx raises the question of the collective deception of anthropological naïveté—the inability to distinguish between ideal and institutionalization, between essence and ideology. There is first the naïveté of the belief that Jesus actually proclaimed the indissolubility of marriage, while in fact the word "indissolubility" is nowhere to be found in the New Testament. There is also the naïve belief that marriage is what modern Western society believes it to be, while the nature of marriage has obviously changed over the three thousand years of Jewish and Christian history.

In patriarchal times, marriage was polygamous. So, polygamy is "indissoluble"? In ancient Judaism, the permanence of marriage was subordinated to the permanence of the clan. A marriage became permanent only after the birth of a child to assure the continuity of the clan; a childless marriage could be dissolved. In the Greco-Roman world, family permanence resided in its sacred hearth. The conversion to Christianity of one of the spouses could seriously threaten the whole household. The Pauline privilege is based, Schillebeeckx reminds us, not just on "disparity of cult," but on the reality of total marital breakdown. For instance, what would happen today to an orthodox kosher-keeping Jewish family if one of the spouses were to convert to fundamentalist Christianity? The life between an orthodox Jew and a fundamentalist Christian might easily break down beyond repair. On the other hand, in agrarian societies the permanence of marriage resides in the economic contribution of both spouses. In case of desertion, non-support, or the death of a spouse, this economic unit can collapse beyond repair. With the advent of romantic love as the basis for marriage, the permanence of the couple is grounded on its mutual love; a loveless marriage is no longer a marriage, but an empty shell. And finally, the permanence of the sacramentality of marriage is shown in the visible manifestation of its Christian faith. According to Schillebeeckx, marriage is "indissoluble not because it is a sacrament, but it is a sacrament because and so far as it carries out . . . the living reality of faith." Or, in Charles N. Davis's words, "Marriage is a sacrament that is carried daily." A church-blessed marriage without Christian faith may only be a sham. Total marital breakdown may be more a sign of hell than of heaven. Hence, to see marriage essentially as a contract is "unhealthy, unfair, and legalistic."

When both church leaders and lay people fail to see the anthropological dimension of marriage, they may deceive themselves in pursuing in marriage what is only a secondary aspect at a given time. Who would define marriage today as a covenant between clans? Who would say that the foundation of marriage resides in its sacred hearth? How deceitful would it be today to see marriage mainly as an economic arrangement? Or as a contract? Or a sacramental marriage because of a ritual that was performed in a few minutes years ago?

5. "The Indissolubility of Marriage in Orthodox Law and Practice" clearly states that "The doctrine of absolute indissolubility cannot be found in Byzantine law" (p. 115). Christian marriages are seen as permanent but can be dissolved in special circumstances. This position is based on a historical rather than a dogmatic interpretation of biblical texts: "The intention of St. Paul and the Synoptics is to adapt the Lord's teaching to times and places to which their writings were destined" (p. 109). This position is in agreement with current scholarship, which believes that the actual words of the historical Jesus cannot be reconstituted with certainty, only interpreted. Such a position has the advantage of not putting scholars and church officials on a collision course.

There was and is also no conflict in Orthodoxy between secular and reli-

gious authorities about divorce. During the Byzantine Middle Ages, canonists did not question the competence of the imperial authority in matrimonial legislation. The collaboration between church and state proved
effective, since the divorce rate then was lower than during late antiquity.
Even today in the United States there is no conflict: once a divorce has been
granted by a civil court, remarriage in the church does not require ecclesiastical tribunal proceedings; legal proof of civil divorce is sufficient. This
collaboration between church and state can be explained historically:
Orthodoxy never held a position of supreme power in matrimonial affairs
as Catholicism did; hence there is no struggle to hold on to past hegemony.

Orthodoxy has also come to grips with the only grounds of divorce that
it has never accepted, namely, divorce by mutual consent. This acceptance
is based on the realization that "once a conjugal union has been broken and
this rupture has been legally ratified, it is difficult to pretend that the marriage continues to subsist in the abstract" (p. 120). This may be a wise position, considering that Eastern churches never attempted to be the moral
police of society. Given the fact that today about one Catholic in four or five
lives in a blended or reconstituted family involving one or two divorced
partners, it makes little sense to pretend that previous marriages still exist.
The contemporary practice of divorce by mutual consent is seen by most
people as preferable to court-contested divorces. The Catholic theology of
marriage will have to come to realize that the church has no power over
most social, economic, and legal factors leading to divorce. If Catholicism
were to give up its juridical control over divorce and remarriage, as Orthodoxy did, there would be little ground for deceit.

6. "Catholic Marriage and Marital Dissolution in Medieval and Modern
Times" covers much ground and allows the reader to see the progressive
shift in the conception of marriage from a social institution of customs and
relationships to an ecclesiastical institution under church control. It is church
control and power that have led to much controversy and resentment.
Among Germanic tribes, marriage was a family affair, an arrangement to
promote family status and alliances. Divorce was rare, since it would
threaten stability and family relations. Under Roman law, marriage was
equally private—no mandatory ritual, no public sanction—as it was in most
countries of the world for centuries. In China and other eastern countries,
marriage remained a private affair until the 1930s. Yet in the West, marriage
became clericalized. In the twelfth century, Gratian first redefined marriage,
from a state of life based on love, as in antiquity, to a wedding contract.
Companionship or friendship is not essential to marriage, reaffirmed
Aquinas, since it is a contract. In scholasticism, marriage became redefined

as an ecclesiastical institution, namely, a legal contract, even if loveless. Such was the power of the clerical elite that no one could object.

The reaction came from scholars, trained in theology and canon law. Luther and Calvin reaffirmed what had been accepted for nearly a millennium, namely, that marriage was a human social institution, although families, church, and state may regulate it. At the Council of Trent, the clericalization of marriage was increased by the requirement, for a marriage to be valid, of two witnesses and a priest (the so-called canonical form). No intellectual justification was given. This greater institutionalization of religion proved fatal in the long run: if it is the canonical form that essentially differentiates a sacramental from a nonsacramental marriage, then the difference is vacuous. For a few more centuries, Catholics agreed to follow the canonical form. Today, however, with the drastic decrease in church attendance, the canonical form itself has come to be seen as empty, at least in European countries.

A drastic setback of the Catholic position followed Pius IX's *Syllabus of Errors,* in which he reasserted in unbalanced terms that the Catholic Church has a monopoly on ecclesiastical marriages, that all marriages (even civil ones) are indissoluble, and that civil authorities have no right to dissolve them. These views were simply ignored by national governments, so that today in most countries of the world (the United States being an outstanding exception), Catholics must undergo two marriage ceremonies, a civil one and a religious one. This latent conflict between church and state has reached an impasse today. While the church does not recognize civil marriages and civil divorces, the majority of divorced Catholics in turn ignore the church tribunals for an annulment. This is not a healthy state of affairs.

7. "Not Made in Heaven: Marriage and Divorce in the Anglican Tradition" describes a balanced situation in divorce proceedings. Looking at history, we first see in the divorce of Henry VIII the state of affairs at the time of the Reformation: marriage was considered an indissoluble institution, but in some cases the pope could dissolve it through an annulment. Moreover, divorce and annulments were political matters. Because the dismissal of Catherine meant great humiliation for Spain, the pope had no choice but to alienate either the king of Spain or the king of England. He made a fatal choice, and the Roman church lost not a king but a kingdom.

The *via media* of Anglicanism is one of compromise. Is marriage a sacrament? The answer is yes and no. It is not a major but a minor one; or maybe it is a "natural sacrament," or maybe the question itself is not important. "Issues of marriage, divorce, and remarriage [are]. . . things indifferent" (p. 158). Never since the Middle Ages has Catholicism taken a fresh look at the notion of sacrament, neither at Trent nor at Vatican II; the old formulas are endlessly repeated. The same seems true in Anglicanism.

The decentralization of Anglicanism allows for greater innovation at the local level. The Diocese of Central Florida offers an interesting example. Its "background statement" explains that "two in one flesh . . . means to regard each other's security, happiness and personal growth as important as one's own." Concrete examples are given about how to achieve this end: "the study of scripture, daily prayer, regular worship and support of consistent Christian fellowship." Divorce is mainly seen as a pastoral task: "The Episcopal Church seeks to help people who make a new life when their marriages are clearly and irreversibly broken." It is words like these that divorced people need to hear in order to rebuild or maintain their faith in themselves and the church.

8. "Divorce among Protestant Clergy" sheds some light on the sociological factors of divorce and pastoral care. Is divorce essentially an individual moral failure? If yes, we would expect it be lower among those who have followed the Lord than among those who, according to Paul, cannot control their sexual desire. This is not the case, however. "Protestant clergy are now divorcing at about the same rate as lay persons in American society" (p. 168). Before the no-fault divorce laws, it was legally necessary to find a guilty party in order to obtain a divorce; then guilt and shame were normally associated with divorce. Now in case of marital breakdown clergy are likely to find sympathy and support on the part of their congregation rather than condemnation.

There are great differences in clergy divorce rates between the theologically conservative and the liberal denominations. Divorce can indeed be repressed and even denied. How reluctant are Episcopal clergymen to tell their bishop about their marital problems? It depends on the bishop's attitude toward divorce. How reluctant are priests to tell their bishop about their alcoholism, their homosexual or child molestation tendencies? Again it depends on whether the bishop will use shame and punishment. In the latter case, the problem can be denied, and the churches can report low rates of divorce, alcoholism, homosexuality, etc. Negating the problem may well be one important explanation (among others) of the lower divorce rate in theologically conservative churches.

One bishop is reported to offer payment for clergy marital counseling. In such a case, marital problems are likely to be acknowledged and helped. Moreover, remarriage in this and other Episcopal dioceses is at the discretion of the individual priest. Divorce and remarriage are nonissues; it is the marital breakdown that is the problem for which individuals need help.

Once the marital breakdown has been solved, hopefully in peace and friendship, remarriage is seen by the congregation as a positive rather than a negative step. In short, marital breakdown can be denied through annulments by stating that a sacramental marriage never existed. Such an attitude is of little help to people going through the trauma of marital breakdown. It is also quite insensitive, leading to feelings of deception. Once a marriage has been dissolved by a civil court, divorce stops being an issue. What is needed, as much by divorced clergy as lay people, is pastoral assistance.

9. In "Church Teaching on Sexuality and Marriage," Edward Schillebeeckx draws on concepts and distinctions already present in his first article, namely, the distinction between the anthropological, historical, and cultural aspects of lived faith, and the universal and transcultural demands of the gospel. In this chapter, church authority itself is seen within the dialectic of gospel universality versus church teachings located in space and time, that is, inspired by political agendas and theological preferences. Because church teachings are always dated in space and time, they are "second discourses"—discourse about discourses—tainted by the cultural biases of given cultures (e.g., Roman or Polish), given theologies (pre–Vatican II as opposed to post–Vatican II), or ideologies of power (e.g., authoritarian versus democratic). This distinction is striking when one reads nineteenth-century encyclicals written by popes fearing the loss of their Papal States.

Of great relevance is the distinction between teachings "from the conviction of the church" and those speaking "from the opinion of the church." The distinction may seem disrespectful. How can church teaching be personal opinions? This question can be countered with another question: Was the condemnation of Galileo really "from the conviction of the church"? To reject the distinction would be deceitful: popes have personal opinions about art, politics, social systems, money, as well as theologies. Many popes have sided with aspects of capitalism against communism; John Paul II rejected both; these are obviously inspired by personal opinions. In the light of this distinction we may come to realize with Schillebeeckx that it is the "quasi-infallible certainty" attached to papal teaching that makes them seen to be coming "from the conviction of the church," while a century later they may appear more clearly as papal preferences and/or theological options. Hence, the most liberating church teaching would begin with "Not the Lord, but I say to you . . . (1 Cor. 7:12).

Let us come to the fundamental questions of this book. How can one be healed from deception? Or from the traumas of marital breakdown? How can a first marriage be a moment of grace for a real second chance? Even more generally: How can one be healed from previous unhealthy relationships? To answer these questions, we turn to attachment research.

ATTACHMENT RESEARCH
AND THE HEALING OF RELATIONSHIPS

Let us begin with a brief overview of the findings. The mother–child attachment style (either secure, anxious-ambivalent, or avoidant) has been found to be stable for life. Moreover, attachment styles affect many aspects of life, for example, communication, marriage happiness, attitudes toward work, patterns of religiosity, and so on. It is likely that those characterized by a secure attachment style will be pleased with these findings, but what about those anxious-ambivalent individuals? What about the avoidants? How can one change one's attachment style? The answer is by changing one's inner working models; and this answer can be applied to other forms of healing, for example, healing deception and healing from marital breakdown.

Attachment Theory

In 1958, Harry Harlow reported that infant rhesus monkeys needed a maternal presence, a terry-cloth mother to cuddle with, rather than a wire-mesh mother who would provide food but no emotional support. In the absence of a maternal presence, these infants did not become mature adults. These findings contradicted the commonly held beliefs and practices of the time. In Freudian theory, for instance, there is no room for the mother, only for the father. The only acknowledged function of the mother was that of proper feeding, which could be provided by others. In the 1950s, parents were not allowed to visit their children in the hospital, since there was no need for them, the hospital providing all necessary care. It was known that infants raised in foundling homes without loving care would wither away and often die, but these facts contradicted commonly held beliefs.

John Bowlby (1969, 1973, 1980) is the intellectual father of attachment theory, but his ideas were only slowly accepted. His theory is based on ethology: animals at birth attach to their mothers not only for food but also for emotional security to be able to explore their environment. Similarly, argued Bowlby, children need a reliable caregiver before they become self-reliant. More specifically, children need a reliable, responsive, and caring attachment figure in order to become secure; those whose mother's attention is inconsistent become insecure; finally those who find inadequate mothering become defensively self-reliant and emotionally detached. In his view, the role of the mother (or primary caregiver) is fundamental. But this raises the question: Shall we blame the mother for the child's poor emotional health? The mother could similarly blame her mother who in turn could blame her mother. Hence the question should rather be: How can we change the damage of poor mothering and improve our emotional life chances?

Mary Ainsworth (1978) made Bowlby's theory acceptable in academic circles by testing it empirically. After observing the mother–child dyad at home during the first months of the infants' lives, she brought them into a laboratory in order to test their relationship in a situation of stress called the Strange Situation. How would the child react to new toys while the mother would temporarily leave the room? As predicted by Bowlby, securely attached infants explored the toys after a mild separation anxiety, insecurely attached children cried intensely and would not be comforted by her return a few minutes later, and those with little attachment to their mother showed little emotion at both her departure and her return. Ainsworth had empirically documented the existence of *three basic attachment types: the secure, the anxious-ambivalent, and the avoidant.*

The three basic attachment styles are stable over time: attachment types measured at age one have been found to be the same at age five or six, and adolescence. They are also present later in life, in work situations and romantic relationships. Thus, secure respondents report relatively high levels of satisfaction with work, income, advancement, and challenge; anxious-ambivalent workers, in contrast, are troubled by job insecurity and lack of appreciation and promotion. Avoidant respondents, finally, thrive in work but not in love; they may become workaholics but feel no need for emotional closeness (see Shaver and Hazan 1994).

Attachment Theory and Marriage

How do attachment types affect romantic relationships? Do most individuals select a mate of their own type? If this were so (e.g., the insecure marrying insecure partners), many relationships would be doomed. But it is not so: romantic choices are not affected mainly by attachment types. The most likely reason is that attachment styles are not easily recognizable. In everyday life, most avoidant and insecurely attached persons show little avoidance and insecurity. It is only in situations of stress that attachment qualities come to the fore. This has been proven in a laboratory situation. Simpson (1994) created a lab situation in which one member of eighty-three couples was made to feel anxious. Husbands and wives were separated. The wife was informed—but not the husband—that she was going to be part of an experiment known to produce considerable anxiety in most people. When she returned to her husband in the waiting room, their interaction was recorded and the anxiety of the subjects rated. As one would expect, when securely attachment females expressed anxiety, they were comforted by their husbands if the latter was also secure. Quite different was the behavior of avoidants. The more anxiety avoidant wives experienced, the *less* likely they were to seek support; greater anxiety inhibited support seeking. The response of avoidant men was similar: the greater the anxiety of their wives, the *less* they offered support. This finding is important because it illustrates a common marriage scene for couples involving an avoidant: the more emotional support one needs, the less one gets, which increases the emotional distance between the two partners. This process can escalate to the point of rupture and separation. What can be done?

The effect of stress on family life has often been noted. Conflict, divorce, single parenthood, and so on, can lead to insecurity and/or avoidance even when the mother–child relationship is secure. It has been estimated that the number of insecure individuals can double in stressed families. Now, how many people are secure and insecure? Research in the United States, Australia, and Israel based on the Hazan and Shaver (1987) questionnaire found that approximately 55 percent of the respondents are secure, 25 percent avoidant, and 20 percent anxious/ambivalent (Shaver and Hazan, 1993:36). Rounding off these numbers so that one individual in two is secure, and one in two is either avoidant or anxious/ambivalent, we realize that only 25 percent of all couples consist of two secure individuals, while 75 percent of families consist of one or two avoidant or anxious partners. What will happen to these families in situations of stress?

Marriage itself is stressful, because the constant proximity of the partners can escalate conflict once started. Attachment types are likely to interfere. Generally speaking, negative emotions are functional if they lead to the satisfaction of needs. Thus, when the mother leaves the room, the infant's anxiety is functional if the mother responds. However, if the mother's response is inconsistent, then the child's anxiety turns into lonely anger and the attachment style becomes anxious/ambivalent. If the mother does not respond most of the time, the child's emotions turn into despair, and the attachment style becomes avoidance; then the negative feelings become dysfunctional, disruptive, and self-destructive. This scene is often seen daily in marriage. For secure partners, negative emotions are functional and seen as such, and they lead to better communication. For avoidant or anxious partners, however, negative feelings often are not heard, and hence tend to be exaggerated and offensive; the response is likely to be negative either through avoidance or overreaction (Kobak and Hazan 1991:861). In this case negative emotions lead to bad communication and conflict. This is the situation for about 75 percent of the couples.

Attachment Types and Communication

Because of socialization, men and women react differently to attachment styles. To the extent that men learn to hide or repress their emotions, they may feel comfortable with an avoidant spouse, but are likely to be unhappy with a hyper-emotional one. Women, on the other hand, may feel comfortable with an emotional man, but are most unhappy with withdrawn and avoidant husband. Attachment research confirms this tendency. Studying seventy-one dating couples in Southern California, Collins and Read (1990) found that females were most happy when their male partner was secure and emotionally close, but indifferent if they were anxious. On the other hand, males reacted most negatively to females' anxiety, but their closeness made little difference to them.

In short, women are turned off and unhappy when men are avoidant and cold, and men are repulsed when women are insecure and anxious. These feelings are shared by both partners: when men are cold and avoidant, both the male and the female give a negative evaluation of the relationship. The same holds when the females are anxious and insecure (see also Feeney et al. 1994). The specter of an insensitive husband and a hysterical wife haunts many couples. What can be done?

Changing One's Internal Working Model

In order to be able to change one's attachment styles we must first learn how they are acquired, namely, as internalized models. According to Bowlby's theory, "internal working models," that is, expectations about self and others, are internalized in early childhood. When the mother provides secure and reliable care, the child is likely to assume (1) that his mother is (and probably all mothers are) warm and caring, and (2) that he or she (the child) deserves such loving care. This logic becomes catastrophic in the case of neglect, because "an unwanted child is likely not only to feel unwanted by his parents but to believe that he or she is essentially unwanted by anyone. Though logically indefensible, these crude overgeneralizations are the rule. Once adopted, moreover, they are apt never to be seriously questioned" (Bowlby, quoted in Shaver and Hazan 1994:112). Objectively, the abandoned child is a victim of abandonment. Subjectively, however, the child sees abandonment as personal unworthiness and deserved punishment, leaving behind feelings of guilt and rage. These working models can be changed; and they will change if and when one becomes aware of them, as in the case of alcoholics and child abusers for example.

Mary Main and her coworkers have established that child abusers have all the characteristics of attachment avoidants. In a controlled experiment, it was observed that abused children avoid the friendly approaches of their caregivers at school, exhibit aggressive behavior toward peers, and show great insensitivity (and even physical aggression) toward crying peers (Main 1984). Being insensitive to the pain of others, they are likely later as parents to be insensitive, even abusive, to their own children. Attachment research has documented that the more avoidant children are, the *less* they show anger toward the mother and the more they exhibit unexplained hostility toward others later in life. Since the avoidant child negates his/her own pain which is turned into shame, guilt, and rage, internalized avoidance can become very destructive, as in the case of alcoholism and criminal behavior.

The mechanisms that allow for the transmission of child abuse are denial and repression. The abused child either represses early memories or denies everything by idealizing the mother. "If the mother insisted that she was unable to recall her childhood, her infant was significantly likely to avoid her. If a mother idealized her rejecting mother, her infant was also likely to avoid her. But if the mother expressed resentment and anger toward her mother during the interview, and if she was coherent regarding her own feelings and experiences surrounding attachment, her infant was unlikely to avoid her" (Main 1984:214). When abusers and alcoholics deny their problem and refuse to face their painful and repressed memories, there is little hope for recovery.

As exemplified by the AA (Alcoholics Anonymous) experience, the first step toward recovery is to end the denial in which one lives. Most alcoholics and their families are in constant denial by pretending to live a "normal" life. But the end of denial creates a crisis of faith about one's confidence in self and others. When ending the denial, the addict opens the gate to the anger that has been repressed since childhood. Instead of idealizing the abuser and identifying with the aggressor, one recognizes oneself as a victim needing help from others. Because the avoidant child has internalized a working model of self-hatred, shame, and guilt, he or she is left with extremely low self-esteem. By bringing denial to an end, the victim is confronted for the first time with his or her own anger, shame, guilt, low self-esteem, and low faith in God. This is a very emotional moment, one of tears over the past and rage toward the aggressors. But it is also the occasion, at the lowest point of one's self-confidence, for a leap of faith in a Higher Power. It is in the flash of these dramatic moments that one's old inner working model is questioned, although it may take years to build a new one. The old model corresponds to the institutionalized self, the self that was expected by one's environment. The new model will allow for personal feelings, including for the first time negative emotions, tears, and the acceptance of one's true individual self.

The social sciences have contributed to our understanding of radical change by showing the importance of internal working models. These internal working models tell us what to expect from life, e.g., from mothers and fathers, from marital partners, or from the church. An abused child is likely to unconsciously expect abuse in marriage, and is likely to inflict abuse on his/her children. Similarly, overcredulous believers are likely to be deceived in their expectations from others, including churches. More generally, the internal working models developed in one's first marriage (a product of childhood expectations) are likely to remain unchanged in one's second marriage. When this is the case, a second marriage is no real second chance.

Most people are not likely to change the internal working models acquired in childhood because they are not aware of them and do not remember. Then, "we are condemned to repeat what we cannot remember" (Main 1984). We may suffer from anger associated with memories that have faded away. Unfortunately this anger is difficult to cure because, in order to cure it, we must go back to the root of it. This principle also holds for negative feelings in marriage, which must be healed before one is ready for second chances.

If divorced people do not see how they contributed to their failed marriage, they are likely to repeat their mistakes. According to David and Joy Rice (1986), development throughout life requires a balance between individuation and community, autonomy and relatedness, faith in self and in the social institutions. But self-awareness must incorporate the secret and wounded self which we may like to repress or idealize. According to Rice, the key marker events of life—marriage as well as divorce and remarriage—require a new adjustment in our balance between self and others. Since half of all marriages fail, how can one improve the success of a second marriage? According to attachment theory, faith in self and others, hope, and styles of loving others are internalized in infancy. Unless we update our internal working models about self and others, there will be little room for divorced Catholics, even divorced and annulled Catholics, in the kingdom of the happily remarried.

TOWARD A THEOLOGY OF SECOND CHANCES

Changes in Marriage and Annulment as a Basis of Deception

When Catholics divorce and want to remarry, they often find themselves in a bind. Their faith in God and in themselves tells them that marrying again would be a legitimate and good thing to do, yet their faith in the Roman Catholic Church forbids this. According to Catholic doctrine, it is against God's law to marry twice (the only exception being marriage after the death of a spouse), and to remarry is in effect to commit the sin of bigamy. Hence the need for ecclesiastical annulments. An annulment is a declaration by a legal authority that a marriage is null and void. It states that a marriage contract never existed, even though one appeared to exist.

The legal grounds for seeking and being granted an annulment used to be few and fairly public, which is why annulments used to be relatively rare (as they still are in civil courts). Discovering that one's spouse was married to someone else or that one's spouse could not perform sexual intercourse (the "marital act") were two traditional grounds for annulments. One could also seek an annulment if one had been coerced into marriage (a "shotgun wedding"). The reasoning behind annulments was that marriage was a contract and that sometimes contracts, although appearing to be valid, could actually be null and void. The two most common reasons for voiding a contract are deception and coercion. If one party cannot "deliver the goods" agreed to by contract, the contract can be thrown out by a court, whether the goods be a piece of property (e.g., a car to which I claim to hold the title) or a person in a certain condition (e.g., unmarried and capable of having sex). The contract can also be thrown out if one of the parties can show that he or she was coerced into the agreement, whether it be an agreement to buy or sell something or an agreement to exchange goods (and marriage was considered an exchange of goods between the parties involved).

Since the 1970s, however, the legal grounds for annulments in the Catholic Church have expanded enormously to include all sorts of hidden psychological factors that can affect a marriage negatively. In 1965, the Second Vatican Council's definition of marriage (*Gaudium et Spes* §48.1) included intimacy (literally, an "intimate community of life and love") between the spouses. From this, canon lawyers reasoned that intimacy was one of the goods that each of the spouses has to be capable of delivering to the other. If, after a marriage has broken down, one can prove to an ecclesiastical court that at least one of the spouses had been incapable of intimacy, the court would grant an annulment. According to attachment theory, this condition may affect 75 percent of first marriages. If one adds other factors (e.g., other psychological factors that prevent intimacy), this figure may be close to 100 percent. Arguably, then, few if any couples are capable of marriage in the sense defined by Vatican II at the time that they are married for the first time. Hence, virtually all Catholic first marriages are potentially annullable.

Being divorced from a spouse who was not able to be a true marriage partner is today an acceptable basis for seeking an annulment. But what if a Catholic woman who finds herself in such a situation does not apply for an annulment? What if she is convinced in her own mind that, on some level at least, her marriage of ten or twenty years was a real marriage? What if she cannot stand the pain of sifting through the ashes of her burned-out marriage in order to satisfy the legal requirements of the Catholic Church?

In such a situation, she is forced to choose between her faith in God and her faith in an institution that claims to speak for God. Like hundreds of thousands of other divorced Catholics, she may decide to remarry without the church's blessing.

At this point, some observations are in order.

The first is that, for many people in the world, the nature of marriage is different today from what it was a century ago. Until the ideal of companionate marriage became widespread, marriage was indeed a public contract entered into for an exchange of goods. Friendship, Aquinas admitted, was not one of these goods. Today, however, marriage without friendship, companionship, and intimacy is unthinkable, intolerable, even repulsive. Few people today would consider the possibility of entering into an arranged marriage, yet arranged marriage was the norm in the Catholic world not that long ago. The very nature of marriage has changed, even though the same word, "marriage," is used to name both the spousal relationship of a hundred years ago and the spousal relationship of today. Is it fair—even honest—to apply the rules of contractual marriage to companionate marriage? Should a theology of marriage that developed when most marriages were arranged by parents for their adolescent children be used legalistically on marriages between autonomous adults? Arguably not.

The second observation is that there is a conflict between the traditional grounds for annulment and the contemporary grounds for annulment. The traditional grounds for annulment, as noted above, were few: mainly deception and coercion. The contemporary grounds for annulment also include self-deception or ignorance: one or both spouses may be self-deceived or ignorant about their psychological ability to enter into an intimate and lasting relationship. Although Catholic canonists like to think that the contemporary grounds are an extension and amplification of the traditional grounds, they are in fact different and in some cases they conflict. Individuals in the past who would have been considered validly married because psychological factors were not taken into account at that time can today apply for and receive annulments because psychological factors are now taken into account. Both what is being measured and the measuring stick have changed.

A third observation is that, although marriage has changed and the grounds for annulment have changed, the treatment of divorced persons in the Catholic Church has not. In canon law, a marriage is presumed to be valid until it is proven that it is not. Hence a divorced person is prevented from remarrying until an annulment is granted, and a divorced person who remarries without an annulment is excluded from the sacraments. He or she is assumed to be "living in sin" (i.e., bigamy) because of having entered into a second marriage without the first marriage having been declared null and void. Yet the grounds for declaring most marriages null today are psychological factors that seem to affect the majority and possibly all marriages, namely, the inability of one or both partners to achieve intimacy. In other words, Catholics are told on the one hand that their marriage is valid until proven otherwise, yet there is ample evidence that many if not most people at the time of their first marriage are not capable of genuine intimacy. Hence they are entering into unions that, if investigated later, are highly likely to be proven invalid. It therefore seems that, from a scientific viewpoint, most marriages today should be assumed to be invalid if the capacity for intimacy is a condition for validity. Surely there is some institutional deception in treating divorced people as still validly married when professionals in the institution (canon lawyers) are aware that many if not most people are not capable of intimacy at the time that they are married—which is why their marriages are annullable.

One would think that if a marriage was invalid at the beginning, it could become valid if the invalidating condition were removed. Thus if a man were healed of his impotence or a woman of her frigidity, for example, or if a couple who were originally coerced came to freely accept their marital union, a once invalid union could theoretically become valid. Reasoning along the same lines, if an individual or couple were originally incapable of intimacy, their marriage may have been invalid at the time of their wedding, but when they develop the capacity for "an intimate communion of the whole of life," their marriage becomes not only healed but also valid. But Catholic canon law does not take these possibilities into account. Thus, a woman who believes that her marriage did not begin with intimacy but later achieved it can feel extremely reluctant to seek an annulment for a marriage that she believes in her heart was valid. At the same time, the unfaithful husband in such a marriage can claim incapacity for intimacy at the beginning of the first marriage as grounds for an annulment so that he can legally leave his wife and children and marry again in the Catholic Church. Again, there is much room here for deception.

Toward a Theology of Second Chances

Catholic psychologist Jack Dominian (1993) has written eloquently about marriage as a healing process. His assumption is that two persons who are initially imperfect, broken, and inadequate can, through the give and take of friendship, the challenge of parenthood, and the difficult quest for intimacy become slowly healed and whole and more fully human. Is it possible that two individuals who naïvely entered into a first marriage thinking that they could "live happily ever after," who have had their lives and illusions shattered by a painful divorce, can enter into a second marriage still imperfect and broken, but more self-aware, so that their second marriage becomes the healing process that their first one was not able to be?

Let us explore this possibility.

The Bible is filled with the theme of second chances under the heading of such terms as salvation, redemption, and forgiveness. Although salvation in postbiblical Christianity came to be thought of as something that happens after death, salvation in the Bible, especially in the Jewish Scriptures, is something that happens in this life. Despite their sinfulness, for example, God gives humans a second chance by inviting Noah to build the ark in which his family can survive the Flood (Gen. 6–9). God saves the Israelites from slavery in Egypt and leads them into the promised land. Not only this, but God repeatedly forgives the sinfulness of the Israelites during the exodus, turning his wrath away from their unfaithfulness, their stubbornness, their unbelief, and their disobedience (Exod. 15:24; 17:1–4; 32:1–35; Deut. 1:34–38; 6:10–25; 9:7–29). When the kingdom of Israel is established in Canaan, God forgives the sins of kings David and Solomon for the sake of the people, calling the monarchs to repent of their greed and to rule justly (2 Sam. 12:1–25; 1 Kgs. 11:1–13). This same pattern is repeated in the period of the divided kingdom, when the prophets combine forebodings of catastrophe with promises of salvation from their enemies if the people and their rulers heed God's law (Isa. 1:2–20; Jer. 2:9–37). During the exile, other prophets speak on God's behalf, assuring the people of God's forgiveness and promising deliverance from Babylonia and a return to their homeland. It is during this period that the theme of a redeemer is first heard, the promise of a savior or messiah who will set right what is wrong and give Israel a second chance at greatness (Isa. 11:1–9; 40:1–41:20; 42:1–7; 51:1–23).

Redemption and salvation are two concepts that are used in the New Testament to explain Jesus' mission and his death on the cross. Peter's first sermons after Pentecost, as presented in Acts 2:22–36 and 3:12–26, explain that the Messiah had to suffer so that the people's sins would be forgiven. Paul in the letter to the Romans contrasts Jesus with Adam, with God offering humankind a second chance at righteousness through Jesus after righteousness was lost through Adam's disobedience (5:12–21). The epistles to the Ephesians and the Colossians both open with early Christian formulations of faith in the salvific work of Christ (Eph. 1:3–14; Col. 1:15–20). The book of Hebrews compares Christ to a high priest in the Jewish temple whose work brings about redemption from sin (5:1–10). The God of the New Testament, like the God of the Old Testament, is one who loves people so much that he offers them second chances after their failures. God does not hold grudges, but he does demand that people change their lives when offered a second chance (Acts 2:38; Gal. 5:1–26; Eph. 4:17–5:20).

Just as Christians are offered second chances by God, so they are to offer second chances to one another. Jesus not only preached God's forgiveness; he also taught mutual forgiveness. Christians are to love one another as Jesus loved (John 13:34), and this implies that they are to forgive one another (Luke 17:3–4). Since God's forgiveness knows no bounds, Christian forgiveness should be unlimited (Matt. 18:21–35).

Love and forgiveness are essential to the healing of relationships and the possibility of second chances. If Jesus' preaching emphasized God's forgiveness, his ministry can be characterized as one of healing. He healed all manner of physical illness, but more importantly he addressed the spiritual illness of estrangement from God and one another (e.g., Luke 5:17–25; 7:36–50). By announcing to all the good news of God's love, and by assuring individuals that their sins are forgiven, Jesus made it possible for people to let go of shame and guilt, anger and resentment, and other thoughts and attitudes that prevent people from loving one another and living in communion with one other. If Jesus' was a ministry of second chances, remarriage that is undertaken with the proper attitude can be regarded as a gift from God to start over again.

Jesus' ministry can also be characterized as a call to conversion (Mark 1:14–15; in the context of healing and forgiveness, John 8:3–11). People in a second marriage need to let go of self-recrimination as well as blame directed toward their former spouse. They can bring healing to one another, perhaps even helping each other to grow out of anxious or avoidant attachment patterns, and to change other attitudes and behaviors that may have led to the demise of their first marriage.

Healing From Deception

Catholics today are aware of the biblical themes mentioned above, even if their knowledge of theology is based only on what they hear in church on Sundays. Catholic theology and preaching since Vatican II have emphasized God's love and forgiveness rather than divine wrath and punishment, and so they do not necessarily feel guilty (as many Catholics did in the past) if their marriage ends in divorce. Many times they do not even think about obtaining an annulment in the church until they begin thinking seriously about a second marriage, and it is here that their personal faith in a loving and forgiving God runs afoul of their institutional faith in what they discover to be (if they did not realize it before) a legalistic church.

Since Catholics' experience of deception can take a variety of forms, some may perceive the apparent discrepancy between the theology of forgiveness they have heard from the pulpit and the theology of forgiveness that they run into when they inquire about an annulment. Others may feel betrayed when a marriage that they were told was indissoluble dissolves despite their best efforts to keep it intact. Still others suffer in an abusive marriage, believing, on the one hand, that they have to stay married and, on the other hand, that it is wrong to remain in this relationship. There are other possibilities as well.

Catholic reactions to the experience of deception can be equally varied. Some may give up on the church in disgust, regarding it as a hypocritical institution. Of these some may seek to nourish their personal faith in another church, while others may reject all forms of institutional religion. Some may find enough strength in their personal faith to disregard with a clear conscience the church's teaching on remarriage, just as the over-whelming majority of Catholics have disregarded the church's teaching on birth control since 1968. These are the ones who remarry without the church's blessing and move to a parish where they can continue to practice their faith openly because their marital status is not public knowledge. Still others may look upon the annulment process as an institutional require-ment that has nothing to do with their experienced reality of marriage; still they consent to go through it for the sake of others for whom observing the church's laws is important (e.g., close relatives or Catholic employers).

Perhaps the most healthy healing from deception—understood here as the self-deception of the Catholic hierarchy which is transmitted wittingly or unwittingly to the Catholic laity—is reaching a point where the church can be accepted as an institution that is truly both human and divine, a means of salvation and sometimes an obstacle to salvation. From this per-spective, one can be grateful for the institution and its traditions without feeling coerced by the institution or bound by its traditions. One retains faith in the institution but it is not blind faith. It is believing with one's eyes open. It is faith that is forgiving.

WORKS CITED

Collins, Nancy L., and Stephen J. Read
1990   "Adult Attachment, Working Models, and Relationship
                        Quality in Dating Couples." *Journal of Personality and
                        Social Psychology* 58, no. 4.
Dominian, Jack
1993   *The Dynamics of Marriage: Love, Sex and Growth
                        from a Christian Perspective.* Mystic, CT: Twenty-Third
                        Publications.

Feeney, Judith, Patricia Noller, and Victor J. Callan
    1994   "Attachment Style, Communication and Satisfaction in
                        the Early Years of Marriage." *Advances in Personal
                        Relationships 5.*
Hazan, Cindy, and Phillip R. Shaver
    1990   "Love and Work: An Attachment-Theoretical Perspec-
                        tive." *Journal of Personality and Social Psychology 59,*
                        no 2.
Kobak, R. Rogers, and Cindy Hazan
    1991   "Attachment in Marriage: Effects of Security and Accu-
                        racy of Working Models." *Journal of Personality and
                        Social Psychology 60,* no 6.
Main, Mary, and Ruth Goldwyn
    1984   "Predicting Rejection of Her Infant from Mother's Rep-
                        resentation of Her Own Experience: Implications for
                        the Abused-Abusing Intergenerational Cycle." *Child
                        Abuse and Neglect 8.*
Rice, Joy K., and David G. Rice
    1986   *Living Through Divorce.* New York: The Guilford
                        Press.
Shaver, Phillip R., and Cindy Hazan
    1993   "Adult Romantic Attachment: Theory and Evidence."
                        Advances in Personal Relationships 4.
    1994   "Attachment." In *Perspectives on Close Relationships,*
                        ed. Ann Weber and John H. Harvey. Old Tappan, N.J.:
                        Allyn & Bacon.
Simpson, Jeffry A., and William Rholes
    1994   "Stress and Secure Base Relationships in Adulthood."
                        Advances in Personal Relationships 5.

Index